TOWARDS

ETERNAL LIFE

Revised Edition

BRITISH LIBRARY CATALOGUING IN PUBLICATION DATA

A catalogue record for this book is available
from the British Library

ISBN: 978-1-78991-078-0 (pbk)

Third Edition

PUBLISHED BY

The World Federation of Khoja Shia Ithna-Asheri
Muslim Communities

Registered Charity in the UK No. 282303

The World Federation is an NGO in Special Consultative Status with the Economic and Social Council (ECOSOC) of the United Nations

Islamic Centre, Wood Lane, Stanmore, Middlesex,
United Kingdom, HA7 4LQ

www.world-federation.org

The moral rights of the author have been asserted.

Typesetting by ZH Designs.

THE WORLD
FEDERATION

بسم الله الرحمن الرحيم

TOWARDS ETERNAL LIFE

Author:

Muhammad Saeed Bahmanpour

Translated by

Abbas Jaffer

CONTENTS

FOREWORD

This book is a small effort to portray the path that a human being must traverse after he leaves this world (*dunyā*) and continues on the journey towards His Lord. It is an attempt to discover the impact of our conduct in *dunyā* on the various stages of that journey which will culminate with the meeting with God. It is an effort to unravel the mystery of man's reality and his ultimate destination.

Raymond Moody, the American physician, philosopher and psychologist, has compiled a large number of reports about the experiences of people who were in the process of dying, or who had been narrowly saved from death. In 1975 he presented his findings in a book called 'Life after Life'.[1]

After observing nearly a thousand of these experiences, he coined a new phrase, "Near Death Experience" which was popularly abbreviated to NDE. In 1981, the International Association for Near-Death Studies[2] was founded with the intention of collecting, studying and publishing reports of near-death experiences.

These experiences are so widespread in American hospitals that according to a Gallup report published in 1992, eight million Americans reported having had them.[3] This is in spite of the fact that many of those who have had this kind of experience are reluctant to talk about it.

While studying the reports of 150 patients who had been declared brain-dead but had subsequently somehow returned

---

1 Moody Raymond. 1975. Life after Life: The Investigation of a Phenomenon – Survival of Bodily Death. Seattle: Mockingbird Books.

2 For more information about this institution see www.iands.org.

3 Mauro, James, "Bright lights, big mystery", Psychology Today, July 1992.

to life, Moody discovered that their near-death experiences could be classified into a few groups.

One group reported that they had emerged from their own bodies while they were in a fully conscious and aware state, and they could observe the actions of the team of doctors from above their bodies. Another group felt that they were in a body that was different from their familiar material body; Moody called this the spiritual body.[4] This spiritual body had all the sensory organs of the material body, except that its movement and perception was not restricted even by stone walls. Other reports described losing all sense of time, entering a state of deep relaxation, and confusion when viewing their own body from outside. Some people reported seeing the souls of the dead in spirit forms welcoming them. Another group reported seeing a holy personality from their religious tradition who had come to guide them on their new journey. Yet others claimed that they were not initially aware that they were in a new body until they realized that their relatives could not see or hear them; meanwhile their own sight and hearing was greatly enhanced, allowing them to see and hear everything.

The foregoing descriptions which are corroborated by other independent evidence make clear to us that we know a lot less about the human being than we think. In the words of Elisabeth Kübler-Ross (d. 2004), who in the course of her work studied countless cases of NDE, "We have to have the courage to open new doors and admit that our present-day scientific tools are inadequate for many of these new investigations."[5]

---

[4] In Islamic philosophy and mysticism this body is called the imaginal body *(al-jism al-mithālī)*.

[5] Life after Life, Introduction, p. xiii.

When we turn to religious teachings, we find that man is presented as a wondrous being whose potentials are greater than his physical body suggests. He is a creature that is constantly growing and changing, and in the course of his journey he passes through many stages. He begins from a drop of liquid and spends the first few months of his life cocooned in a dark and hidden world. At this stage of his life, he does not do anything of his own volition; natural processes alone govern his development, transforming his form and features and colour without consulting with him. This phase of life is very long when compared to his previous existence as a drop of fluid, but very short when compared to the next phase when he will step out into the world. For a new-born baby who has just come from its mother's womb the world is surreal, a huge and exciting place, full of dazzling features; mountains and valleys, oceans and forests, cities and hamlets, foods and clothing, skies and stars, and most importantly, human beings; other people like him, whom he can talk to, ask for assistance, get to know and get used to; more than that, he can grow to love them and make sacrifices for them.

All this variety is quite dazzling for the baby who has just left his brief life in a tiny and dark space. However, this exciting and seemingly everlasting world will gradually lose its charm for him, and the days will come when his wonder will change to disappointment and anxiety. In time his vision will deteriorate, his hearing fade, his teeth will fall out, his bones will turn brittle, his muscles will become weak, his face will age, and his memory will begin to fail. Once more, he will become like a child and all the beauty he was familiar with will pass and disappear; soon he will have to leave again.

Where will he go to this time? To a bigger world or a smaller one? Better or worse? Or none at all? What was the purpose of his life here? Is there anyone who can answer these questions? Can anyone truly know? Is there really another world or worlds after this one? And is it at all important for us to know about what is to come in the future? Is there actually anything that is waiting for us? Who can tell, and who has the master map for this journey?

Some people become convinced that there is nothing after death, but they don't have any proof for it. But why should this journey, that has already taken us through several stages, come to a sudden halt without a satisfactory outcome? This group does not speak from knowledge; rather, they base their assumption on a lack of knowledge about the future. So, should we trust their lack of knowledge?

On the other hand, there has always been a small group of people who stated that they knew what was to come. They claimed that they did not speak from themselves, but on behalf of the One Who has created this path and laid it out. They said that they do not speak out of conjecture or lack of information; rather they speak of what they know and perceive. They said that the Creator of mankind had informed them of these realities and directed them to inform others. Their words were compelling, their personalities noble, their hearts pure and their morals sublime. Their speech rang with honesty and many in their audience acknowledged the truth of their words and found them to resonate with their inner disposition. Their words not only appealed to those of their own time but reached out to attract future generations of people also.

Amongst them was Muhammad (s), the son of Abdullah, who become famous for his scrupulous honesty and righteousness, earning him the title al-Amīn (the trustworthy). He left no stone unturned in his attempts to make his followers understand the road that they would need to walk on after death and the provisions that they would require for it.

He would say, "O mankind! Indeed you are labouring painfully towards your Lord and one day you will meet Him."[6] He would say, "Your objective should be to grow to an extent that you become ready to meet God, and thereafter eternally abide "in a seat of honour in the presence of an Omnipotent King."[7] He would say, "God waits to meet you and wants you to live near Him for eternity."[8] He would say, "God forbid that on the Day when you meet Him you carry the burden of wrongdoing (ẓulm), because, "he who bears iniquity on that Day would indeed despair",[9] because your Lord does not despise anything more than wrongdoing." He would say, "Your Lord is the Purest of the Pure, and if you enter into His presence in a pure state, He will envelop you in His mercy and send you a greeting of peace.[10] Yes, all this is for you, the one who sprang from a small drop of fluid, do you remember your insignificant beginnings?

But Muhammad (s) did not just talk about the final destination; he also defined for us the path towards it as clearly as he could. Although it was not possible to truly describe it, he spoke of it often, in the hope that we would realize its significance. He taught us that whatever we do in this world will have a great impact on the future stages of our journey and our ultimate destination.

---

[6] Surat al-Inshiqāq, 84:6.

[7] Surat al-Qamar, 54:55.

[8] Surat Āl-ʿImrān, 3:198.

[9] Surat Ṭā Hā, 20:111.

[10] Surat al-Aḥzāb, 33:44.

What you shall read in this book is an effort to explore what Muhammad (s) told us about this journey. It is not possible to accurately describe a world whose dimensions remain yet hidden to us. Even for one who is intimately conversant with that world, it is impossible to explain its features to someone who has no experience of it. A three-dimensional being can never understand a world of four dimensions, let alone one that is multi-dimensional. Therefore, that which I shall try to describe hereunder is only a brief sketch so that we may get a notion of this journey, and more importantly so that we may prepare the provisions that we shall need along the way.

We are grateful and indebted to Muhammad (s) and all the noble individuals who devoted their lives to making us familiar with this indispensable knowledge.

TRANSLATOR'S PREFACE

The question of the life after death has always fascinated mankind. And even for those who believe that life continues after death, the nature and detail of that existence has remained a mystery, largely because no one has ever returned to tell us about it. Our limited understanding comes mainly from the descriptions left behind by the special servants of God, to whom He has granted some knowledge about the next worlds that man will encounter on his journey towards his Creator.

Of course, it is not possible in the material realm to fully appreciate the immaterial worlds that we are heading towards after death, but it is important to know the challenges that lie ahead so that the requisite preparations can be made for it while we still live in this world.

What makes this work different is that the author, Sh. Muhammad Saeed Bahmanpour, has succeeded to a reasonable extent in unravelling these mysteries by carefully analysing the relevant Qur'anic verses and traditions of the Prophet (s). He has made use of both Sunni and Shiʿi hadith texts, as well as considered the opinions and experiences of both Islamic and Christian mystical philosophers. In this way he has prepared a very compelling and plausible description of the road that lies ahead.

I have been privileged to attend many of Sh. Bahmanpour's discourses on Islamic eschatology over the years and he has always generously made himself available to answer my questions about life after death. When I first came across the book he had written on the subject, entitled *Nasīm-e Abadiyyat* (The Breeze of Eternity), I was struck by the systematic approach he had adopted in discussing each stage after death. I felt that English readers would also greatly benefit from its fresh and novel approach, and it was an honour to be asked to translate the work by the The World Federation of the KSIMC.

I would like to acknowledge with gratitude the patient assistance of Sh Bahmanpour during the translation.

From God is all succour and to Him is the return.

Abbas Jaffer

Jan 2016, London UK

CHAPTER 1

DEATH - THE PORTAL TO A WONDROUS WORLD

The Imaginal Realm after Death

After birth, death may be considered as the most momentous experience that a human undergoes. Death can be described both as dying and being reborn. Dying from this world and being reborn in another world. Death is not the end of existence; rather, it is a continuation towards maturation. It is the evolution of the human soul as it journeys towards a more enhanced and beautiful existence.

Man is a much more complex being than we realise or that our scientific knowledge and philosophical endeavours have made us imagine. In truth, the reality of the world and the human being still remains a mysterious iceberg whose tip we have barely recognised and whose vast expanse remains yet to be uncovered. When we consider the universe around us, we imagine that it is just confined to the sky and its constellations, and to the earth and its mountains and plains and seas, and to its vegetation and forests and animals. We regard the human being in the same way and consider him to be no more than his limbs and organs and brain and flesh and bones. However, what we see is just the tip of the iceberg. This world has countless layers and dimensions which are hidden from our sight and cannot be perceived by physical eyes. In order to see these layers, the various dimensions must be illuminated for us, and we must travel through them. In the course of life in *dunyā*, this is only possible for a select few whose souls have undergone and withstood stiff trials; for most people, however, these layers only become accessible after death. The layers are still dimensions of this same *dunyā*, and only when the universe enters its final stage (*ākhira*) will these layers also undergo fundamental transformations.

At death we enter a wondrous and dream-like dimension of this world, which is very different from the dimension we currently live in. This new dimension has been called by various names, such as the realm of imagination (*'ālam al-khiyāl*), the realm of similitudes and images (*'ālam al-mithāl*), the isthmus or intermediate realm, and the barrier (*barzakh*).

We call it the isthmus or intermediate realm because it is a stage between this world (*dunyā*) and the world of the Hereafter (*ākhira*).

It is the *barzakh* because between that dimension and the dimension that we currently inhabit, there is a strong barrier that can only be breached with the aid of the angel of death; once one has crossed over, no return is possible except by the permission of God. *Barzakh* means barrier, and it is called *barzakh* because once humans enter into that realm, "*behind them is a barrier until the Day they are resurrected.*"[11]

It is the world of images or the imaginal world (*'ālam al-mithāl*) because what is found there is an image of this world but without a body or matter.[12] Or a better explanation would

---

[11] Surat al-Mu'minūn, 23:100.

[12] According to Suhrawardī, the founder of Illuminationist Philosophy (*Ḥikmat al-Ihshrāq*), *'ālam al-khiyāl* or *mithāl* is a stage of existence that is non-material but not free from the influence of matter; it is a stage between the sensible (*maḥsūs*) and the intelligible (*ma'qūl*), or it is both material and immaterial, and consequently contains some properties of both. He believes that it is not possible to cross over from the sensible (phenomenal, *dunyā*) realm to the intelligible (noumenal, *ākhira*) realm without an intervening agency. Therefore, there must exist a realm between these two which can draw on the properties of both

be that what exists in this world is a material image of the pure existence of that world. "*Mithāl*" means an image or similitude, but it is not like an image that is seen in a mirror; rather, it is an image whose reflection is more expansive and whose existence, capability and life-force is more powerful than the object itself. Colour, smell, taste and every other sensation that we experience in this world exists there also, except that the sensations are not limited by the restrictions of matter and consequently are stronger, more vital and more beautiful. Compared to that realm, what we experience here of sorrow and joy and pain and ease is just a pale image cast on the dusty and coarse mirror of our material world. In that realm, the heaviness of matter does not restrict movement and sap one's strength. It is a place of lightness and subtleties, similar to our dreams or thoughts. There, the soul of man becomes freer and more active than it has ever been.

For this reason, that world is also called *'ālam al-khiyāl* – the world of imagination. This is because what we have described above is very close to what we experience in our dreams and imagination; not in the sense that it is not real, but in the sense that it is a world in which the imagination can have a free rein and every material property can be conceived and perceived, without the need for matter itself. Our contemplations in *dunyā* are relatively weak and have little impact because they are "connected" to us; however, in the imaginal world, because they are an existence in their own right and "disconnected" from us and every material constraint, our thoughts gain tremendous strength and potency.

---

phenomena and noumena. (Syed Khalil Toussi, *Mabānī Falsafey-i Akhlāq-i Mullā Ṣadrā*, p. 73)

One can only picture man's amazement when he first enters this dream-like world. It is so expansive and rich and awe-inspiring that the soul will remain stunned and bewildered for long moments. The feeling is somewhat similar to the moment a baby is born into this world, with the difference that the new-born does not remember much of the dark confines of its life in the mother's womb, and is not fully aware of the vastness and radiance of the world it has come to. However, when the soul enters *barzakh*, it is much more alert and aware, and the realities of the new world cause it great amazement. With its passage, the soul evolves one degree higher and consequently its ability to perceive the true nature of its surroundings is enhanced. In this way it takes a step forward and begins to experience the wonders of the final leg of the journey towards the meeting with God.

How Death takes Place

As far as this world is concerned, death means the stilling of the heartbeat and the blood flow in the body. However, this is only part of the story. The event of death is something much deeper and elaborate; when the heart stops, the soul of man – which is in fact his essence – must decouple from the body, which has long been its vehicle and means of action. As we will see later, this procedure cannot take place without the mediation and assistance of the angel of death.

Death can be viewed from two aspects: it could be said the human soul accompanies the body so long as it can draw on the host's vitality to benefit itself; and when the body becomes a corpse and is of no further use, the soul leaves it. On the other hand, it could be said that when the soul leaves the body, the body is no longer able to sustain itself and becomes lifeless. In either case, it appears that the connection between the soul and body is very complex and any attempt to simplify it will not do justice to the intricacy of their relationship.

But what is the soul?[13] It is not easy to describe, but in simple terms it can be considered to be the part of ourselves that we refer to when we say, "I". It is the part of us that makes intentions and decisions, decides what it loves, and what choices to make. It is the power that governs the body and uses it to achieve its ends and manifest its will. It sees and hears and travels by prompting the body. With its assistance it makes analyses and arrives at conclusions, displays love and hate, and a host of other things besides. We often imagine that these things are to do with our body and in particular our brains, but in truth, the body and brain are just composed of cells; these tissues are not aware of each other, in the sense that a group of cells cannot decide something by consulting with another group of cells, although they can act in concert to create effects that are perceived by the soul.

Through the body, the human soul is able to know the world and undergo countless experiences. If the body was not available, the soul could not become familiar with this material world at all and would remain forever like a blank page. In the same way if the soul was absent, the body would not have the ability to carry out any work, because work requires movement and movement needs volition and that is a faculty of the soul.

However, we are more interested to know how the soul subsists once it decouples from the body and leaves the material world and in what manner and in which body it enters into the realm of *barzakh.* Evidently, just as the soul needed to occupy a material body in *dunyā* to interact with the world of

[13] For ease of understanding, we have assumed that the spirit (*rūḥ*) and the soul (*nafs*) refer to the same thing, although there is a subtle difference between the two.

matter, it will require a suitable body in the imaginal world to interact with imaginal existences. It therefore activates an immaterial or imaginal body.[14] Just like its physical body, its non-material body also has eyes, ears and a mind by which it can perceive and analyse what it experiences in that world. Rumi writes that these vastly superior non-material senses when contrasted with the physical senses are like "burnished gold compared to copper."[15]

Most people cannot use their immaterial senses in this world and only become aware of them at death. However, many people do use these powers, although without realizing it. There are some who see God's signs in everything around them, others who bring faith on hearing the verses of God's revelation, and others who learn lasting lessons from the experiences of former generations; all this occurs because a part of their immaterial (*malakūti*) intellect is active. As for those in whom this intellect is dormant, they see and hear nothing of this. It is by this means that the Prophets (a) communicated with angels; and Prophet Muhammad (s) went on his heavenly ascension (*mi'rāj*) in this non-material body.

But where does this non-material, imaginal body originate from and how does the soul attach itself to it? The imaginal form resembles the physical body in colour, size, features and expressions; the only difference is that it has no material substance. It is similar to a reflection seen in a mirror, or a thought passing in the mind, or a dream seen in sleep. In fact, our true dreams occur during a type of connection

[14] Majlisī writes that, "The imaginal body has been mentioned in so many reliable narrations that we have no choice but to accept its existence." *Biḥār al-Anwār*, 6:270.

[15] Rūmī, *Mathnawī Ma'nawī*, Introduction to the second volume, verse 49 | "There are another five senses apart from these five; but while those are like burnished gold, these are just like copper."

with the imaginal world, while false dreams arise from our own imagination or stray thoughts. The fact that we can connect with the imaginal world in our sleep indicates that the imaginal world is not in a universe different from the material world; rather it is the opposite face of the same coin and a deeper dimension of the *dunyā*.[16] Therefore, even while we live in this world, we have a presence in the imaginal world about which we are unaware. At each stage of our physical life, from our conception and our subsequent birth and development into adulthood, our imaginal bodies are being formed and shaped also. In fact, our souls in *dunyā* live in two bodies, an imaginal body and a material one; and both are coincident and synchronized with each other. However, since the imaginal body exists in a subtle and hidden dimension, most human beings are oblivious of it. At the time of death, the soul leaves the material body, which is temporary and frail, and enters the realm of *barzakh* clothed only in its stronger, non-material, imaginal body.[17] Therefore, when we talk of death and the decoupling of the soul from the body, we are talking of ourselves in our new imaginal body.

Contrasting Experiences of Death

What kind of experience will death be? Sweet or bitter? Beautiful or ugly? This will depend on what kind of life we

[16] The reality of man, even though he is a being of one identity, is that he has a rank in the visible as well as a rank in the invisible world; in his rank in the natural and visible world, he is a physical being, but in the realm of imagination and pure perception, he is an imaginal (*barzakhi*) being; while in the dimension of intellects, he is absolutely immaterial. (Mullā Ṣadrā Shīrāzī, quoted by Syed Khalil Toussi, *Mabānī Falsafey-i Akhlāq-i Mullā Ṣadrā*, p. 58)

[17] Majlisī, *Biḥār al-Anwār*, 6:268 quoting Imam al-Sadiq (a) |

فِي أَبْدَانٍ كَأَبْدَانِهِمْ

have led. In truth, everyone will die in the same manner as he lived. This seemingly trivial and fleeting life of *dunyā* is actually the most important and influential stage of human existence, because from the moment of death onwards, everything that happens to an individual has been shaped and earned in some way during this stage.

The angel of death is the first mirror in which a human being sees his true nature and is the first being of the higher realms that the soul meets with its non-material body. Depending on an individual's personality, the angel of death can be beautiful or ugly, kind or cruel, loveable or hateful. It has been reported from Imam al-Sadiq (a) that, "One day when Ibrahim (a) returned to his home he saw an individual whose beauty and countenance was the like that he had never encountered before. He asked, "Who are you?" "I am the angel of death", he replied. He said, "Glory be to God! How can someone who sees you dislike you, when you are so beautiful?" The angel replied, "O Friend of the all-Merciful! When God desires goodness for an individual He sends me in this form to him. But when He desires to punish him, He sends me in a different form."[18]

Therefore, the angel of death and his assistants can take our life with mercy and tenderness or with harshness and roughness. When we leave this world, we may either feel as if we are being released from a stifling prison and are going towards a world of freedom, or we may feel that we have been captured and are being led to a place of torture. It all depends on the kind of life we have led. Have we been filled with despair or hope, have we been harsh or compassionate, have we been grateful or ungrateful, have we hurt others or extended a helpful hand to them, have we worshipped God or been neglectful of Him;

---

[18] Ṣadūq, *'Ilal al-Sharāya'*, 1:38.

in short have we led a noble life or a corrupt one. "*Those whom the angels cause to die while they led pure lives, they say to them, "Peace be upon you. Enter Paradise because of what you used to do.*"[19] However, "*But if you could only see the angels take the souls of those who disbelieved; they smite their faces and their backs (saying), "Taste the punishment of the burning fire! That is because of what your hands have sent forth. And certainly, God is not unjust to His servants.*"[20] Indeed, whatever happens to them is only due to what they have created, prepared and sent forth themselves; this is who they are.

Entry into the World of the Angels

In truth, as we come to the world of the angels we enter into a sanctified and pure environment; if our own souls are polluted, then we will experience severe discomfort in that world. The more polluted we are, the more acute and painful this discomfort shall be. The closer we get to God, Who is the epitome of purity, the more severe is the reaction of our polluted state to that purity.

By contrast, the purer the soul, the greater the comfort it experiences in that world. Liberated from its former constraints, it flourishes and soars to even higher levels of purity. Its attachment to that world and what it contains becomes stronger.

Therefore, the experience of the next world, which is also the world of angels, is different for every individual. For the arrogant and the guilty, "*On the day when they shall see the angels, there shall be no joy for them and they shall say: Get away from us and do not come close.*"[21] They shall see these pure

[19] Surat al-Naḥl, 6:32.

[20] Surat al-Anfāl, 8:50-51.

[21] Surat al-Furqān, 25:22.

beings as their enemy, and the evil of their own acts will become evident, causing them to be ashamed.

By contrast, the virtuous will consider themselves amongst new friends in the world of the angels. These are friends whose friendship is perpetual, and whose nature is filled with warmth and mercy, and knowledge and wisdom. They are friends who are constantly attentive to the needs of their new charges, and fuss around them trying to remove every unhappiness and anxiety from them.

They gently whisper into their souls not to be afraid or distressed, and comfort them with the glad tidings that the heaven that had been promised to them awaits them. They assure them that they will be their constant guides and companions in the journey that is to come, "*The angels descend upon them, saying: Fear not, nor be grieved, and receive good news of the Paradise which you were promised. We are your guardians in this world's life and in the Hereafter.*"[22]

For the righteous, death thus becomes a great gift from God and the most pleasant experience of their life.

The Angels of Death

The angels of death are charged with two responsibilities with regards to *barzakh*. The first is to detach the souls of individuals from their material bodies, and the second, to settle these souls into the imaginal bodies which will house them in their lives in *barzakh*. The relationship of the soul to the material body is so deep and strong that to separate them is often a difficult and painful process. In any case, the angels know their task well, and in the end, the ease or difficulty with which their mission is accomplished depends on the willingness of the dying person to give up his soul.

[22] Surat Fuṣṣilat 41:30, 31.

However, the actual task at hand is to activate the immaterial or spiritual body. As we have said, the imaginal body is a semblance of the material body but in a non-corporeal form, just as the immaterial world is composed of sights and sounds of a non-corporeal nature. The *barzakhi* body possesses eyes and ears that can perceive the sights and sounds of that world. Similarly, it possesses a mind that can understand the concepts of that world, which are complicated and deep. In fact, in comparison, the complex issues and serious matters of this world appear trivial and frivolous.

This stage is also different for every individual. For those whose spirit was active in this world, especially the Prophets (a) and the close servants of God, the activation is easy and swift. However, for ordinary individuals, the process takes longer. In order to understand this stage more clearly, we will consider the different experiences that await three broad categories of people:

1. **The People of the Middle State**

This group encompasses the vast majority of human beings. Although they generally have faith in the Hereafter, they are not familiar with its details. Their initial encounter with the angels of death, and their exposure to the next world fills them with confusion, especially because they still see themselves in a similar body to their usual one. The angels of death assist them to become acquainted with the faculties of their new body, showing them how to open their eyes and ears. It is as if they have removed a veil from their eyes and ears. Thereafter, they reveal to them some information that is vital to their existence in their new environment. This understanding is quicker for some, and gradual for others. The angels are manifestations of the mercy of God; they are filled with sincere love and care and are eager to instruct the new soul about the world it has entered; however, the success of their efforts requires the soul to be receptive, and not resistant, to their instruction.

The soul is a creation belonging to the timeless world of God's command (*ʿālam al-amr*), and like God Himself, it cannot be defined or seen; "*They ask you about the soul, say it is from the command of my Lord, and you have not been informed about it except a little.*"[23]

The soul can only be known by its effects, which are manifested through the body. This is true during its existence in the world, as well as after death.[24] In this world, the soul acts through the body to manifest its whims and desires. In fact, it is not incorrect to say that the soul of an individual is the same as his likes and dislikes; all his actions, conduct and personality derive from it. In this world, we humans mould our souls. What we call personality, or in Qur'anic terms, *shākila*, shapes our decisions, our attitude towards the situations we face in this world, the manner of our interactions with one another, our personal preferences, our expectations from this world, how we utilize its bounties and even the way we view our existence. All this stems from the proclivities of our souls, which gradually shape our personality. Once our personality or *shākila* is formed, it influences every decision and choice we make.[25]

As we get older in the course of our lives in this world, it becomes harder and harder to reshape this personality; once we die though, it is no longer possible, or at least, it is

---

[23] Surat al-Isrāʾ, 17:85.

[24] Of course, there are other ways to achieve cognizance, by which both God and the soul can be better understood, but this discussion is outside the scope of our present work.

[25] Surat al-Isrāʾ, 17:84.

out of our hands and requires other means. What we carry forth with us from this world is this personality and nature of the soul that we have shaped; its competency will now reveal itself with increasing clarity in the backdrop of the various worlds we will traverse through in the long journey towards our Lord. The nature of our encounters with the diverse beings that inhabit these worlds will be based on this personality - a personality that can be either pleasant or repulsive.

Mulla Sadra has demonstrated the foregoing through his philosophical principles. He states that, in this corporeal world, the soul flourishes through the body, and in the next world it transfers the habits it has formed to create and give shape to the body that it will occupy there. The imaginal body will be beautiful or ugly depending on the nature of the soul. It is in the process of this creation that an individual - with his particular temperament, disposition, virtues and vices - gives shape to an imaginal body with the same dominant characteristics.[26]

In *barzakh* the human soul flourishes; it is a place where mental constructs gain external forms and bodies. The soul carries an imprint of every atom's weight of good and evil that an individual has done, and in *barzakh* it is embodied externally as well; "*So whoever does an atom's weight of good shall see it, and whoever does an atom's weight of evil shall see it.*"[27]

The encounter of the soul with the angels of death[28] and the kind of reception it receives and the manner in which

[26] Mullā Ṣadrā, *Asfār*, 9:227.

[27] Surat al-Zilzāl, 99:7-8.

[28] Probably not one, but several angels are involved in the transfer of the soul to the realm of *barzakh*; each angel shall have a specific task in the process. The Qur'an speaks of the numbers of these angels; "When

it reacts to the realities of that world all depend on the nature and personality that the individual has formed in life. Amongst the people of the middle state, there are those whose faith and spiritual progress was less and their affinity to *dunyā* greater; when their imaginal senses awaken and they see the angels and begin to receive instructions from them, they become alarmed and uneasy and desire to be free of their presence as soon as possible. This is why they resist the well-meaning and kindly directions of the angels. The angels realize that their efforts are futile at this stage and depart, leaving the individual alone.

In contrast, those whose faith and spiritual progress was greater, take comfort and delight in the presence of the angels; they willingly follow their affectionate advice about the potentials of their new bodies and their new environment. And as a result, as we shall see later, their lives in *barzakh* are much more comfortable than the first group. For them the experience of death was, "like casting off a soiled and shabby garment and putting on a perfumed and fine one."[29] It is like, "a bath that washes away grime and sores from the body and dispels every pain and sorrow from the soul and fills the heart with happiness and excitement."[30] Or as the Prophet (s) said, "Like the birth of a baby from the dark confines of its mother's womb into the wide expanse of the world."[31]

---

death comes to one of you, our messengers take his soul, and they never neglect their duty." (Surat al-Anʿām, 6:61)

[29] Ṣadūq, *Maʿānī al-Akhbār*, 1/289

لِلْمُؤْمِنِ كَنَزْعِ ثِيَابٍ وَسِخَةٍ قَمِلَةٍ، وَالْاِسْتِبْدَالِ بِأَفْخَرِ الثِّيَابِ وَأَطْيَبِهَا رَوَائِحَ.

[30] Ibid, p. 290 |

فَقَدْ نَجَوْتَ مِنْ كُلِّ غَمٍّ وَهَمٍّ وَأَذًى، وَوَصَلْتَ إِلَى كُلِّ سُرُورٍ وَفَرَحٍ.

[31] Muttaqī al-Hindī, *Kanz al-ʿUmmāl*, trad 42212, quoting the Prophet (s) |

2. **Pure Individuals**

By pure individuals we mean those whose love in this world was sincerely reserved for God and their souls had become empty of self-conceit and pride to the extent humanly possible. Since conceit and self-love are the roots of all vices, by controlling themselves these individuals had managed to cleanse their hearts of every trace of impurity and had adorned their souls with purity and righteousness out of their love for God. It is about these individuals that God has revealed in the Torah that they "love God with all their hearts, all their souls, all their strength and all their mind."[32] For these individuals, their imaginal body is already half-awake at the time of death, and with the assistance of the angels it quickly becomes fully alert and prepared to ascend to the higher stages in proximity to God. Understanding the deeper realities and profound truths of the realm of *barzakh* is not too difficult for the receptive souls and prepared minds of this group; and their eagerness to learn makes the angels keen to show them more. For such individuals death is, "the most fragrant scent they have ever enjoyed; they will be intoxicated with their own perfume and instantly and eternally become free of every pain and sorrow."[33]

The moment of death of a pure individual is full of honour. When the angel of death approaches him, "he comes and stands by him like a respectful servant and greets him with a

مَا شَبَّهْتُ خُرُوجَ الْمُؤْمِنِ مِنَ الدُّنْيَا إِلَّا مِثْلَ خُرُوجِ الصَّبِيِّ مِنْ بَطْنِ أُمِّهِ، مِنْ ذَلِكَ الْغَمِّ وَالظُّلْمَةِ إِلَى رَوْحِ الدُّنْيَا.

[32] Gospel of Luke, 10:27.

[33] Ṣadūq, *Ma'ānī al-Akhbār*, 1/287 |

لِلْمُؤْمِنِ كَأَطْيَبِ رِيحٍ يَشُمُّهُ، فَيَنْعَسُ لِطِيبِهِ، وَيَنْقَطِعُ التَّعَبُ وَالْأَلَمُ كُلُّهُ عَنْهُ.

greeting of peace and gives him the glad tidings of Paradise."[34] "Angels stand at his head, each carrying a glass containing the water of *Kawthar* and a glass of purifying wine so that they may cleanse his soul and ease the agony and bitterness of death. At the same time, they give him the glad tidings of the greatest reward and say, "You have been purified and so has your station; now you will go towards God, the Mighty, the Wise, the Loving and the Intimate."[35] They say to him, "Welcome, O friend of God! Receive the good news of God's pleasure and His Paradise. God has even forgiven those believers who have accompanied your bier."[36]

A Vision of the Future and Entry into the Presence of the Virtuous

At this point the soul forgets all its pain and sorrow; it is as if a huge weight has been lifted from the shoulders,[37] or heavy fetters have been removed from the leg. Then the angels -who behave with him like close friends - illuminate new dimensions for him and remove the heavy veils of location and time that cover his sight. This is so that he may see his place in Paradise, from which he is yet far away.

---

[34] Ṣadūq, *Man lā Yaḥḍuruhu'l Faqīh*, 1:135, quoting the Prophet (s) |
إِنَّ مَلَكَ الْمَوْتِ لَيَقِفُ عِنْدَ مَوْتِهِ مَوْقِفَ الْعَبْدِ الذَّلِيلِ مِنَ الْمَوْلَى، فَيَقُومُ وَأَصْحَابُهُ لَا يَدْنُونَ] مِنْهُ حَتَّى يَبْدَأَهُ بِالتَّسْلِيمِ وَيُبَشِّرَهُ بِالْجَنَّةِ.

[35] Majlisī, *Biḥār al-Anwār*, 74:27, quoting the Prophet (s) |
إِذَا كَانَ الْعَبْدُ فِي حَالَةِ الْمَوْتِ يَقُومُ عَلَى رَأْسِهِ مَلَائِكَةٌ، بِيَدِ كُلِّ مَلَكٍ كَأْسٌ مِنْ مَاءِ الْكَوْثَرِ وَكَأْسٌ مِنَ الْخَمْرِ يَسْقُونَ رُوحَهُ حَتَّى تَذْهَبَ سَكْرَتُهُ وَمَرَارَتُهُ، وَيُبَشِّرُونَهُ بِالْبِشَارَةِ الْعُظْمَى وَيَقُولُونَ لَهُ: طِبْتَ وَطَابَ مَثْوَاكَ، إِنَّكَ تَقْدِمُ عَلَى الْعَزِيزِ الْحَبِيبِ الْقَرِيبِ.

[36] Muttaqī al-Hindī, *Kanz al-'Ummāl*, trad 42212, quoting the Prophet (s) |
أَوَّلُ مَا يُبَشَّرُ بِهِ الْمُؤْمِنُ أَنْ يُقَالَ لَهُ: أَبْشِرْ وَلِيَّ اللهِ بِرِضَاهُ وَالْجَنَّةِ، قَدِمْتَ خَيْرَ مَقْدَمٍ قَدْ غَفَرَ اللهُ لِمَنْ شَيَّعَكَ.

[37] Muhammadī, Ray Shahrī, *Mīzān al-Ḥikma*, 4:2973, quoting Imam Ali (a):
فُرِّغَ مِنْ كُلِّ شُغْلٍ، وَوُضِعَ عَنْهُ كُلُّ ثِقْلٍ.

At this point, the soul, which has been liberated from its cage and has been given indescribable bounties, says excitedly to the angels, "Return me to my family so that I may describe to them what I am seeing here." However, they inform him with loving smiles that, "This is no longer possible!"[38] At the same time, the purest individuals who inhabit that realm, like the Prophets (a) and their successors (a) appear before his eyes and his eagerness to proceed to the world beyond increases a hundredfold. There is no longer anything he desires more than disconnecting from the *dunyā* and hurrying to the next world.[39]

3. Corrupt Individuals

Corrupt individuals are those who allowed their souls to become polluted in this world and placed their bodies at the service of vices; they displayed disbelief and disobedience, ranging from defiance of God's dictates to oppressing and usurping the rights of fellow human beings.

For them nothing is more painful than the sight of the angels of death, just as nothing is more hateful for these angels than to be in the presence of such polluted people. Everything and everyone in the world of purity cannot stand them because corruptness has filled their entire beings.[40] The angels of

---

[38] Kulaynī, *al-Kāfī*, 3:135 |

رُدُّونِي إِلَى الدُّنْيَا حَتَّى أُخْبِرَ أَهْلِي بِمَا أَرَى، فَيُقَالُ لَهُ: لَيْسَ إِلَى ذَلِكَ سَبِيلٌ.

[39] Muhammadī, Ray Shahrī, *Mīzān al-Ḥikma*, 4:2973, quoting Imam al-Ṣādiq (a) :

فَمَا مِنْ شَيْءٍ أَحَبَّ إِلَيْهِ مِنْ إِسْتِلَالِ رُوحِهِ وَاللُّحُوقِ بِالْمُنَادِي.

[40] Trans-substantial motion (*al-ḥarakat al-jawharīya*) ... is not always a move-ment towards human perfection and is not exclusive to the virtuous; the souls of the wicked are also in the state of motion towards immateriality (*tajarrud*), and it is not necessary that all movement towards immateriality is a movement towards perfection. In fact, the

death cannot disguise their disgust at such a person and appear before him with harsh and fearsome faces. The dying individual is overcome with great fear and remorse at the sight.[41] The pain and hardship of death will course through every cell of his body, "every moment of the process of dying would be as agonizing as a hundred fatal strikes of a sword."[42] "Being cut to pieces with a pair of scissors or being dissected by a saw or being battered with large rocks would be easier for him to bear than a single moment of the process of his death."[43] These are only descriptive metaphors while in fact, "the pangs of death are beyond description and cannot be fathomed by the inhabitants of this world."[44]

---

soul may undergo an intensified substantial motion (*al-ḥarakat al-ishtidādī*) towards animal tendencies. This occurs when the motion of the soul is not under the guiding control of the power of the intellect. As an example, if the power of anger or of lust is the constant dominant focus and inspiration, and a person can do whatever he desires, then one of these two powers will gradually come to control him. After a while it will draw most of the soul's attention towards it and will bring other powers under its influence also and overcome the entire soul. In this manner, instead of the power of the intellect - which is the noblest power – being in control, it will become subservient to the powers of anger and lust. In this situation the development of the immaterial soul will be towards becoming animalistic. Such a soul has departed from the state where its powers are balanced and employed logically; it will become like an ailing body in which some organs are weakened due to sickness or poor health management while other organs are engorged due to excessive fat. In the end this imbalance will destroy the body. (Syed Khalil Toussi, *Mabānī Falsafey-i Akhlāq-i Mullā Ṣadrā*, p. 72, 73.).

[41] *Nahj al-Balāgha*, sermon 109.

[42] Muttaqī al-Hindī, *Kanz al-'Ummāl*, trad 42158, quoting the Prophet (s) |

أَدْنَى جَذَبَاتِ الْمَوْتِ بِمَنْزِلَةِ مِائَةِ ضَرْبَةٍ بِالسَّيْفِ.

[43] Majlisī, *Biḥār al-Anwār*, 6:152, quoting Imam al-Sadiq (a) :

إِنَّهُ أَشَدُّ مِنْ نَشْرٍ بِالْمَنَاشِيرِ وَقَرْضٍ بِالْمَقَارِيضِ وَرَضْخٍ بِالْأَحْجَارِ.

[44] *Nahj al-Balāgha*, sermon 220 |

He understands absolutely nothing of the instructions that the angels are giving him; everything appears strange and incomprehensible to him. On the one hand he has just been wrenched away from the world to which he was so attached, and on the other he has been brought to a world which he does not recognize or understand, where everybody else despises him; he is both bewildered and horrified at the turn of events. He dearly wants to return to *dunyā* but the angels of death strike him from the back and pull him forward; and as he is unwillingly driven deeper into that realm, the angels of *barzakh* strike his face in disgust, "*But if you could only see when the angels take the souls of those who disbelieved; they smite their faces and their backs.*"[45]

Now he is left alone with his corrupt and unpleasant personality, by which he himself is also nauseated. His heart is filled with sorrow, a sorrow that he knows will never be dispelled except if God wills so; but all his life he had harboured hostility towards God and now he is unable to call out to Him because he cannot withstand His limitless Purity. At this time, the purest of individuals of the realm like Jesus (a) and Moses (a) and Muhammad (s) and Ali (a), who had sincerely called to God throughout their lives, appear before his eyes.[46] However, they do not invite him towards God anymore because the time for guidance has passed and the time for consequences has arrived. Seeing them only increases his distress and sorrow and intense remorse courses through him.

إِنَّ لِلْمَوْتِ لَغَمَرَاتٍ هِيَ أَفْظَعُ مِنْ أَنْ تُسْتَغْرَقَ بِصِفَةٍ، أَوْ تَعْتَدِلَ عَلَى عُقُولِ أَهْلِ الدُّنْيَا.

[45] Surat al-Anfāl, 8:50.

[46] Muhammadī, Muhammad Ray Shahrī, *Mīzān al-Ḥikma*, 4:2973, quoting Imam al-Sadiq (a)

No Chance for Repentance and Return

At this point, he is desperate to reform and repent, "*But repentance is not accepted from those who continue with their evil conduct until, when death comes to one of them, he says, "Now I repent"; nor for those who die while they are disbelievers. For them we have prepared a painful torment.*"[47] This is because his personality has already taken shape and his inner form is already fixed on a foundation of impurity. "*The repentance accepted by God is only for those who do wrong in ignorance and repent soon afterwards. It is they to whom God will turn in forgiveness; and God is all-Knowing, all-Wise.*"[48] The time for repentance is now and here, before death. We can repent while we still breathe, while we can still think and speak, while we can still weep; but once the identity and personality is sealed and the cup of life shatters, it is too late. How can he reform now when he is no longer even able to move of his own accord? He can no longer make up his lapsed prayers or come to the aid of anyone. He cannot show compassion to the orphan, or feed the hungry, or help the weary, or even weep in remorse. He forsook all the goodness of the world and filled his life with its vices. That which will perplex him the most is that it will appear that death was no more than crossing from one side of a wall to the other; his eyes and ears and limbs and body seem to be intact, except that what these angels are teaching is exactly the opposite of what he used to do in the world. It is at this point that he dearly wishes he could return and live his life differently. If only he had another chance, he would bring back with him something that would be useful here; perhaps he will be allowed to return for one week, one day or just a single

[47] Surat al-Nisā' 4:18.

[48] Surat al-Nisā' 4:17.

hour. Despair courses through him when his wish is denied, "*When death comes to one of them (the disbelievers) he says, "My Lord! Send me back so that I may act righteously to put right that which I left behind." Never! These are just vain words.*"[49] This is because the tree of his existence has borne no fruit of worth. Its rotten produce is apparent and there is no reason to believe that such a tree would ever produce anything else. In any case, what he now desires is against the system of creation; once a soul has travelled into that realm there is no way for its return back to *dunyā*, until the day when the entire universe evolves and *dunyā* is transformed into *ākhira.* But till then, "*Behind them is a barrier until the Day they are resurrected*".[50] Every bridge behind him has been destroyed. All that remains with him now is his repulsive personality with which he has to live and travel on, a long journey in a land of misery.

[49] Surat al-Mu'minūn, 23:99,100.

[50] Surat al-Mu'minūn, 23:100.

CHAPTER 2

BARZAKH - THE INTERMEDIATE REALM

The Entry of the Soul into *Barzakh*

The soul's entry into *barzakh* is in some ways similar to arriving in a new country and encountering a foreign culture; everything appears strange and intriguing. It is very disconcerting for the soul to observe the physical body that it was long accustomed to lie lifeless before it, while it itself remains healthy and vital in a new body. However, although it now occupies a new body, it cannot yet separate its identity from the lifeless corpse that remains before it. This fills it with both wonder and fear.[51]

In addition, the enhanced abilities of the imaginal body are initially very confusing for the soul; the new body is lighter, suppler, and much more perceptive. The soul can now see and hear things that were imperceptible to it in the material world. The body has no sign of flesh and bones, or nerves

---

[51] Mullā Ṣadrā explains this phenomenon in this way, "After the soul leaves the physical body it still maintains a weak connection to it, because forms and figures are retained in its memory. This is due to the fact that when the soul separates from the body it takes with it the imaginal faculty which is the source of particular perceptions and it can employ this to perceive physical forms." (Mullā Ṣadrā, *al-Mabda' wa'l Ma'ād*, p. 474) Therefore, after death the soul perceives material entities like its former body through the faculty of imagination. At the same time, it can perceive beings from the afterlife who do not reside in the material realm. When the soul leaves the body as a person dies, it is cognizant of its independent existence and of its perceptive ability. It views its own existence within its faculty of imagination but imagines itself as one with the body that has been put in the grave. As a result, it initially imagines that the punishments and rewards experienced in *barzakh* are being administered to its former physical body.

or a brain, yet the soul can feel and see and hear and sense. Its perceptive organs are made of materials and systems completely unfamiliar to it. It is like a new-born child, except that it has intelligence and is very aware of the world around it. A world that is so different from the one it has thus far experienced that it cannot fathom much of it at all.

The soul will soon become familiar with this new world but interestingly, at this stage, its bond with the previous, material realm is not yet severed. Although it no longer has access to physical eyes, ears and limbs to see, hear and touch, it still continues to think in material terms in those first moments. The phenomena that it encounters are seen and processed as we do in our dreams. However, this hazy sense of reality is different for different individuals. The alertness and insight of souls is greater or lesser in proportion to their levels of purity.

Although the soul now resides in the imaginal body, it still retains a strong empathy and bond with its former material body. In fact, the soul's awareness of events of the material world is made possible by this persistent relationship with its previous body. Perhaps that is why many souls witness all the stages of washing, shrouding and burial of the corpse.[52]

Burial

With the exception of the case of the sincere and purified servants of God, the burial of the body is one of the most difficult experiences that the soul undergoes as it enters the intermediate realm of *barzakh*.

After the angels have transferred the soul into the imaginal world (*'ālam al-mithāl, barzakh*), and activated its new subtle body, the soul remains in its new form like a person in the

[52] Refer to the previous footnote.

middle of a vast desert with no knowledge of his destination or resources. It is not aware of other souls because it has not yet been taken to the place where they reside. It is in a quarantine of sorts. As we have mentioned, at this point its attention is still directed towards the realm it has just left and the place where the body it used to occupy is resting. It witnesses many of the events that the body goes through and follows his corpse wherever it is taken.

It is very difficult to understand the nature of the relationship of the soul to the body at this stage, however many traditions and reports inform us that the thought of the body being buried into the ground fills the soul with fear and anxiety. It sees the place of burial of the body as its new residence also. Although it knows that it has another place and position in the new world it has entered, the thought of being confined in this small grave fills it with dread. We will discuss later the issue of time and space in the relationship of the inhabitants of the imaginal world with those yet in the material world.

Every stage of the burial is distressing and frightening for the soul, but the most terrifying time is when the body is finally lowered into the ground and the soul witnesses the depths of the grave. As we have mentioned before, when the soul is separated from the body, it is aware of its identity and is completely conscious throughout. But when it thinks of itself, it still considers itself one with the body in the grave; in fact, it mistakenly imagines that it is still in the body and identifies completely with whatever is being done to it.

It is for this reason that the soul in the *barzakhi* body imagines that the pain or pleasure that it is experiencing is actually being visited onto its former, material body. Therefore, it is frightened of being covered underground because it feels that it is being buried alive. At this time, it begins to realize the truth of what has happened; it realizes that they are truly preparing to send him to the next world.[53] It is unable to do anything and helplessly accompanies the body, as if it is still attached to it.

The Squeezing of the Grave

When a person's grave is filled with earth, it does not cover him, because his soul is already living in another dimension, and viewing the grave from the imaginal world. Nevertheless, as the soil begins to pour down on his former body, he experiences an indescribable choking and crushing. It is of a severity that is proportional to that world, not this one. Once more, he is unable to distinguish between his material body and his imaginal one and finally understands what people meant when they talked about the squeezing of the grave. Now he experiences a terrible bone-crushing compression which feels like his entire body is being squeezed through the eye of a needle. We do not know how this squeezing happens and what its purpose is, but very few people will be excused from it, "There is no believer who will not experience the squeezing".[54]

It is as if the squeezing is designed to wring out every last trace of impurity and pollution from the person. In fact, this process is of benefit to the believers whose righteous faith is mixed with traces of pollution from their wrongful thoughts and deeds and is "an atonement for squandering God's bounties"[55] and wasting opportunities. However, for

[53] This is what is referred to in traditions as the "terror of the time of vision (of the grave's depth)" (*hawl al-maṭṭla'*) (See Ṣadūq, *'Ilal al-Sharāya'*, 1/306.

[54] Majlisī, *Biḥār al-Anwār*, 6/221, quoting Imam al-Sadiq (a):

إِنَّهُ لَيْسَ مِنْ مُؤْمِنٍ إِلَّا وَلَهُ ضَمَّةٌ.

[55] Ṣadūq, *Thawāb al-A'māl*, p. 190 |

ضَغْطَةُ الْقَبْرِ لِلْمُؤْمِنِ كَفَّارَةٌ لِمَا كَانَ مِنْهُ مِنْ تَضْيِيعِ النِّعَمِ.

those whose entire beings are impure, the process results in nothing but excruciating suffering. The dead person does not know how long the squeezing will last and when it will end, but it consumes him completely, rendering him oblivious of what is happening in the world around him.

The Loneliness of the Grave

When the squeezing abates and his relatives and friends have long departed from the graveyard, the soul is overcome with a deep sense of isolation and loneliness in the imaginal world of the grave. He is no longer aware of the happenings of the material world, or of the angels, or even the dead in other graves. The environment in the grave is unfamiliar and frightening. He has no idea how long he will remain trapped in this desolate chamber, nor does he know what will happen in the next moment. It is at this point that the experiences of people vary. Those who held no belief in the afterlife are absolutely unable to understand how they are still alive in their own bodies after having died and been buried. Those who believed in an afterlife but had only a vague understanding of its reality are awestruck by the mysterious world that they have entered into.

The isolation of the grave affects everyone. They have witnessed strange and mysterious events and they do not know what other wonders to expect. They do not know whether they will move from this place. Have they been abandoned in this bleak chamber for eternity? Will God, with all His Majesty and Grandeur bother with this insignificant and worthless creature? It is at this moment that the faith of the believer and his intimate relationship and constant reliance on God give rise to a flame of hope, while the ingratitude and faithlessness of the disbeliever envelops him in the cold cloak of dread.

The Activation of the Spiritual Memory

We have mentioned that even in our material world, human beings possess two bodies, a corporeal or material body and a spiritual or imaginal body. At the time of death, the soul disconnects from the material body and enters into the world of *barzakh* clothed in its imaginal body. This body also possesses eyes and ears to see and hear the entities of the imaginal realm. However, the most important faculty that it possesses is the individual's spiritual memory which is installed in the imaginal body and preserves all that had happened in the material world. In *dunyā*, the access of the material body itself to its stored memories is limited; the memories themselves are subject to limitations of detail and furthermore, recall becomes erratic or impossible as brain cells fail with age and illness. However, the accuracy of the spiritual memory in comparison is strikingly precise. No event in the individual's entire life is forgotten; no scene, no deed, no word, no intent, no thought or influence remains except that every detail of it is indelibly etched in the spiritual memory. In fact, these memories are embedded into the soul, becoming a permanent part of it and giving it shape.

While the individual occupies the material body, he is unaware of the existence of the spiritual memory and has no access to it, except occasionally in an unconscious state. After death, this memory needs to be activated, but the individual must have the aid of an angel to accomplish this.

Rūmān, the Angel who Reminds

The arrival of Rūmān, the angel who "enlivens graves and rouses the dead" (*fattān al-qubūr wa malakun munabbih*), brings the vigil in the grave to an end and transforms it into a solemn and ethereal scene.[56] The imaginal grave begins to expand and becomes dazzlingly bright. A handsome and imposing angel enters the grave. The individual who has recently departed the world is yet unsure of the functions of the fascinating beings he has begun to see and does not know what they will want of him. Each new encounter is a source of increased trepidation. In some, this new arrival causes fear, in others apprehension, and in some, relief and solace. The splendour of Rūmān is beyond description; certainly no one like him could have been imagined in this world.

Every description of grandeur known to human beings could not do him justice. It would be like trying to compare the stars to earthly lights. It would seem that after having seen the angels of death, the individual should have become somewhat familiar with the sight of them; however, these angels are wondrous creatures, each unique with its own imposing qualities. The arrival of Rūmān confirms the fact that in spite of His Majesty, God has not forgotten this small creature who is waiting in his narrow grave.

The angel begins to speak, and introduces himself as Rūmān, the examiner in the grave. All understand his words because in this new world there is only one language. The variety of languages that were stored in the material memory of individuals all vanish, and everyone communicates in the innate language of the soul, which is already coded into the spiritual memory. This language has more to do with the exchange of concepts rather than words and phrases.

The Swedish Christian scholar, thinker, and mystical philosopher, Emanuel Swedenborg (1688 – 1772) wrote a

[56] In Shīʿī traditions there are allusions to Rūmān in very general terms. For example, Imam Sajjād (a) has mentioned him in one of his supplications in *Ṣahīfat al-Sajjādiyya*. What has been mentioned here is from Sunnī sources. (Ref: *Biḥār al-Anwār*, 56:234).

valuable work about life after death and claimed that the contents of his book were entirely based on his personal visions and observations of the after-world.[57]

He has explained these visions in an eloquent and compelling style and the conviction and honesty in his words are evident.

According to his experience, the language of the people of *barzakh* is such that single words communicate complex details; it would require several volumes in our current languages to achieve the same result. Information is transferred in an instant, while the same task would perhaps require hours of explanation in our world.[58]

This is achieved by the imparting of wisdom and information in a compressed form which can be deciphered and understood by the imaginal senses and mind. Furthermore, the language allows for a much more accurate and deeper transfer of thoughts and feelings.

In any case, the function of Rūmān is to activate the spiritual memory of the individual in the grave. He does this by instructing the new arrival to write down the details of his life, "Write down every deed that you committed in the world, every good and evil that issued from you, everything that you should have done but did not - write it all down." The individual does not know what writing means in that world and remains still and confused. But Rūmān teaches him how. Writing paper is not required here, because he will not be writing down words. Rather, he will be recording events, just as they occurred. It is as if he is reliving every moment

[57] Some excerpts from his work are mentioned in this section, especially when they conform to the Qur'an and traditions. For further information, see: Emanuel Swedenborg, *Heaven and its Wonders and Hell: From Things Heard and Seen*, Philadelphia: Lippincott company, 1892.

[58] Swedenborg, p.239, 240.

of the past once more, more vividly and fully than before. It will seem surreal, but what he saw in three dimensions before will now come forth from his memory in all its multi-dimensional aspects, revealing every layer of the act. Indeed, it is an amazing night, this first night in the grave.

He will say, "I cannot mention everything, I am ashamed of writing my sinful deeds." On hearing this Rūmān will reply in a tone that will shake the individual to the core of his being, "You were not ashamed in front of the Lord of the universe, but you say that you are ashamed in front of me?"

The whole countenance of Rūmān changes when he utters the words, "Lord of the universe". His striking presence is transformed into a posture of humility, meekness and adoration. Then, he says flatly, "I will make you recollect everything. I am the angel who makes you relive your life." Rūmān forces him to focus and with his help, his spiritual memory awakens and every moment of his life, from his birth to the instant of his death, is arrayed before his eyes.

What he sees is not a picture from his memory; rather every moment is experienced again. Not only does he relive his words and his deeds, but he also recalls the thoughts and intent at the moment of acting; the delight, the sorrow, the anticipation and in short, he feels again every emotion that accompanied that particular deed. What a wondrous creature Rūmān is, effortlessly drawing the deepest memories to the surface. And the individual writes down everything helplessly. He transfers his whole life into the book that Rūmān has brought for him; he fills it, not with words and phrases, but with entire events.

The deeds he records are not in the form he has known in the world, rather, they assume forms that are more mysterious and cryptic. In fact, the deeds we produce in this world find existence in three states or three dimensions; the first has effects in this material world, the second has its effects in the imaginal world or *barzakh*, and the third exists in the intellectual world in *qiyāma* or the Day of Judgement. Every act that we do assumes a shape in all three worlds simultaneously. The effects in the material world can be witnessed by all but the other two forms are veiled behind the curtains of *barzakh* and the Day of Judgement, and will only be witnessed and understood as these curtains are removed in time.[59] Therefore, what is now becoming apparent to him and what he records in his book is the *barzakhi* form of the actions he committed in the world. It is not the material form, nor is it yet the ultimate form which will only be visible on the Day of Judgement.

Rūmān takes the book and hangs it around the owner's neck. The book disappears, becoming a part of the individual; it is as if Rūmān has inserted it into him, making it one with him. The effects of his entire life have been collected in one place and melded with his being. What he perceives now is not his personality at that particular moment but his personality spanning his entire lifetime handed to him in a compressed form. Before this, and before the activation of his spiritual memory, he could never have imagined the net effect of his entire lifetime of thoughts, words and deeds. It is for this reason that no one in this world can truly know themselves fully and in depth.

Rūmān informs him that, "This is your book of existence and it shall remain closed inside you until the day that God brings mankind forth from their graves; and then the book will be opened."[60]

---

[59] Tehrānī, Muhamad Husain Husaini, *Maʿād Shināsī*, 4:26.

[60] Abdallah b. Salām narrates: I asked the Prophet (s) about the first angel

For most people these words would be difficult to assimilate, because Rūmān has caused the deceased to see for the first time the achievement of his life, which has hitherto remained hidden to him.

In fact, at this stage this is only the display of the *barzakhi* aspect of his book, and the true reality of his existence, which is the *qiyāmati* aspect, has not yet been revealed to him. This book and its contents are still in a cocoon state awaiting the advent of the Day of Judgement when they will emerge in their final state. Only on that Day will the true worth of an individual's existence be realized.

After accomplishing his role, Rūmān departs, and the grave becomes lonely again. Once more its occupant waits, but this time the vigil is different. The one whose book was full of virtuous and worthy deeds is filled with an indescribable

---

to appear in front of the deceased before Munkar and Nakīr. He replied, "It is an angel whose face is as radiant as the sun, whose name is Rūmān. He enters the grave and commands the deceased to write down all his deeds, the good and the bad. The deceased asks, "With what shall I write? Where is the pen and the ink?" He will reply, "Your saliva is your ink and your forefinger is your pen." He will ask, "On what shall I write, for I have no paper?" He will be told, "Your shroud is your paper, so write!" So, he begins to record his good deeds, but becomes embarrassed to write his bad deeds. The angel says to him, "O sinner! You were not ashamed when you committed these acts in front of your Creator, and you are ashamed now?" And the angel lifts a club to strike him. The deceased pleads, "Do not punish me, I will write it down!" And he records on it everything he ever did, good and bad. Then the angel commands him to close the record and seal it. He asks, "How shall I seal my record when I have no seal?" The angel instructs him to seal it with his fingernail, and then hangs the record on his neck, where it shall remain until the Day of Judgement. This is as God has stated in the Qur'an, "*And We have made every man's actions to cling to his neck, and We will bring forth to him on the resurrection day a book which he will find wide open.*" Surat al-Isrā' (17:13). (Madanī, Syed Ali Khan, *Riyāḍ al-Sālikīn fī Sharḥ Ṣaḥīfatu Sayyid al-Sājidīn*, 2:66,67).

relief and peace. The beauty of his book of deeds suffuses his entire being. After his loneliness and anxiety, he is now aware of the company of a comforting presence. He notices a beautiful countenance and asks, “Who are you?” It says, “I am the embodiment of your good deeds.”[61]

However, for the one who was only reminded by Rūmān of the vileness of his conduct, and whose book is full of evil, the grave now becomes a place of fear and dread. He becomes aware of the presence of a noxious and repulsive being, whose company adds to the terror of the narrow and dark confines of the grave.

The Prophet mentioned to Qays b. Mālik in this regard, “Know that you have no choice, O Qays, except to be buried with a companion who is alive, while you are dead. If the companion is noble, then he will honour you, but if he is of evil character, then he will overpower you. He will only be resurrected with you, and you will only come forth with him. You will not be questioned about anything other than him. Therefore, do not allow your companion to be anything but good, so that you may form a close bond with him, because if he is evil, you will not be repulsed by anything more than by him... And he is nothing other than the embodiment of your actions.[62]

Ranking of Human Beings

[61] Majlisī, *Biḥār al-Anwār*, 8:209, quoting the Prophet (s) |

فَتَجِيءُ صُورَةٌ حَسَنَةٌ فَيَقُولُ: مَا أَنْتَ؟ فَيَقُولُ: أَنَا عَمَلُكَ الصَّالِحُ.

[62] Ṣadūq, al-Khiṣāl, p. 114 |

وَإِنَّهُ لَا بُدَّ لَكَ يَا قَيْسُ مِنْ قَرِينٍ يُدْفَنُ مَعَكَ وَهُوَ حَيٌّ، وَتُدْفَنُ مَعَهُ وَأَنْتَ مَيِّتٌ، فَإِنْ كَانَ كَرِيمًا أَكْرَمَكَ، وَإِنْ كَانَ لَئِيمًا أَسْلَمَكَ، ثُمَّ لَا يُحْشَرُ إِلَّا مَعَكَ وَلَا تُبْعَثُ إِلَّا مَعَهُ وَلَا تُسْأَلُ إِلَّا عَنْهُ، فَلَا تَجْعَلْهُ إِلَّا صَالِحًا فَإِنَّهُ إِنْ صَلَحَ أَنِسْتَ بِهِ، وَإِنْ فَسَدَ لَا تَسْتَوْحِشُ إِلَّا مِنْهُ ، وَهُوَ فِعْلُكَ.

After the summoning of the spiritual memory and the determination of the *barzakhi* persona of human beings – which is formed from their deeds in the world – people are divided into three broad groups. The first is the group of those who led an exemplary life; any pollution that they may have had has been cleansed by the process of death.

The second is the group of those who are completely impure and any virtue they possessed is lost in their impurity. The third is the group in the middle, with evil and virtue both present. Within this last group there is a great diversity of levels. This third group is left alone after their encounter with Rūmān,[63] and allowed to begin their *barzakhi* life. Later we will talk about this group in some detail.

As for the first two groups, they have to pass another stage, and that is the questioning in the grave.

Questioning in the Grave

The fate of the people in the first two groups in *barzakh* is quite different from those of the third group, who have been left alone. The first group, who were completely pure, are immediately admitted into the Paradise of *barzakh* and given the glad tidings of heaven in the Hereafter as well. As a consequence, all fear and sorrow leave them. As for the second group, who are completely impure, they are led directly to the Hell of *barzakh* and are promised the torment of Hell in the Hereafter. Consequently, they are filled with remorse and despair.

The people in the third group will remain in a state between hope and fear until the Day of Judgement when their fate would be decided. When the Commander of the faithful (a)

---

[63] Kulaynī, al-Kāfī, 3/235 | فَيُلْهَى عَنْهُمْ.

was asked about death he replied, "Death is one of three states: it is the receiving of good news of eternal bliss, or the bad news of eternal torment, or it is the sorrow and fear of one who does not know which group he belongs to."[64]

Since the fate of the first two groups becomes clear at the first stage and in the first night, they move to a further stage which is not experienced by the third group. This is the questioning in the grave. In fact, this is just a final stage to confirm their permanent abodes.

Therefore, most people – who make up the third group – do not experience the questioning in the grave. It has been narrated from Imam al-Sadiq (a) that he said, "Only the exemplary believers and the absolute disbelievers are questioned in the grave. All others are left alone."[65]

The questioning in the grave which is carried out by designated angels is actually a validation of the personalities of the people of the first and second groups so that they can be sent to their eternal abodes.

In other words, everyone who enters into the world of *barzakh* is met by angels who cater to their needs and who attempt to familiarize them with God and the after-world and the new life of *barzakh*, and to introduce them to a deeper understanding of reality.

Since the people of the middle group are yet unable to affirm or reject these truths, they are left alone until they have spent sufficient time in the world of *barzakh* for their

---

[64] Ṣadūq, *Maʿānī al-Akhbār*, p. 288 |

هُوَ أَحَدُ ثَلَاثَةِ أُمُورٍ يَرِدُ عَلَيْهِ، إِمَّا بِشَارَةٌ بِنَعِيمِ الْأَبَدِ وَإِمَّا بِشَارَةٌ بِعَذَابِ الْأَبَدِ، وَإِمَّا تَحْزِينٌ وَتَهْوِيلٌ وَأَمْرٌ مُبْهَمٌ لَا يَدْرِي مِنْ أَيِّ الْفِرَقِ هُوَ.

[65] Kulaynī, *al-Kāfī*, 3 /235 |

إِنَّمَا يُسْأَلُ فِي قَبْرِهِ مَنْ مَحَضَ الْإِيمَانَ مَحْضًا، وَمَنْ مَحَضَ الْكُفْرَ مَحْضًا، وَأَمَّا مَا سِوَى ذَلِكَ فَيُلْهَى عَنْهُمْ.

situation to become clearer. It is for this reason that this group does not experience the presence of the interrogating angels in the first instance.

Nakīr and Munkar

The corrupt individuals used to mock these truths in *dunyā*, both by word and deed. They spent their days in self-serving and vain activities, making no attempt to understand the deeper reality of their existence. But now they are subjected to a difficult examination; this is because instead of submitting to the truth, they chose the path of obstinacy and resistance, thus manifesting their true personality.

For them nothing is more distressing and painful than their encounter with these two angels, whose terrifying appearance causes them to lose any remaining sense of composure and control. The angels petrify them when they suddenly materialize from the surrounding earth, appearing to cleave through the ground with their teeth.[66] Their voices reverberate like thunder while their gaze is as piercing as lightning.[67] In appearance these two angels are truly Nakīr and Munkar, meaning "ugly" and "fearsome", because the individuals' inner pollution has distorted their perception – they see beauty as ugliness and vileness as pleasant.

The role of these angels is quite different from that of Rūmān. They are not there to remind, rather they have come to both evaluate and validate that which Rūmān has brought out so that the worthiness of the deceased individual can

---

[66] Majlisī, *Biḥār al-Anwār*, 6/225 |

يَبْحَثَانِ الْأَرْضَ بِأَنْيَابِهِمَا.

[67] Ibid |

أَصْوَاتُهُمَا كَالرَّعْدِ الْقَاصِفِ وَأَبْصَارُهُمَا كَالْبَرْقِ الْخَاطِفِ.

be assessed, and an appropriate abode and provision be assigned to him in the world of the dead.

However, what does worthiness mean in this place and what are the parameters for assessing it? In the *dunyā*, their worth and status was directly linked to several factors: their wealth, their clothes, their houses and their cars. It was related to their social and political links, their friends and who they knew. It was related to their education, their qualifications, their manner, the books that they had read, the languages they knew, the amount of travelling they had done. However, here it is doubtful whether Nakīr and Munkar would be impressed with these accomplishments. This is the realm of *malakūt* of God and here everything is to do with Him, first and last. It is for this reason that they open their questioning by asking, "Who is your God?"

This question is not meant to distress the new arrival, rather its purpose is to gauge the level of their understanding so as to be able to evaluate accordingly. In reality, these angels are not actually frightening at all; it is the individual's Satan-tinged soul and self-absorption that makes everything related to God appear frightening and bleak.

The poor soul searches into the depths of his being for an answer. Rūmān is not present here to prompt him and he does not know how to reply. He did not worship God during his time in the former world, nor did he bother to ask about Him. God was never relevant in his life, and he did not feel any adverse effects as a result. But now everything has changed. In this world God is the only important reference and yet he cannot perceive any trace of Him anywhere. The explanations offered by the two angels are not helpful either. Their efforts only perplex him further. No matter how hard they try, he does not understand what they are saying.

His silence and incomprehension enrage the angels and with angry faces they ask him who his Prophet was and what religion did he follow and what Scripture did he read. However, he cannot recall any prophet or any religion or any scripture. Nakīr and Munkar try to explain these things to him, but he does not understand. They ask him about his priorities in the world, how he passed his days, how he earned his living and where he spent his wealth.[68]

In the course of their lengthy interrogation, they gradually expose the deepest features of his character. Every question forces him to face the unpleasant truth that is reflected within the *barzakhi* manifestation of his actions. However, every time he tries to answer in a manner that is contrary to his true nature, desperately lying to justify his actions in this new world, he experiences a fiery response from Nakīr and Munkar in the form of a whip of fire lashing across his face, turning his grave into a blazing inferno. These two angels cannot be deceived in the least and lying to them brings immediate and painful retribution. It is almost as if they know the individual better than he knows himself. In that world, lying yields no result except grief and chastisement.

In any case, they continue to inspect every aspect of his conduct in the world, prodding his conscious and unconscious memory to examine the intention behind every good and evil deed he performed during his life, until he becomes aware of every inner layer of his character. Alas, this revelation fills him with nothing but despondency and remorse.

[68] You will be first asked about the God that you worshipped, then about the Messenger sent to you, and the religion you lived by and the Book that you followed, and about the Imam who was your authority. Thereafter, you will be asked about how you spent the years of your life, and how you earned your wealth and where you spent it. (Majlisī, quoting the Prophet (s), *Biḥār al-Anwār*, 6:221, from Ṣadūq who quotes Imam Zain al-ʿĀbidīn (a).

What he worked for day and night in *dunyā* is totally useless and incompatible with what is of value and meaning in this *barzakhi* phase of his life. He is shown once more his original human form; beautiful and pure and noble. It is as if these two angels have opened a window that overlooks Paradise, and he glimpses within it the beautiful vistas that were meant to be the eternal abodes of human beings. But soon these scenes are clouded over by the pollution that he has brought upon himself – seeing all this causes a burning remorse to suffuse his being. And then he experiences a deep sense of suffocation and darkness – it is as if Nakīr and Munkar are causing the walls of the grave to close tightly over him.

Suddenly, within the depths of his being a window opens towards the fire of Hell. He now experiences a terrible premonition about his future, and this fills his entire being with terror. Nakīr and Munkar create an opening between his grave and Hell, through which he begins to immediately feel its burning heat and punishment.[69]

He wants to be rid of the company of these angels as soon as possible. He does not want to hear their constant attempts to teach him about God anymore. He realizes that the punishment is more compatible with his nature than the remembrance of God. When the angels see that this is the case, they withdraw, and leave him in the Hell of his own creation. He who could not face the truth now turns

[69] He will see a door from heaven open into his grave through which its bounties are visible. Munkar and Nakīr will say to him, "Look at what you denied yourself." Thereafter, a door from Hell will open into his grave through which its punishment will be felt, and the deceased individual will cry out, "Lord, do not bring about the Day of Judgement, Lord do not bring about the Day of Judgement." (Majlisī, *Bihār al-Anwār*, 6:176). Similar traditions are found in Sunnī sources, for example, see a lengthy tradition of Barā' ibn 'Āzib from the Prophet (s) (al-Ṭabarānī, *al-Aḥādīth al-Ṭiwāl*, p. 65-67, trad. 25).

his mind away from it and defiantly ventures into the Hell of *barzakh*, turning his back on God and heading off in the opposite direction.

He will look for others like him and try to get to know them. It is as if there is a strong rope drawing him inexorably forward. It seems as if he wants to break free of God, Who was calling him to Himself, and get away as far as he can. However, because the essence of human beings is based on the love of God, and the heart's comfort only comes from His remembrance and proximity, every step he takes away only increases his misery, pain and frustration. His heart will not find peace with anyone else. *"Indeed, God is not unjust to men in the least, but men are unjust to themselves."*[70]

His being forms a black cloud that veils him from God, blocking the light of His grace – the grace that is available everywhere and to everyone. And in this manner, these polluted souls enter the Hell of *barzakh*.

Bashīr and Mubashshir

Let us now look at the pure souls. For them the two angels are not Nakīr and Munkar, but Bashīr and Mubashsher. In the words of Mufīd, "The two angels who come to the believers are called Bashīr and Mubashshir because they are messengers from God bringing the good news of eternal happiness and reward. These are not their names, but their titles, signifying the role that they perform."[71] Their appearance is not ugly and fearsome, but beautiful and

[70] Surat Yūnus, 10:44.

[71] Majlisī, *Bihār al-Anwār*, 6:280 |

قَالَ الشَّيْخُ الْمُفِيدُ: وَسُمِّيَ مَلَكَا الْمُؤْمِنِ مُبَشِّرًا وَبَشِيرًا، لِأَنَّهُمَا يُبَشِّرَانِهِ مِنَ اللهِ تَعَالَى بِالرِّضَا وَالثَّوَابِ الْمُقِيمِ، وَإِنَّ هَذَيْنِ الِاسْمَيْنِ لَيْسَا بِلَقَبٍ لَهُمَا، وَإِنَّهُمَا عِبَارَةٌ عَنْ فِعْلِهِمَا.

friendly.[72] Every question that they ask and every layer of his life that they expose to him is good news for him. He is able to reply confidently because the truth has saturated his heart and soul. There is nothing sweeter and more satisfying for him than witnessing the imaginal forms of the truths that he had learned and practised in his life as taught to him by God and mentioned in His Book and which the angels now recount before him. In fact, the angels reveal to him the deeper significances of his beliefs which cannot be grasped by those who have not yet entered that world.

Their language is vastly different from the languages of mankind, each word transferring to the heart of the listener wisdom that could not be contained even within several volumes in the corporeal world. They unravel truths which can only be comprehended in that world, as a result of which the deceased gains the deepest realization of the Majesty of God that he has yet experienced. And this greatly increases his eagerness to continue on the long journey ahead.

The horizons of his thoughts and comprehensions continue to expand, and the new arrival does not tire from listening to the illuminating murmur of the angels and learning from their great and wondrous wisdom.

Now that they have made him aware of every layer of his being and introduced him to a deeper cognizance of God, they open for the deceased a window to Paradise through which the breeze of God's mercy fills his grave with perfume and light and happiness. The angels enlarge his grave in proportion to his character and goodness until it resembles

---

[72] Kulaynī, *al-Kāfī*, 1:65 | Abu Baṣīr narrates that he asked Imam al-Sadiq (a), "May I be your ransom, is their appearance the same to both the believers and the disbelievers?" The Imam (a) said, "No."

a garden from the garden of Paradise. And in this way the pure souls enter the heaven of *barzakh*.[73]

The size of their new abode is different for everyone depending on their insight and cognizance of God. Of course, the expansiveness of their gardens is not in physical terms, just as "the grave" does not refer to the physical resting place; rather, the grave refers to the *barzakhi* life of the believer and its expansiveness is in spiritual and imaginal terms.[74]

The newly arrived soul is wonderstruck and elated. He does not know what to do or say next. He wonders whether it is possible to inform his friends and his community of how well God has dealt with him.[75] However, the angels tell him that this will not be possible. He will need to remain in this place in peace until God brings the dead to life once again. He is automatically drawn towards the window that connects his grave to the eternal Paradise beyond and wants to experience the bounties that lie in wait, but the two angels gently tell him that this also is not possible.

He must be patient and wait for all those who yet live to join him in this world and wait for the Day of resurrection. For him the sweetest anticipation is the coming of this Day and he prays with all his heart, "My Lord, bring about the Day of resurrection without delay."

---

[73] Majlisī, *Biḥār al-Anwār*, 6:275, quoting the Prophet (s) | "The grave is either a garden from the gardens of Paradise or a pit from the pits of Hellfire."

[74] Ṣadūq, *Amālī*, p. 365 |

فَيَفْسَحَانِ لَهُ فِي قَبْرِهِ مَدَّ بَصَرِهِ.

[75] *Rejoicing in what God has bestowed upon them of His bounty and desiring to share the good tidings with those who have not yet joined them...*" (Āl-'Imran, 3/170). This has been mentioned in the traditions also, for example, "His grave is expanded by seventy cubits on all sides, and it is filled with a brilliant light. Then he is told, "Sleep!" He asks, "Can I go back and inform my family about these blessings?" (Majlisī, *Biḥār al-Anwār*, 5:276, quoting the Prophet (s).

Meeting with Friends and Relatives

As he enters the Paradise of *barzakh*, the soul encounters his friends and relatives who had preceded him and is drawn to the group whose souls most closely match his own. Immediately on arrival, acquaintances gather around him, welcoming him and eagerly enquiring about mutual friends and he shares the news about each of them. If they find out that their relative or friend is still alive, they are delighted because they hope to be reunited with them after their death. But if he informs them that the person that they are asking about has already died, they are saddened because they realize that he has somehow been prevented from entering Paradise. It has been reported from Imam al-Sadiq (a) that, "Souls occupy forms that resemble human bodies and live in gardens of Paradise; they recognize and communicate with one another. And when a new arrival joins them, they leave him alone for a while to recover after his difficult experience. Then they ask him about different individuals: if he says that they were alive when he died, they become hopeful that he may join them, but if he says that they had died, they cry out, "He has fallen, fallen."[76]

The soul begins to explore the Paradise of *barzakh*. He meets with different groups of believers, finally attaching himself to the group with which he is most compatible. Imam Ali (a) said to a companion, "If the veil fell away from your eyes, you would see them congregated in small clusters."[77]

---

[76] Kulaynī, *al-Kafī*, 3:244, reporting from Imam al-Sadiq (a) |

إِنَّ الْأَرْوَاحَ فِي صِفَةِ الْأَجْسَادِ، فِي شَجَرَةٍ فِي الْجَنَّةِ، [تَ]تعَارَفُ وَ[تَ]تَسَائَلُ، فَإِذَا قَدِمَتِ الرُّوحُ عَلَى الْأَرْوَاحِ يَقُولُ: دَعُوهَا فَإِنَّهَا قَدْ أَفْلَتَتْ مِنْ هَوْلٍ عَظِيمٍ، ثُمَّ يَسْأَلُونَهَا، مَا فَعَلَ فُلَانٌ وَمَا فَعَلَ فُلَانٌ؟ فَإِنْ قَالَتْ لَهُمْ: تَرَكْتُهُ حَيًّا، اِرْتَجُوهُ، وَإِنْ قَالَتْ لَهُمْ: قَدْ هَلَكَ، قَالُوا: قَدْ هَوَى قَدْ هَوَى.

[77] Kulaynī, *al-Kafī*, 3:243 |

لَوْ كُشِفَ لَكَ لَرَأَيْتَهُمْ حَلَقًا حَلَقًا.

He recognizes members of his own group from their outward appearance because in that world, one's outward aspect is the mirror of one's inner nature. As soon as he finds this group, he experiences a deep affinity and attachment to them, as if he has known them all his life. He feels a greater love for them than he does for his own parents and siblings. It is at this point that he chooses his place in Paradise. "*He says: All praise is due to God, Who has made good to us His promise, and He has made us inherit the land; so that we may abide in the garden wherever we please...*"[78]

He feels completely at home here and cannot imagine better company to spend his days with. This feeling is because in *barzakh* and the afterlife, the factor that cause attraction or repulsion between people is the similarity in their previous deeds and their inner characteristics, and these two qualities mould their outward features. It is for this reason that the members of these individual groups resemble one another, as if they are children of one father and mother.

In the same way, the soul that has entered the *barzakhi* Hell meets and gets to know its inmates. However, in Hell there is no welcome, only hate and malevolence - everybody tries to intimidate and subjugate everyone else. Here also the new arrival wanders amongst the different groups until he encounters one whose members match his own status. He attaches himself to this group even though every one of them is the enemy of the other.

The People of the Middle State

As we stated previously, the people of the middle state do not experience the questioning of the grave or meet the angels who expose the soul's true nature to itself. This is because

[78] Surat al-Zumar, 39:74. Although this verse is about the eternal Paradise of *akhīra*, it is nonetheless quite relevant to the Paradise of *barzakh* also.

their nature has not yet crystallized into pure good or pure evil and consequently, they are not entered into heaven or Hell. They will inhabit a place between the two and live a limited degree of life in *barzakh*. The level of their existence is proportional to the goodness or evil that they possess and can be a time of relative comfort and contentment or one of constant anxiety and dejection. In other words, those souls that are purer will be drawn towards the Paradise of *barzakh* and will begin to experience comfort and joy as a result. According to a report, Imam al-Baqir (a) said about these people that, "A passage will be created between their graves and the Paradise that God has created in the west (that is, of the *barzakhi* realm). Through this they will experience comfort and peace until the Day of Judgement when they will meet their Lord and account for their good and evil deeds. Thereafter, they will go to heaven or Hell. These are the people whose fate depends on God's decree."[79]

And those who are more impure will similarly be attracted to the Hell of *barzakh* and its flames will burn them, "A passage will be created between their graves and the Hell that God has created in the east (that is, the Hell of the *barzakhi* realm). Through this they will feel its scorching heat; smoke and scalding water will enter into their graves."[80] What these passages may mean and how they connect people to either Hell or Paradise shall remain unknown to all but those who experience it. This situation will persist until the Day of Judgement arrives and their ultimate fate is decided.

---

[79] Kulaynī, *al-Kāfī*, 3/247, reporting from Imam al-Baqir (a) |
يُخَدُّ لَهُ خَدٌّ إِلَى الْجَنَّةِ الَّتِي خَلَقَهَا اللهُ فِي الْمَغْرِبِ، فَيَدْخُلُ عَلَيْهِ مِنْهَا الرَّوْحُ فِي حُفْرَتِهِ إِلَى يَوْمِ الْقِيَامَةِ، فَيَلْقَى اللهَ، فَيُحَاسِبُهُ بِحَسَنَاتِهِ وَسَيِّئَاتِهِ، فَإِمَّا إِلَى الْجَنَّةِ، وَإِمَّا إِلَى النَّارِ، فَهَؤُلَاءِ مَوْقُوفُونَ لِأَمْرِ اللهِ.

[80] Ibid |
يُخَدُّ لَهُمْ خَدٌّ إِلَى النَّارِ الَّتِي خَلَقَهَا اللهُ فِي الْمَشْرِقِ، فَيَدْخُلُ عَلَيْهِمْ مِنْهَا اللَّهَبُ وَالشَّرَرُ وَالدُّخَانُ وَفَوْرَةُ الْحَمِيمِ.

They too meet and recognize the people who have arrived before them.

Emanuel Swedenborg, whom we have mentioned before as someone who frequently witnessed the realm of *barzakh* in his visions, calls this place the "world of spirits". He describes it as a valley between a maze of mountains. From this world, guarded doorways lead off to heaven and Hell, but these entrances are only visible to those who are being prepared to pass through them.[81] He says that after some time these groups enter the Paradise of *barzakh* or are driven towards the Hell of *barzakh;* but according to our traditions they remain in these valleys until the Day of Judgement, except for a very small group which are the exception. What we have in the traditions is just that a passage or window is opened between the grave and the *barzakhi* Paradise or Hell; it is possible that Swedenborg saw the same thing but described it as an entry into Paradise or Hell.

Swedenborg says that during this period the people of the middle state go through three stages: an outer life, an inner life and a period of preparation. The outer or exterior life may last from a few days to several months after death. At this time the soul lives in a manner similar to its life in *dunyā*. In our world, an individual normally masks his inner thoughts and intentions from others, and usually his outward actions do not reflect his real inner convictions.

In the *dunyā* he was so habituated to outwardly conforming to social norms and etiquettes that he ignored or was even unfamiliar of his inner nature, hardly thinking about what he really stood for. However, in *barzakh* this dichotomy between inner and outer states cannot continue. Gradually and unwittingly, the soul is influenced by his true inner

---

[81] Swedenborg, Section 429.

nature and is drawn towards other souls whose inner nature matches his own. After a while, his movements, his expressions and even his outward appearance changes to reflect his inner reality. What had always remained hidden during his life in the *dunyā* now becomes manifest. At this second stage, those who possessed an evil nature take on demon-like features and a window from the Hell of *barzakh* is opened into their abode.[82]

As for those whose inner nature was good, they must pass through a third stage before a window from the Paradise of *barzakh* is opened into their grave, and this is the stage of preparation. During this time, the angels instruct them about the meaning of Paradise and proximity to God and the blissful life in heaven, so that they are able to take delight when they have a small window opened into their grave from the Paradise of *barzakh*. Such instruction is not possible for those who have been connected to the Hell of *barzakh*, because they would only understand these meanings when a camel could pass through the eye of a needle. For the righteous, the transition from the outer to the inner life will be like awakening from sleep, or like walking into the light from the darkness. For the evil though, it will be exactly the opposite.

Furthermore, here every type of vice will create a particular effect on the soul and the imaginal body. For example,[83] an individual who considered himself superior to everyone else, was immersed in self-love and always acted only in self-interest will find himself intensely dull-witted and in fact, insane. This is because self-love takes a person away from Paradise, and the further one is from Paradise, the more distant he is from intellect and wisdom.

---

82 According to Swedenborg, they enter into the Hell of *barzakh*.

83 These examples are from the visions of Swedenborg. (Swedenborg, passage 508).

There will be some who added deviousness to their self-love and used deceit and guile to raise their station in the eyes of people; these will be in the company of the vilest of creation and such will be their madness that they will even hatch plots to storm into heaven and try to lay it to waste!

Their insane behaviour will bring down on them severe punishment. It can be said that the lashes of punishment that are visited upon them are either due to their behaviour in *barzakh* or their acts during their life in *dunyā*; in fact, there is no difference, because what he does in *barzakh* is an echo of his deeds in *dunyā*. In any case, the punishment is designed to deter them from acting on their mad impulses.

Another group is that of religious authorities who used religion to further their own ambitions and arbitrarily forgave the sins of the people and claimed for themselves that position that belongs only to God. Such people, aside from insanity will also be immersed in a darkness that will cause them pain.

Those who attributed creation to a natural accident, and thus denied God's role, will gather with like-minded individuals and will exhibit animal-like behaviour. If they encounter anyone who exhibits some power, they will begin to worship him. Swedenborg further states that he has even seen individuals who had been considered learned and wise scholars in the world reduced to this demeaning state.

It should be emphasized that the souls in *barzakh* are much freer to act than they were formerly, because in the *dunyā*, an individual may not act according to his innermost desires for many reasons. His outward behaviour is not always freely chosen by his inner self. However, in the life of *barzakh* these restrictions are absent, and everyone's behaviour is exactly according to their inner desires and inclinations, which were formed in *dunyā*. Here, admonition and education are not enough to stop the soul from acting out according to its real nature and the only thing that forestalls their Satanic impulses is not the fear of punishment but the punishment itself.

From the foregoing, we can conclude that every individual finds his place in *barzakh* and lives a life according to his character and disposition. He seeks out like-minded companions for himself and settles in their company. The function of angels such as Rūmān and Munkar and Nakīr and Bashīr and Mubashshir is merely to guide him to a place that is suitable for him and facilitate the path for him. The Qur'an says: *I swear by the night when it draws a veil over everything, and the day when it shines in brightness, and the creating of the male and the female; your striving is indeed diverse. Then as for him who shares his wealth, and is God-wary, and believes in the reward of the good (heaven), We will soon prepare for him an easy passage. And as for him who is niggardly and considers himself free from need (of God) and rejects the reward of the good (heaven), We will soon prepare for him a difficult passage.*[84]

Whatever we desired and loved in the *dunyā* will remain with us in the next world and it is these inclinations that will elevate or lower the station of our souls in *barzakh*. And this attachment will be even stronger on the Day of Judgement with the manifestation of the ultimate (*qiyāmati*) face of our deeds.

It is true that it is God who assigns each individual his particular station in *barzakh*; however, it becomes clear from what we have mentioned above that these assignations are not made at whim. For instance, it would never happen that those who possess evil natures are placed in the stations of the righteous or that the righteous are transferred to a place

[84] Surat al-Layl, 92:1-10

of evil. In the same manner that a fish would die outside water and land animals would perish if submerged in water, evil individuals could not survive in the abodes of the righteous, and vice versa. And this is the actual meaning of the reward and punishment that is mentioned in the Divine books.

Just as the reward for taking a breath is life, and the consequence of not breathing is death, the reward for worshipping God is to live in His proximity while the consequence of turning away from Him is eternal sorrow and remorse.

The *Barzakhi* Countenance

One issue that is often mentioned is the resemblance in *barzakh* between the physical features and the inner character of the individual; Swedenborg says that when the people of the middle state first enter *barzakh* their features remain unchanged even in their new imaginal body.

Gradually however, as they manifest their true nature, their features and bodies begin to alter to resemble their inner realities. They transform into forms that are either fearsome or enchanting. This is because in that world, no one can conceal their true nature for long and personalities are accurately reflected in facial features. In other words, their inner self is revealed. He further states that the impulses and desires of human beings are of no consequence and do not have an impact on their features unless they have been acted upon in the *dunyā*. Therefore, only deeds, which arise from intention and deliberation, have any effect on the *barzakhi* countenance of individuals. Desires which are not acted upon have no effect.[85] This startling observation of Swedenborg is very much in line with Islamic tradition.

[85] Swedenborg, passage 475.

In addition, these scenes are widely reported in narrations and anecdotes. An example is that which the Prophet (s) saw on his night ascension (*miʿrāj*) when he passed through *barzakh*. Amongst his reports from that part of his journey, he is quoted as saying:

"I passed by a group of people who had lips like those of a camel; their flesh was being cut away from their sides and fed into their mouths. I asked Jibra'il about them. He said that they were those who sought out the faults of others and spread scandal. Then I saw a group in whose mouths fire was being poured and which was coming out of their backs. I asked Jibra'il about them. He said that they were those who had unjustly consumed the inheritance of orphans; they consumed nothing but fire and soon they would enter Hellfire. Then I saw a group of people whose bellies were so large that they could not stand up even when they tried to rise. I asked Jibra'il about them. He said that they were those who engaged in usury. Now they are unable to stand, like one driven by Satan into insanity (see 2:275), and they have been placed in the ranks of the people of Pharaoh who are brought to the fire every morning and evening. They continually cry out "O Lord! When will the Day of Judgement come about?" Then I saw women who were hung up by their breasts. Jibra'il informed me that they were women who had committed adultery and then allowed their illegitimate offspring to inherit from their husbands."[86]

---

[86] Majlisī, *Biḥār al-Anwār*, 18:324 |

ثُمَّ مَضَيْتُ فَإِذَا أَنَا بِأَقْوَامٍ لَهُمْ مَشَافِرُ كَمَشَافِرِ الْإِبِلِ يُقْرَضُ اللَّحْمُ مِنْ جُنُوبِهِمْ، وَيُلْقَى فِي أَفْوَاهِهِمْ، فَقُلْتُ: مَنْ هَؤُلَاءِ يَا جَبْرَائِيلُ؟ فَقَالَ: هَؤُلَاءِ الْهَمَّازُونَ اللَّمَازُونَ، ... ثُمَّ مَضَيْتُ فَإِذَا أَنَا بِأَقْوَامٍ تُقْذَفُ النَّارُ فِي أَفْوَاهِهِمْ، وَتَخْرُجُ مِنْ أَدْبَارِهِمْ، فَقُلْتُ: مَنْ هَؤُلَاءِ يَا جَبْرَائِيلُ؟ قَالَ: هَؤُلَاءِ الَّذِينَ يَأْكُلُونَ أَمْوَالَ الْيَتَامَى ظُلْمًا، إِنَّمَا يَأْكُلُونَ فِي بُطُونِهِمْ نَارًا وَسَيَصْلَوْنَ سَعِيرًا، ثُمَّ مَضَيْتُ فَإِذَا بِأَقْوَامٍ يُرِيدُ أَحَدُهُمْ أَنْ يَقُومَ فَلَا يَقْدِرُ مِنْ عِظَمِ بَطْنِهِ، فَقُلْتُ: مَنْ هَؤُلَاءِ يَا جَبْرَائِيلُ؟ قَالَ: هَؤُلَاءِ الَّذِينَ يَأْكُلُونَ الرِّبَا لَا يَقُومُونَ إِلَّا

In contrast, the believers are found in various levels of *barzakh* with luminous faces and beautiful countenances, enjoying a life of comfort and peace. Those who died in the way of God and sacrificed their lives in His way, appear as if their faces have been created from pure light. They occupy the most elevated levels of *barzakh* in its highest realms (*al-malakūt al-a'lā*). About them God states in the Qur'an, "*Do not think of those who were slain in the way of God as dead. No! They are alive, receiving their sustenance beside their Lord.*"[87] In this same journey of *mi'rāj* the Prophet (s) traversed through several levels of the imaginal world on his way towards God's proximity. He witnessed the stations of some of the righteous and virtuous believers. The Qur'an refers to the seven layers and aspects of this world as the "seven heavens" and the Prophet (s) too, when recounting his journey of *mi'rāj* and his travels through the various layers of *barzakh*, employed the same term, "Then we ascended to the fifth heaven (meaning the fifth layer of this world). There I saw an elderly man with piercing eyes with a nobility I had never seen before. He was surrounded by a huge multitude of his followers, and I was amazed by their number. I asked Jibra'il about him and he informed that he was Aaron (Hārūn), the son of 'Imrān. I saluted him with a greeting of peace, and he replied to my greeting."[88] "Then we ascended to the seventh heaven. There

---

كَمَا يَقُومُ الَّذِي يَتَخَبَّطُهُ الشَّيْطَانُ مِنَ الْمَسِّ وَإِذَا هُمْ بِسَبِيلِ آلِ فِرْعَوْنَ يُعْرَضُونَ عَلَى النَّارِ غُدُوًّا وَعَشِيًّا، يَقُولُونَ: رَبَّنَا مَتَى تَقُومُ السَّاعَةُ؟ قَالَ: ثُمَّ مَضَيْتُ فَإِذَا أَنَا بِنِسْوَانٍ مُعَلَّقَاتٍ بِثَدْيِهِنَّ، فَقُلْتُ: مَنْ هَؤُلَاءِ يَا جَبْرَائِيلُ؟ فَقَالَ: هَؤُلَاءِ اللَّوَاتِي يُوَرِّثْنَ أَمْوَالَ أَزْوَاجِهِنَّ أَوْلَادَ غَيْرِهِمْ.

[87] Surat Āl-'Imrān, 3:169.

[88] Majlisī, *Biḥār al-Anwār*, 18:325 |

ثُمَّ صَعِدْنَا إِلَى السَّمَاءِ الْخَامِسَةِ، فَإِذَا فِيهَا رَجُلٌ كَهْلٌ عَظِيمُ الْعَيْنِ لَمْ أَرَ كَهْلًا أَعْظَمَ مِنْهُ، حَوْلَهُ ثُلَّةٌ مِنْ أُمَّتِهِ، فَأَعْجَبَتْنِي كَثْرَتُهُمْ، فَقُلْتُ: مَنْ هَذَا يَا جَبْرَائِيلُ؟ فَقَالَ: هَذَا الْمُجِيبُ فِي قَوْمِهِ هَارُونُ بْنُ عِمْرَانَ، فَسَلَّمْتُ عَلَيْهِ، وَسَلَّمَ عَلَيَّ.

I saw a man with brown hair and beard seated on a throne. I asked Jibra'il, "Who is this who has a favoured position at the doorway of the place of visitation of angels (*bayt al-ma'mūr*) in the seventh heaven and in the proximity of God?" He replied, "This is your father Abraham, and this will be your abode and the abode of the Godwary from your nation."[89]

The Connection between *Barzakh* and this *Dunyā*

It is very difficult to understand and describe the life of *barzakh*, because its dimensions and realities are completely different from our experiences in *dunyā*. As a result, whatever we say about it can only be a simile and approximation of that life. There is great diversity amongst the people of *barzakh* and they differ between each other far more than people do in *dunyā*. Their food, diet, drink and clothing are different from one another, and they all live in various stages of comfort or difficulty. In *barzakh*, the human being has evolved into a new stage of life; his existence has expanded exponentially, and he has come one step closer to the grand meeting with God. However, before that there is a long road yet to travel, and his capacity needs to grow before he can do so.

As we mentioned before, for everyone in that world – except a very select few – their abode is their own grave which is connected to a layer from the layers of *barzakh*; this causes their grave to transform into a new home which may be an expansive or a constricted space, pleasant or loathsome, beautiful or ugly. However, what is the nature of the link between the realm of *barzakh* and the space and time of this

---

[89] Majlisī, Biḥār al-Anwār, 18:326 |

ثُمَّ صَعِدْنَا إِلَى السَّمَاءِ السَّابِعَةِ..... وَإِذَا فِيهَا رَجُلٌ أَشْمَطُ الرَّأْسِ وَاللِّحْيَةِ، جَالِسٌ عَلَى كُرْسِيٍّ، فَقُلْتُ: يَا جَبْرَائِيلُ، مَنْ هَذَا الَّذِي فِي السَّمَاءِ السَّابِعَةِ عَلَى بَابِ الْبَيْتِ الْمَعْمُورِ فِي جِوَارِ اللهِ؟ فَقَالَ: هَذَا يَا مُحَمَّدُ أَبُوكَ إِبْرَاهِيمُ، وَهَذَا مَحَلُّكَ وَمَحَلُّ مَنِ اتَّقَى مِنْ أُمَّتِكَ.

dunyā, and what do we mean when we talk of a connection between people's graves in *dunyā* and their own *barzakh*? The meaning of this is beyond the comprehension of our ordinary minds. What we do know is that the Prophet (s) said, "Between my grave and my pulpit is a garden from the gardens of Paradise."[90] From the scriptures and the teachings of God's prophets (a) we can deduce that there is a type of correspondence (*tanāẓur*) between this world, the realm of *barzakh* and the world of the Hereafter (*ākhira*). Everything we see in this world has a corresponding counterpart in *barzakh* which represents it. That counterpart does not need to be similar to the thing it represents, however there is a link between the two. Even abstract things like intentions, actions, emotions and moods have representations in *barzakh* which we cannot fathom.

As an example, the moon, sun, mountains and skies do not exist in *barzakh* and its inhabitants cannot see these objects anymore, because their access to the material world (except in the cases which we will mention later) has been cut off. However, there are things that exist in that realm that if they were to describe them for us, they would use the words moon, sun, mountains and skies. The reason for this is that whatever is in this world is material, and whatever exists in *barzakh* is imaginal and consequently cannot be truly described to us. However, they have a correspondence with material objects and can be matched to them. The sun and the moon that exist in the material world are pale and lifeless compared to the brilliance of their representations in the realm of *barzakh*. The difference in the radiance of our sun compared to that of *barzakh* is like night and day. In that

---

[90] Ṣadūq, Maʿānī al-Akhbār, p. 267 |

مَا بَيْنَ قَبْرِي وَمِنْبَرِي رَوْضَةٌ مِنْ رِيَاضِ الْجَنَّةِ.

world it illuminates those wonders in God's creation that the sun of this world is not capable of doing.

In the same way, the eyes, ears, brain and body of everyone in *barzakh* has a type of correspondence to their physical body but is not identical to it; the imaginal body can see and hear and reflect in a manner that cannot be imagined in this world. The Ka'ba, Bayt al-Maqdas, Mina, 'Arafat and Karbala and Mount Sinai all have their own correspondences in the realm of *barzakh*. Therefore, when we say the abode of everyone is their grave, we are referring to a place that is the correspondence and representation of this grave in *barzakh*; and when we say that the souls of the believers are transported to Wādī al-salām in Najaf and the souls of the disbelievers to Barahūt in Yemen, we mean they go to the representations of these valleys in *barzakh*. This matter is both amazing and hard to believe, yet deep and worthy of contemplation.

The Gardens of *Barzakh*

The specific gardens of *barzakh* which are within the graves of the pious are, as mentioned earlier, proportionate to the nature of the soul of the believers; they have been constructed by their actions and principles and are the result of their deeds. They vary in size, beauty and provisions but if we were to describe one of these gardens in general terms, we would say that it is enormous, with plants and trees which seem to have been painstakingly planted and looked after by expert hands. In the prime locations within this garden, there are palaces which we may imagine have been constructed of gold, emeralds and other valuable gems. Each palace contains many halls and rooms, and the craftsmanship of its construction is beyond description. Its magnificence gives delight to both the eye and the spirit. It is pleasing to the eye because of the beauty of its design and colour and pleasing to the spirit because it is a creation from the higher realms and a manifestation of the beauty of God; a beauty that is appreciated in the depths of the heart and soul in a mysterious manner, saturating the being with love and elation. In the same manner as such opulence causes neglect of God in this world, in that realm it only increases the remembrance and cognizance of God. Every building has countless servants, whose charm and demeanour are exemplary; their entire purpose of existence is to serve their masters, because they have been created for them and due to their deeds. Of course, all these blessings befit the all-Generous Lord, and do not reduce from His limitless treasure in the slightest.

Although there is no issue of offspring and children here, nevertheless there is marriage and socialization, and love manifests itself in its purest and most beautiful form; it is an expression of that part of human nature that shows the true meaning of his attachment to both God and His creation.

There is no pain or fatigue in this place; everything is easy and accessible; travel and transfer is instantaneous - a simple intention to travel by the individual finds him at his desired location. One might ask, what then is the difference between this garden and the gardens of Paradise in the *ākhira*? It is as we said before; at this stage the universe is still developing and has not yet evolved into the perfect state. What is experienced in *barzakh* is but a shadow of life in the *ākhira*, it is only a semblance of life, not real life itself.

In any case, the believers will eat and drink within these gardens and visit one another.[91] However, their food and

[91] Kulaynī, *al-Kāfī*, 3:244, quoting Imam al-Sadiq (a) |

يَأْكُلُونَ مِنْ طَعَامِهَا وَيَشْرَبُونَ مِنْ شَرَابِهَا وَيَتَزَاوَرُونَ فِيهَا.

drink are quite different from ours; just as the measure of time for them is different. They have reached a stage of being that is higher than ours and their existence is stronger and more vital.

As for those who were ungrateful for God's favours, they reside in pits within their graves; they receive food and clothing that befits their corrupt souls and they visit one another in the valley of Barahūt. Every grave is a pit resembling the pits of Hell, full of despair, misery, torment and fear. The inhabitants of these graves continually pray that the Day of Judgement does not arrive because then they will be transported to a life that will be even worse.[92]

The Landscape of *Barzakh*

There is endless diversity within the life in *barzakh* and no two groups, or even two people, have the same experience. Catering for this diversity and allocating the various lands of *barzakh* is a complex process; as a result, we can really only gain a general idea of the geographical details of this vast realm.

The primary division in *barzakh* is between the land of the virtuous, the land of the sleepwalkers, and the land of the evildoers; these are three different continents or three distinct realms that are completely unlike each other. It might be asked what relevance land and geography has in *barzakh*.

Land in *barzakh* is to be thought of as an internal feature not an external one; its limits and geographical boundaries are not like those of this world. Locational references there are defined by the inner nature of individuals. People are housed in various abodes depending on the direction that their soul

[92] *Ibid*, p. 245.

is pointing towards. Those whose hearts are inclined to God are in a different place from those who turned their backs on God, even though they may be buried in one graveyard next to each other. Therefore, the limits and boundaries in *barzakh* are actually the different orientations of human souls and nothing else. Visualizing the geography of such a realm is difficult for us because it so different to what we are used to; however, we must not think that everything that our material intellects cannot perceive cannot exist.

The Land of the Virtuous

The land of the virtuous is itself divided into two areas; the *barzakh* of the servants that God has brought near (*muqarrabūn*) and the *barzakh* of the righteous. The *muqarrabūn* are those that in *dunyā* led lives that were completely and sincerely devoted to God; they divested themselves of every desire except Him and preferred Him over everything else. They exemplified the directive to, "love your God with all your heart, all your soul, all your strength and all your mind."[93] They had no trace of selfishness, which restricts the ability to receive ultimate mercy. As a result, their hearts were suffused with love for God and their souls became prepared to receive His special mercy. They were drawn close to His vicinity and became acquainted with His secrets; they removed every impediment that could prevent them from enjoying His grace. Their *barzakh* is generated by an internal discernment, meaning that they receive God's grace in the depths of their souls in a manner which is not possible for the rest of the inhabitants of *barzakh* to perceive. This grace, which swells in their souls, transforms their external life, giving it an indescribable beauty, grandeur and power; in fact, both in *barzakh* as well as in *ākhira*, beauty, grandeur

[93] Gospel of Luke, 10:27.

and power always flow from inner to external realities. The *muqarrabūn* may be considered to be the elite of the people of *barzakh* of the virtuous; their wisdom and intellect, and their understanding of God's secrets means that nobody else could be compared with them.

Wherever they go in *barzakh*, their grandeur and pre-eminence is evident, and their presence is constantly bathed in light and accompanied by splendour. This is because they have connected to God's own splendour and beauty and light from the depths of their being, and this continually nourishes them. However, it should never be imagined that all this grandeur makes them arrogant for even an instant; rather, it is because they have no pride that they are able to manifest such grandeur. Splendour and beauty and majesty belongs to God alone, and it is only when man walks on the hidden path towards Him, and adores him, and strives to remove every trace of self-love and egoism from himself, that that beauty and majesty adorns his soul.

But the level of humbleness of the *muqarrabūn* was something that the righteous, could not achieve despite their goodness. The righteous are those who lived pious and faithful lives; they worshipped God and were people of charity and good works and as a result they immediately found their way to the Paradise of *barzakh*. However, they could not achieve the high levels of inner sincerity, utter humility and constant remembrance of God that the *muqarrabūn* possessed. As a result, the cognizance of God of the *muqarrabūn* did not enter their souls. Their love for God did not reach the completeness that it should have, and their souls were consequently not prepared enough to fully receive the majesty and beauty of God. In the *dunyā*, they were inclined to goodness and were grateful for God's blessings, but they worshipped God due to faith and not out of love; they believed in Him but were not in love with Him, because they did not recognize Him properly; and there is a world of difference between faith and love. For this reason, although they enjoy a comfortable and immensely rich life in *barzakh*, they are unable to connect to God's grace through their hearts and souls because the path of love remained unopened by them. Consequently, they do not possess the inner receptivity of the *muqarrabūn*, or their detailed knowledge of the secrets of creation. They are the middle rank of the inhabitants of *barzakh*.

These two areas, the *barzakh* of the *muqarrabūn* and the *barzakh* of the righteous, are like two different countries and can be referred to as the land of the *muqarrabūn* and the land of the righteous. The *muqarrabūn* are free to come and go within the land of the righteous and when they come to that land, it resembles the majestic arrival of kings. However, the righteous cannot enter the land of the *muqarrabūn* except in rare instances and with special permission. This is because entry into that land is beyond their capacity. The visits of the *muqarrabūn* to the land of the righteous are pleasant and memorable because such visits are always accompanied by an increase in the blessings and mercy of God.

As we mentioned, "land" in *barzakh* refers to a place where the imaginal manifestation of an individual's grave occurs. Depending on the closeness or remoteness of the person from the majesty and power of God, it can be a place of splendour and honour or a place of darkness and misery. What is apparent is that people do not remain constantly at the location of their graves, whether it is a garden and palace of Paradise or a pit and torture chamber of Hell. They possess homes there from which they visit other places and return when they desire solitude and rest. However, everyone can only travel within the boundaries of their own territory in *barzakh*.

The land of the righteous is divided into different areas according to the type of virtue. However, this does not mean that people living in different areas cannot see one another and enjoy each other's company. On special occasions the souls of the believers gather in locations that are more beautiful and grander than their own; here they socialize and converse and discuss any new bounty that they have received from God or a greater realization they have gained of Him. When they hear of each other's experiences, its sweetness brings them closer and strengthens their bonds further. Sometimes, they also get to meet and enjoy the company of the elite and close servants of God. Occasionally, these meetings take place in Wādī al-salām in Najaf, whose *barzakhi* manifestation is one of the most magnificent gardens in the imaginal world,[94] and sometimes near the Dome of the Rock (*qubbat al-ṣakhra*) at Bayt al-Maqdas in Palestine.[95] Perhaps they also meet the righteous from other religions every now and then. If we imagine them, we would see them gathered around each other busy in conversation, "There is no believer in the east or west of the world except that God transfers his soul to Wādī al-salām...it is as if I can see them at this moment sitting together in groups talking with one another."[96] However, we could never imagine what

[94] Kulaynī, *al-Kāfī*, 3:243 quoting Imam Ali (a) | "Indeed Wādī al-salām is part of the Garden of Eden." |

وَإِنَّهَا لَبُقْعَةٌ مِنْ جَنَّةِ عَدْنٍ.

[95] Majlisī, *Bihār al-Anwār*, 6:286.

[96] Kulaynī, *al-Kāfī*, 3:243 quoting Imam al-Sadiq (a) |

أَمَا إِنَّهُ لَا يَبْقَى مُؤْمِنٌ فِي شَرْقِ الْأَرْضِ وَغَرْبِهَا إِلَّا حَشَرَ اللهُ رُوحَهُ إِلَى وَادِي السَّلَامِ ... أَمَا إِنِّي كَأَنِّي بِهِمْ حَلَقٌ حَلَقٌ قُعُودٌ يَتَحَدَّثُونَ.

they are saying to each other, because their talk is not the idle chatter of the business of this world, rather it is about affairs that shall remain hidden from us until we die.

When we speak of the delights enjoyed by the inhabitants of the Paradise of *barzakh* it is natural for us, who have not yet stepped into that realm, to imagine that they will be similar to the pleasures that we enjoy in this world. This couldn't be further from the truth; the delights of that world are spontaneously generated externally from within the soul of an individual and not from outside to inside. It is for this reason that we cannot really imagine them except by attempting to make comparisons with what we have experienced in our world. Swedenborg claims that he was permitted in his visions to experience that type of delight. He goes on to say that there is no way to adequately describe these "pleasures of heavenly joy". All he could say was that each experience was a unified effect of bliss that contained a "harmony of countless affections, all elements so beautifully arranged as to defy description". He observed that, "the joy and delight seemed to be coming from my heart, spreading very subtly through all my inner fibres ... and everything I perceived and felt around me was alive with bliss." Next to these delights, "the joy of physical pleasures is like crude and irritating dust compared to a pure and gentle breeze." The most interesting thing is that this pleasure can be transferred to others as well; whenever someone, out of love and affection, would try to convey his pleasure to his friends, "God caused a deeper and fuller pleasure to flow in its place."[97]

However, despite living this happy life, there is one prayer on everyone's lips, "Our Lord! Bring about the Day of Judgement

[97] Swedenborg, *Heaven and Hell*, section 413.

so that you can grant us that which You have promised."[98] The window that has been opened between their *barzakh* and the Paradise of the *ākhira*, and the breeze of Divine mercy and pleasure that blows into their luxurious graves, captivate and intoxicates them and fills them with impatience. What they have and the type of life they lead is already beyond our imagination, but what they can sense through the window to Paradise is something else again. It is an elevated level of existence that nothing in this world or the realm of *barzakh* can compare with.

The Land of the Sleepwalkers

At a lower level than the land of the righteous lies the territory of the people of the middle state. They are the ones who were neither completely righteous nor completely evil. Just as we mentioned before, Swedenborg calls this the land of souls; here we have named it the land of the sleepwalkers, because their level of existence compared to that of the righteous or the evildoers is like that of sleep compared to wakefulness.

These are people who were not very good or very evil either; some of them were unable to differentiate truth from falsehood in the *dunyā* because the criteria for righteous conduct was not known to them and no one corrected their mistakes.[99] Or their faith was weak and despite their knowledge, they mixed good and sinful conduct; all these people live in this land. Naturally, they do not belong to either the land of the righteous or the land of the evildoers

[98] Kulaynī, *al-Kāfī*, 3:244, quoting from Imam al-Sadiq (a) |

رَبَّنَا أَقِمِ السَّاعَةَ لَنَا وَأَنْجِزْ لَنَا مَا وَعَدْتَنَا.

[99] In religious terms these people are known as "*mustaḍ'af*", meaning weak or vulnerable.

in *barzakh*, "They remain in their grave and do not leave it; in return for their good acts in the *dunyā*, a window is opened between their grave and the Paradise of *barzakh*, through which a pleasant and comforting breeze flows in."[100] We do not know what this window means and how it connects them to the pleasures of the Paradise of *barzakh*, but we are told that secure and peaceful, they enter into a relaxed slumber. But if they were more inclined towards evil conduct in the *dunyā*, then a window is opened between their grave and the Hell of *barzakh* at Barahūt, through which they feel a blistering and harsh wind blow into their lonely home. This state continues until the Day of Judgment arrives, when God makes known the fate of both groups. What is meant by "remaining in their grave" in the narration is that they live in the land of the souls and are unable to find the way into the Paradise of *barzakh*.

In this region of *barzakh* life passes as in sleep; although their experience is much richer and opulent compared to the life of this world. However, compared to the life of the righteous and their knowledge, freedom of movement and joy, they might as well be sleeping. Most of their experience of joy is confined to the material aspects of *barzakh* and has very little to do with its spiritual richness. In fact, they are quite unable to perceive or understand the experiences of the righteous.

The Window to Paradise

Swedenborg makes some observations about the type of connection that the righteous in *barzakh* have with the Paradise of *ākhira* which can be considered as the same thing as the window that has been opened into their graves from the Paradise of *barzakh* and which has been mentioned in Islamic traditions. He says that sometimes the righteous

[100] Kulaynī, *al-Kāfī*, 3:246, quoting from Imam al-Sadiq (a).

enter a peaceful state rather like sleep and during that time they witness Paradise. When they wake up, they are so full of wonder and amazement at what they saw that they cannot put the feeling and beauty of it into words. Everything that exists there sparkles brilliantly as if it was made of gold and silver and precious gems; objects have amazing and stunning forms. However, he saw that the inhabitants of Paradise did not take any particular delight in these objects but were more engrossed in what they represented of Divine flashes of infinite wisdom that human language could not describe. They see delights there that could not be described even briefly, concepts that are outside the reach of our material minds. When they return to consciousness the memory of what they have seen is etched in their soul and fills them with great joy. Sometimes their hearts are suffused with a strange and indescribable elation, which is reserved for the people of Paradise, and sometimes they are taken to a state of innocence which they sense in the deepest layers of their soul. In this way they are made to realize the real joy and delight of the Paradise of the Hereafter and what kind of innocence and purity is required to enter into it.[101]

The Land of the Evildoers

At a lower level than the land of the sleepwalkers lies the land of the evildoers. It is the abode of the disbelievers and the arrogant. They are those who only loved themselves and they know no other love, whether for God or for virtue. Their preoccupation with their own desires closed their path to gain any virtue and, because they are themselves devoid of any goodness, jealousy drives them to hate the virtues found in others. They constantly strive to destroy all goodness but because God has confined them to the land of the evildoers,

---

101 Swedenborg, *Heaven and Hell*, sections 411 and 412.

and they are unable to do what they want; they are always restless with rage and bitterness. They harbour hate in their hearts for everything and everyone, especially God, Who is the source of all goodness. His mention and remembrance remind them of their insignificance, and they know they are powerless in front of Him. In *barzakh*, power stems from the truth (*ḥaq*), and truth is a reality that flows down from God. Whoever is more unified with this truth is more powerful and whoever is distant from it is weaker. Therefore, power here belongs to the righteous and the *muqarrabūn*, and the arrogant inhabitants of the land of the evildoers are the weakest of all, despite all their bluster and rage.

The land of the evildoers is divided amongst its inhabitants according to their levels of evil and wickedness. Each area is associated with a particular vice; and there is a punishment, misery and stench that is unique to it. It is as if the inhabitants of this land are organized in different tribes, each immersed in the torment befitting its particular evil habit.

However, there is one trait here that is common to all, and that is that each person despises everyone else, and each tries to enslave the other and force them to serve him. This is an instinct that arises from their self-love. The only thing that controls the situation from getting out of hand is Divine retribution. The angels are constantly involved in the affairs of this land and whoever crosses the bounds in harassing anybody else is immediately subject to harsh punishment. However, the effect of this chastisement is short-lived and does not deter them for long from acting rebelliously once again; this is because bullying, meanness and cunning has become ingrained in their nature and controls them like the instincts in animals. In fact, they experience two kinds of punishment, one that they bring onto each other and the second that is visited on them by the angels when restraining them. There is no other way to control their viciousness except through punishment.

The inhabitants of the land of evildoers gather every night to try to overpower each other; they boast about themselves and humiliate one another. They want everyone to do what they want, and not only do they desire domination over every man, angel and creature in the land, they desire that God too, should act according to their wishes. Of course, since such desires are futile, these meetings and socializing serve nothing except to increase their rage and frustration, and when day breaks, they return beaten and disappointed back to their graves. The location of their meetings is a desolate desert in Yemen which is known as Barahūt. The imaginal representation of this place in *barzakh* is a scorching desert; in it dry winds blow which are more searing than the fire of *dunyā*.[102] And its pools are filled with the most repulsive water.[103] And the interesting thing is that the souls of the evildoers willingly rush to this place, imagining and hoping that they will be able to wrest some benefit from the other wretches in *barzakh*, and force them to become their abject servants.

Although they have themselves become used to their features and forms, if an outsider were to see these souls, they would appear to be monstrous. The imaginal world is an amazing place. Every quality and trait, good or evil, assumes an external form. Jealousy gives rise to one form and altruism to another. Turning towards God illuminates a man's face while turning away from Him darkens it. Hatred alters a man's features one way and love in another. Therefore, one

[102] Kulaynī, *al-Kāfī*, 3:247, quoting from Imam al-Baqir (a).

[103] Kulaynī, *al-Kāfī*, 3:246, quoting from Imam al-Sadiq (a).

should not be surprised that the features of the people in the land of the evildoers more closely resemble savage animals than human beings. In addition, just as siblings look alike in *dunyā*, the features and habits of those in *barzakh* whose evil natures were similar resemble each other as well.

According to Swedenborg's visions, the features of the evildoers are generally frightful and resemble the faces of morbid corpses. Some faces are pitch-dark, some are fiery red, while others have faces disfigured by large ulcers and sores. Others have no visible face, only some hair or bone in its place; in some others only, teeth show and nothing else.

Their bodies are equally misshapen and hideous. Their speech embodies rage and hatred, and their tone is full of evil intent. In short, they all portray the image of their inner Hell.[104] Swedenborg also says that the people of this land remain in it willingly, and although they occasionally have access to the land of the righteous, they never travel there. This is because firstly, their own land is shrouded in a semi-darkness in which the light of truth does not enter. The darkness of this land, which is only faintly lit by glowing coals, is a blessing for them because in its dimness they look almost human to each other. It is only when a ray of light from the higher realms illuminates them that their repulsive faces are revealed. Swedenborg believes that the darkness of this land is a gift of God's mercy to these wretched people.[105] Secondly, the land of the righteous appears in total darkness for them, because that land is illuminated by God's light, and this light cannot be received by the inhabitants of the land of the evildoers; they are blind to it, just as they were blind to

[104] Swedenborg, *Heaven and Hell*, section 553.

[105] Ibid.

God's truths in *dunyā*. As a consequence, they prefer to stay in their lonely caves.[106]

To gain a better picture of this community, we may imagine a place where every member is completely self-absorbed and is only interested in working with others if they can jointly visit harm on another group. At the same time as they work together, the heart of each is full of hate for his comrades. As soon as their objective is met and they overcome the weaker party, they turn on one another and quarrel to a point where they are ready to kill each other and feast on their bodies. And this is nothing more than the viciousness of their evil nature becoming manifest, "*Indeed the quarrelling of the people of the fire is the truth.*"[107] Because they are completely selfish, and because they were never grateful to God during their lives in *dunyā*, they have never learned appreciation. Although they may speak of justice, but in their hearts, they have only scorn for justice, honesty, compassion and virtue. God's light does not penetrate their hearts because any light is immediately distorted into self-love and thoughts of wrongdoing.

The Landscape of Barahūt

Barahūt itself is divided into two areas: the land of darkness and the land of fire. Those who live in the land of darkness are the people who were under the influence of evildoers, while the people who live in the land of fire are those who were evil themselves and now their entire being has been transformed to pure evil. In the realm of *barzakh* of Barahūt, they live in different levels within underground caves and pits whose depths cannot be imagined. Some of these caves

---

106 Swedenborg, *Heaven and Hell*, section 584.

107 Surat Ṣād, 38:64.

are like the dens of wild animals while others are in the form of vertical or spiralling caverns of unknown depths. In some areas there are burnt ruins of houses and cities situated in deep valleys and dry, blistering deserts dotted with springs of hot and putrid water; all of this is a manifestation of the inner corruptness of the souls of those who live here. One might ask how these external realities reflect their inner state. The answer to this was discussed before, both from the traditions as well as the philosophy of Mulla Sadra. In our material world we observe the effect of inner states on the external world too, but it is nothing compared to the same process in the imaginal world. As an example, in *dunyā*, no matter what they eat, people with a certain illness will find the taste bitter; or for someone whose vision is weak, everything appears dim, and to a depressed person, everything appears cheerless, and for a jealous person, the blessings of others cause resentment. These effects are intensified a hundred-fold in *barzakh* and a thousand-fold in *ākhira.* What then will be the fate of the Godless people whose souls are closed to the most beautiful realities of the universe?

Swedenborg says that he witnessed that some of the districts of Barahūt were full of brothels filled with filth and excrement, with women whose faces only add revulsion to adulterers.

The streets here are full of violence and hostility. Some areas are hidden by dark forests with unsightly trees where Hellish souls roam like wild beasts; when they are threatened by other souls they flee and hide in their underground caves.[108]

[108] Swedenborg, *Heaven and Hell*, section 586.

The Social Order in *Barzakh*

That most people in *barzakh* live together in communities is beyond doubt. However, is there any social order that governs their lives? Is it possible for a group of free people with different inclinations and abilities to live together in one place, without there being any system to govern them? Or will the same system apply in *barzakh* which was used to regulate societies in *dunyā*, each with its own rules based on diverse social ideologies?

As a rule, in every community where there is freedom on the one hand, and a difference of views and inclinations on the other, some sort of social system must exist. Such a system is even found in the realm of angels. For example, all angels must follow the commands of Jibra'il, the angel who is, "*a noble messenger, possessed of power and high rank with the Lord of the Dominion. He is obeyed (in the heavens) and faithful in trust.*"[109] Usually, most of the angels are under the command of senior angels who in turn, take instructions from angels of a higher rank. For example, during his *mi'rāj*, the Prophet (s) saw an angel who, "had a group of seventy thousand angels under his command, each of whom was in charge of a further seventy thousand angels."[110] In short, in the social order of the angels, every angel has a designated and known position, "*There is not one of us (angels) but has his own assigned place.*"[111]

Therefore, in *barzakh* too, a social system exists, and this system varies across its different regions. However, before we discuss these differences, we must define the meaning of a social system – a part of which is leadership and rule –

[109] Surat al-Takwīr, 81:19-21

[110] Qummī, *Tafsīr 'Alī b. Ibrāhīm*, p. 371.

[111] Surat al-Ṣaffāt, 37:164.

in reference to *barzakh*. Rulership in the *dunyā* is exercised in a variety of ways, but it is always based on power and authority. This authority sometimes comes from military prowess, sometimes from a hereditary transfer which is acceptable to the subjects, and sometimes by the vote of the majority. This is the actual sort of social system that prevails in the land of the evildoers in *barzakh*. Those who are more powerful and cunning gang together and subjugate weaker souls and make use of them in their personal fights and other corrupt objectives. We will discuss this again when we discuss the Hell of the Hereafter (*ākhira*), because that which transpires in *barzakh* is nothing compared to what will be seen in the *ākhira*.

However, in the land of the *muqarrabūn*, which is the domain of the Prophets (a) and close servants (*awliyā*), authority is only based on love. There, everyone is the recipient of God's grace directly, and whoever has the capacity to receive the most grace is more beloved to the rest and obeyed in every matter by them.

In the land of the righteous the social order is more complex and follows a hierarchy of authority. Whoever possesses more knowledge and virtue naturally occupies a higher rank in authority, because his decisions conform better to the beauty of existence and contain more goodness and virtue.

As was indicated earlier, the realm of *barzakh* has a representation in the realm of *ākhira*, therefore whatever happens in the Paradise or Hell of *barzakh* is a pale shadow of what will occur in the *ākhira* and the higher realms; the only difference there will be the availability of the indescribable mercy of all Merciful, which we will talk about later. Therefore, it may be assumed that the hierarchy that exists in the Paradise of the righteous in the *ākhira* is similar to that found in the Paradise of *barzakh*. About the hierarchy in the Paradise of *ākhira*, the Prophet (s) has said, "Those who possess the knowledge of the Qur'an shall be administrators in Paradise, and those who strived in God's path shall be governors in Paradise and the Prophets shall be leaders in Paradise."[112]

And this means each prophet will rule over a group of governors and administrators in the Paradise of the righteous; therefore, the final authority in the Paradise of the righteous is in the hands of the *muqarrabūn*, who themselves are under a single authority in their own Paradise.

It is very likely that a similar system will exist in *barzakh* of the righteous also. However, those who run this social system will not be chosen due to their power, charisma or family; rather there will be total freedom of choice which will be based on the perception that that which comes from above is only goodness. In addition, following their guidance will result in greater delight, happiness and development of their souls. The term *'urafā'* which has been used in the tradition above for those who possess knowledge of the Qur'an is the plural of *'arīf*, which is used for a person who is responsible for the administration of a district in a large city. From this meaning we can conclude that social framework of life in Paradise will be based on a well-organized and orderly system.

---

[112] Kulaynī, al-Kāfī, 2:606

حَمَلَةُ الْقُرْآنِ عُرَفَاءُ أَهْلِ الْجَنَّةِ، وَالْمُجْتَهِدُونَ قُوَّادُ أَهْلِ الْجَنَّةِ، وَالْأَنْبِيَاءُ سَادَةُ أَهْلِ الْجَنَّةِ.

This narration, with slight variation in words has been ; reported in many sources, both Shī'ī and Sunnī, for example: Muttaqī al-Hindī, *Kanz al-'Ummāl*, trad. 2288 – 2290; Qāḍī Nu'mān al-Miṣrī, *Da'ā'im al-Islām*, 1:343; Ṣadūq, *al-Khiṣāl*, p. 28; Mawlā Muḥammad Ṣāliḥ Māzandarānī, *Sharḥ Uṣūl al-Kāfī*, 11:30 has mentioned other ranks in addition to these three.

These matters are confirmed by Swedenborg's visions. He says that the population of the Paradise of *barzakh* is divided into communities of various sizes and although all the people in one community are involved in good activities, they are not similar in their wisdom. Therefore, there necessarily must be a form of government to maintain order. And this government is solely based on mutual love.[113]

Rulership there is not about control and command, but about serving out of love and concern for the welfare of the community. Since the rulers have more wisdom and understanding than the rest, they know how to apply the law according to God's will to bring about the welfare of each individual.[114]

Children in *Barzakh*[115]

Humans who die in childhood have one advantage and one disadvantage when compared to those who die after adulthood. Their advantage is that they are yet sinless and consequently their souls are completely open and prepared to receive everything that the angels want to teach them about God, His Lordship and His expansive mercy. Their soul has not been made defiant by egoism, arrogance and sinful conduct and its receptivity to knowledge and wisdom is intact. However, their disadvantage lies in the fact that they left this world before they could understand the truths

[113] Swedenborg, *Heaven and Hell*, section 213.

[114] Swedenborg, *Heaven and Hell*, section 217.

[115] Most Christian theologians are of the opinion that only Christian children who have been baptized will be admitted to Paradise. A minority of Muslim theologians believe that children will follow their parents in Paradise or Hell. Shīʿa theologians consider this view to be against God's Justice (*ʿadāla*) and believe that all children without exception will be in Paradise.

and concepts that would ignite the cognizance of God in their hearts, and before they could pass through the various stages of life during which an individual experiences God's mercy and grows to love Him. As a result, their initiation in *barzakh* into the deeper realities of existence is possible only to a certain extent. Of course, the sinlessness of children is vastly different to the sinlessness that an adult manages to maintain. In the latter case, the soul is open and submissive and consequently receptive to God's grace and mercy but also at the same time, it has also perfectly realized the truths and concepts that are to be learned in *dunyā*; this is because sinlessness in adulthood can only be achieved by those who ponder and reflect with knowledge and wisdom.

As we have seen, children cannot immediately enter the Paradise of *barzakh* after their death. They are initially taken to a beautiful and comfortable location where they stay for a time receiving guidance from angels who are more loving towards them than their own mothers. Thereafter, they are taken to meet the people of Paradise. This guidance has two functions. Firstly, it is to impart to the children the knowledge and understanding that is required to live in the Paradise of *barzakh*; secondly, it is to cleanse their souls of any false ideas and values that they may have received from their parents and society during their brief stay in *dunyā*. This is because, contrary to the view of most people who believe that the Paradise of *barzakh* or that of *ākhira* is a collection of material blessings which can be granted to anyone, Paradise is actually identical to an individual's level of closeness to the Source of goodness and love and knowledge and wisdom. It is different for every single person depending on the amount of goodness, love, knowledge and wisdom he has acquired. Material blessings are in fact external manifestations of these matters, and expressions of God's names and attributes through the human soul in the world external to it.

After their period of training, depending on their receptivity and their different levels of purity, children enter either the land of the *muqarrabūn* or that of the righteous. According to the visions of Swedenborg, the imaginal bodies of children when they first leave *dunyā* are identical to their material bodies, but gradually, as they develop mentally and the capacity of their souls is increased through the teaching of the angels, their bodies grow as well. That which nourishes their minds also nourishes their bodies, until they reach adolescence. However, their development stops at this stage, and they never grow beyond the prime of youth.[116] This is because further development requires one to exercise their free will and act and react in the *dunyā*, which children did not get an opportunity to do. In addition, Swedenborg believes that because children who die in infancy have no recollection of *dunyā*, they imagine that they have been born in the imaginal world and display a complete dependency on God.[117]

The foregoing is a simplified idea of the destiny of children in *barzakh*; otherwise, its details and the variation amongst individual children is much more complex than can be imagined by our material minds.

The People of *Barzakh* and the Material World

Is our material world hidden to the people in *barzakh* in the same manner as their realm is hidden to us, or can the dead see our world and be aware of events here? This is not an easy question to answer.

[116] Swedenborg, *Heaven and Hell*, section 340.

[117] Swedenborg, *Heaven and Hell*, section 345.

As a rule, the entities of the realm of *barzakh* are correspondents of the entities of this world. As we have already mentioned, representations of the sky and the earth, mountains and valleys, rivers and oceans, space and time and distances, all exist in *barzakh* just as they do in this world; however, just as man occupies an imaginal body in *barzakh*, everything else there is similarly in an imaginal state also. That is, although they exist, they are non-material in nature. Being immaterial actually adds to their colour, radiance and richness and elevates them to a higher level of existence. In truth, what we see in this world is a pale expression of what exists in the imaginal world. As long as the human being occupies a material body, he cannot see objects in the imaginal world, except if his soul is extraordinarily strong, or his soul disconnects from the body and enters an imaginal body. Conversely, when the soul moves into the imaginal world, the material fades before its eyes and it remains unaware of the lives of the living, except if the soul is extraordinarily strong, or for some reason its connection to the material world is not completely severed.

In addition, the soul's means to view the material world was through the physical senses of the material body; with the disintegration of the material body and its sensory organs, the soul's connection with the world of matter is cut off and its means of perceiving it disappears. Therefore, we can say that in normal circumstances the dead are unaware of the goings-on in our world; it is hidden to them, but not as completely as the realm of *barzakh* is hidden from the eyes of the living. For the friends of God who are called the *awliyā*, there is no question of a veil between *barzakh* and *dunyā*; they can see whatever they choose and whenever they choose. Their knowledge was far superior to the knowledge of the ordinary man in *dunyā*, and they could often even see the realm of *barzakh*; similarly, in that world also, their knowledge is a level apart from the rest of the dead and they are aware of whatever happens in the *dunyā*. Of course, the understanding of the dead in *barzakh* should not be compared to the understanding of the living; their knowledge encompasses dimensions of space and time that cannot be imagined by those who yet live in this world. They no longer need material eyes and ears to see and hear things of this world because their knowledge is now obtained through higher means.

As for the ordinary people, depending on the level they occupy in *barzakh*, on special occasions they can perceive some of the events of this world; this is similar to the glimpses that some of the living have about the next world. These events are usually to do with the souls themselves or their family members who are still alive. For some souls this perception and knowledge may only come once a year, for every month, and for others every week or even every day. This interval varies according to "the status of the dead person."[118]

According to some narrations, this awareness and witnessing normally occurs at midday (*ẓuhr*) and, "when the believers see their living relatives doing acts of goodness they become happy and thank God; and when the disbelievers see their living relatives doing acts of goodness they are filled with regret."[119] However, the sinful conduct of relatives is usually

[118] Kulaynī, *al-Kāfī*, 3:230 | Isḥāq b. ʿAmmār says that I asked Imam al-Kazim (a), "Does the dead person visit his relatives?" He replied, "Yes." I asked, "How often?" He said, "Every Friday, or every month, or every year, depending on his status."

إِسْحَاقَ بْنُ عَمَّارٍ، عَنْ أَبِي الْحَسَنِ الْأَوَّلِ (عَلَيْهِ السَّلَامُ) قَالَ: سَأَلْتُهُ عَنِ الْمَيِّتِ يَزُورُ أَهْلَهُ؟ قَالَ: نَعَمْ، فَقُلْتُ: فِي كَمْ يَزُورُ؟ قَالَ: فِي الْجُمْعَةِ وَفِي الشَّهْرِ وَفِي السَّنَةِ عَلَى قَدْرِ مَنْزِلَتِهِ.

[119] Kulaynī, *al-Kāfī*, 3:230 |

hidden from the eyes of the dead, and the souls are not able to see it. Sometimes the connection is so strong that some souls in *barzakh* gain permission to influence and guide their relatives on important and decisive matters by coming in their dreams.

Another method by which the people of *barzakh* can connect with this world is when the relatives visit their graves. At such times the dead usually sense the presence of their relatives, and are happy to see them and it increases their love for them, "Visit your deceased, because they are pleased when you do so."[120] And, "I swear by God that they are aware of your presence and are gladdened by it and your visit increases their love for you."[121] They are also affected when their relatives pray for them and seek forgiveness for them, or do a good deed on their behalf and in their memory. If this prayer or good act is done with a sincere intention and reaches fruition, it is like a gift that is presented by the living to the dead, "Those who have died become happy when someone prays for mercy and forgiveness for them, just as the living are happy when they receive gifts."[122] It seems that these matters have a great impact on the quality of their lives in the realm of *barzakh*, and sometimes it can transform the narrow and dark confines of their graves into wideness

---

عَنْ أَبِي عَبْدِ اللهِ (ع) قَالَ: مَا مِنْ مُؤْمِنٍ وَلَا كَافِرٍ إِلَّا وَهُوَ يَأْتِي أَهْلَهُ عِنْدَ زَوَالِ الشَّمْسِ، فَإِذَا رَأَى أَهْلَهُ يَعْمَلُونَ بِالصَّالِحَاتِ حَمِدَ اللهَ عَلَى ذَلِكَ، وَإِذَا رَأَى الْكَافِرُ أَهْلَهُ يَعْمَلُونَ بِالصَّالِحَاتِ كَانَتْ عَلَيْهِ حَسْرَةً.

[120] Kulaynī, *al-Kāfī*, 3:229, quoting Imam Ali (a) |
زُورُوا مَوْتَاكُمْ فَإِنَّهُمْ يَفْرَحُونَ بِزِيَارَتِكُمْ.

[121] Ḥurr al-Āmilī, *Wasā'il al-Shī'a*, 2:878 quoting Imam al-Sadiq (a) |
وَاللهِ، لَيَعْلَمُونَ بِكُمْ، وَيَفْرَحُونَ بِكُمْ، وَيَسْتَأْنِسُونَ إِلَيْكُمْ.

[122] Ḥurr al-Āmilī, *Wasā'il al-Shī'a*, 2:878 quoting Imam al-Sadiq (a) |
إِنَّ الْمَيِّتَ لَيَفْرَحُ بِالتَّرَحُّمِ عَلَيْهِ وَالْاِسْتِغْفَارِ لَهُ كَمَا يَفْرَحُ الْحَيُّ بِالْهَدِيَّةِ تُهْدَى إِلَيْهِ.

and light[123] and earn their appreciation and gratitude. Of course, the effects of the prayers and good acts of the living for the dead are to do with their life in the realm of *barzakh*; however, the Day of Judgement is another matter entirely, and one that we will discuss in due course.

The People of *Barzakh* and the World of the Angels

Entry into the world of *barzakh* is actually entry into the world of the angels also. Although the greatest angels cannot be seen here, nonetheless, there is still a bewildering variety of angels whose numbers are simply beyond count. The angels are wondrous creatures and *barzakh* itself is a wondrous place. In this strange place, human beings and angels can understand each other's speech, because here only one language exists and that is an unspoken inner (*fiṭrī*) language that has been embedded in the imaginal memory of both human beings and angels. This language is a direct expression of the inner nature of individuals which reflects perfectly their perceptions, emotions and intentions. It is for this reason that there is no possibility of lying or duplicity here and if someone tries to express something contrary to their inner feelings and thoughts, it immediately becomes evident to the listener.

However, what is more amazing is that although the language in *barzakh* is instinctive and everyone has the ability to speak and hear, there are many human beings here who are deaf and mute; in fact, many more than existed in the *dunyā*. This deafness and dumbness are because the thoughts that run in the minds of this group are so conflicting with reality that they cannot be expressed. As a result, they appear as

---

[123] Ḥurr al-Āmilī, *Wasā'il al-Shī'a*, 2:655 quoting Imam al-Sadiq (a) | حَتَّى إِنَّهُ يَكُونُ فِي ضِيقٍ، فَيُوَسِّعُ اللهُ عَلَيْهِ ذَلِكَ الضِّيقَ.

mutes or that which comes from their minds sounds like the senseless raving of a lunatic. And neither is it possible to make them understand anything because their minds have lost the ability to receive information; for this reason, they are unable to communicate themselves and cannot hear what others say. And since their minds are confused and the hearts dark, they cannot perceive the radiant realities around them, and so they are blind as well. "*And We shall gather them on the Day of Judgment, prone on their faces, blind, dumb and deaf.*"[124]

The angels are creatures who are highly intelligent and very sensitive at the same time. Their lives, thoughts and devotions are exclusively dedicated to God. If you were to praise them in their presence, they would turn away in annoyance because they consider every goodness and beauty as being due to God; their happiness lies in His remembrance and glorification rather than in their own excellences. To them, paying attention to themselves is limiting, while paying attention to God is to turn to unlimited beauty and glory. When they encounter people of evil inclination they are deeply distressed and try to distance themselves from them as soon as possible. However, if they are commanded to spend time with them, they assume a manner that fills the evil with foreboding. We mentioned earlier how the evil perceived the appearance of Munkar and Nakīr and the angel of death as fearsome indeed. The angels who shall be assigned to Hell are likewise, "harsh and severe",[125] because their task is to control vicious criminals. As we said, the features of every creature in that world manifest their inner state, and because the angels feel nothing but aversion and distaste for these evildoers, they cannot mask these feelings

124 Surat al-Isrā', 17:97.

125 Surat al-Taḥrīm, 66:6.

from their faces. Of course, this is how we analyse them from afar and God knows best.

There are more angels than the entirety of other creatures and God has not created any creature more numerous than the angels.[126] Their types, ranks and functions are likewise more varied than the rest of creation; basically, one can say that no two angels are similar. On the whole, the angels can be divided into two groups: the angels of the dominion (*malakūt*) and the angels of the exalted assembly (*mala' al-aʿlā*). *Mala' al-aʿlā* is a Qur'anic term[127] and refers to a group of high-ranking angels. In some narrations they are referred to as the angels of the realm of Compelling Power (*jabarūt*). These angels are closest to God and their knowledge, power, beauty, and proximity to God cannot be compared to the angels of *malakūt*. That which this exalted assembly of angels understands and receives from God can never be perceived by the other angels. The angels who attend to the dead in the realm of *barzakh* are the angels of *malakūt*, and they exist in countless different forms. Of course, those whose faith has penetrated into the depth of their souls are able to harness this strength and see the angels of *jabarūt* as well. This is because faith serves the heart in the same manner that eyes serve the head; and the stronger and more ingrained this faith is, the further it can see into the depths of God's kingdom and can even perceive the throne (*ʿarsh*) of God itself.

Angels do not marry or have offspring. Each is created separately, and this creation continues endlessly as God creates more angels at every moment; the procedure of this creation is unknown to us, however. Angels do not require

---

126 Majlisī, *Bihār al-Anwār*, 56:175 |

مَا مِنْ شَيْءٍ خَلَقَهُ اللهُ أَكْثَرَ مِنَ الْمَلَائِكَةِ.

127 Surat Ṣād, 38:69.

nourishment and are sustained by a breeze that blows from the *'arsh;*[128] they possess non-material eyes and ears and tremendous intelligence.[129] An angel is defined by the work it does, just as in that world people are defined by the deeds that they have performed. All the angels who perform a specific task belong to the same tribe[130] and their features resemble one another, although just like human beings, they can be told apart. Since the work they carry out is always pure goodness, their faces are also beautiful; and since the good acts they carry out are different, their faces are also different from one another.

The beauty of the angels cannot be described to the people in our world; in fact, Imam Ali (a) has said that some angels are such that even if all the *jinn* and mankind assembled together, they would not be able to describe their grandeur and the beauty of their features.[131] Of course, as we have mentioned before, features in that world are quite different from those in our world; in that world every feeling, emotion and inner reality is reflected in the face of every human being and angel and radiates from it and gives it shape. No one there can display a face that is different from their inner reality; the more beautiful they are on the inside, the more beautiful their features appear, and the uglier they are on the inside, the uglier their features appear. It is for this reason that, "*the guilty will be recognized by their marks.*"[132] Because beauty belongs only to God, the beauty of the angels and

[128] Majlisī, *Biḥār al-Anwār*, 56:174. This phrase is metaphorical of course, and its meaning is not clear for us.

[129] *Ibid*, p.175.

[130] Surat al-Ṣaffāt, 37:164. Many traditions talk about the tribes of the angels also.

[131] Majlisī, *Biḥār al-Anwār*, 56:178.

[132] Surat al-Raḥmān, 55:41.

human beings is a reflection of His beauty, while ugliness is a manifestation of the ugliness of the human souls and other sentient creatures such as the *jinn* and Shaytān.

The tribes of the angels vary in size. Some consist of hundreds of thousands of angels while others do not exceed a few hundred. The members of every group worship together and stand in congregation to glorify God, "*There is not one of us (angels) but has his own assigned place, and indeed, we stand in rows for prayers.*"[133] Occasionally, legions of angels who number in the millions, will come to the senior angels such as Jibra'il, Mika'il or Israfil and act on their behalf and under their direction, just as flanks of an army obey their commander. Perhaps this is the meaning of the "wings or flanks of the angels" which have been mentioned in the Qur'an, "*All praise is due to God, the Creator of the heavens and the earth, Who made the angels messengers having two, three or four flanks...*"[134]

To make this discussion more complete, it will be beneficial to refer to parts of the tradition of *mi'rāj* which talk of the meeting of the Prophet (s) with some of the angels:

"Jibra'il went up to heaven of *dunyā* and I also ascended with him. An angel named Ismā'īl was in charge there and his instructions were to stop any eavesdropping, about which God has said in the Qur'an, "*Except such* (jinn) *who try to snatch (some words), but they are pursued by a flame of piercing brightness.*" Seventy thousand angels stood watch under his command, each with a further seventy thousand angels under him. He asked Jibra'il, "Who is this person with you?" Jibra'il replied, "This is Muhammad." He asked, "Has Muhammad been appointed to his mission already?" Jibra'il

133 Surat al-Ṣaffāt, 37:164, 165.

134 Surat Fāṭir, 35:1.

replied, "Yes." At this time, he opened the door[135] and greeted me with a salutation of peace; I returned his greeting and prayed for his forgiveness, and he prayed for mine in turn, and said, "Welcome O righteous brother and O righteous messenger!" Thereafter, angels came forward to welcome me until I entered the heaven of this world. Every angel who met me along the way was smiling in delight, and in this manner, we reached a huge angel. He was a creature bigger than any I had ever seen before; he had a stern face and a fearsome appearance. He welcomed me like the rest and prayed for me, but he did not smile, and I did not observe in him the happiness and delight of the other angels. I asked Jibra'il, "Who is this angel? Truly he is intimidating!" He replied, "You should be intimidated; we are all afraid of him. This is Mālik, the angel in charge of Hell who has never smiled all his life...."

Then I met an angel that God had created in an extraordinary fashion. Half his body was made of fire and the other half of ice;[136] neither did the fire melt the ice nor did the ice extinguish the fire. The angel was calling out in a loud voice, "All praise belongs to the One who has held back the heat of this fire from melting the ice and kept this ice from extinguishing the fire! O God, Who has kept a balance between fire and ice! Make the hearts of Your believers compassionate towards one another." I asked Jibra'il, "Who is this?" He replied, "It is a type of angel that God has assigned to all corners of the heavens and around the earth. He is the greatest well-wisher

[135] Surat al-Ḥijir, 15:18. As we have mentioned previously, the seven heavens are all dimensions of the realm of *malakūt*; "opening the door" here means granting permission to enter the dimension that the Prophet (s) was allowed access to during the *miʿrāj*.

[136] Of course, these substances are not made of material, but imaginal components. And as mentioned in other reports, there is a large number of this type of angel. See Majlisī, *Biḥār al-Anwār*, 56:174.

for the believers; from the day he was created he prays for them by continually invoking God with the same words that you hear." Then I saw two angels who were supplicating together; one was saying. "O God! Increase the wealth of everyone who spends in charity", while the other was saying, "O God, take away the wealth of every miser..."

Then we passed by a group of angels whose form and features defy description.[137] Every part of their bodies was engaged in the praise and glorification of God, each with a different melody. Their voices were raised in praise and in weeping out of awe of God. I asked Jibra'il about them. He said, "They have been created just like this. None of them have ever spoken to the angel next to them, and they have never raised their heads out of fear and awe of God and have never looked down either." I greeted them with a salutation of peace. Without looking at me they replied with a slight nod. Jibra'il said to them, "This is Muhammad, the messenger of mercy; he is a Prophet of God whom He has sent to guide His servants. He is the last of the Prophets and the best of them. Will you not speak with him?" Because they heard this from Jibra'il, they came towards me and greeted me warmly and prayed for goodness for me and my nation...

Then we ascended to the second heaven...It was full of angels who were overcome with complete humility and awe before God and their faces were beyond description. Every one of them was engaged in glorifying and praising God, each in a unique manner and voice... In the third heaven also, there were angels who were cloaked in humility and awe just as in the first and second heavens. Once more Jibra'il introduced

[137] The words of the tradition are, "God made them the way He desired and shaped their features the way He desired." |

خَلَقَهُمُ اللهُ كَيْفَ شَاءَ، وَوَضَعَ وُجُوهَهُمْ كَيْفَ شَاءَ.

me as he had earlier, and they likewise greeted me in the same manner as the other angels had...

Then we ascended to the fourth heaven. Just as in the other heavens, this too was also full of humble angels who prayed for goodness for me and my nation." And this was his experience in the fifth, sixth and seventh heavens also.[138]

[138] Qummī, *Tafsīr of ʿAlī b. Ibrāhīm*, p.369 – 374.

CHAPTER 3

THE BLOWING OF THE TRUMPET

The Death of the World

All the messengers of God have informed us that one Day this present world (*dunyā*) will come to an end, and the entire world of creation will enter a new phase which is called the Hereafter (*ākhira*). *Dunyā* encompasses the realms of the living as well as the dead; therefore, the life of those living on the earth as well as those living in *barzakh* will both come to an end on that Day and everything that has been granted life will die.

The end of the world will come about violently and terrifyingly such that every sentient being including the souls of human beings, the *jinn* and the angels will be stunned, "*On the day that the trumpet will be blown everyone in the heavens and the earth shall be petrified.*"[139] It will create an enormous cataclysm causing the earth to go through unprecedented convulsions, "*The earthquake of the final hour is a tremendous thing.*"[140] The supports of the earth will shake,[141] the sun will be extinguished, the stars will fade and the seas will burst into flame.[142] The skies will be rent asunder and the ground will be pounded to an extent that it will become featureless.[143] Mountains will crumble away.[144] The sun will darken, and the

[139] Surat al-Naml, 27:87.

[140] Surat al-Haj, 22:1.

[141] Gospel of Matthew, 24:29.

[142] Surat al-Takwir, 81:1-3.

[143] Surat al-Inshiqaq, 84:1-3.

[144] Surat al-Muzzammil, 73:14.

moon will shine no more, the stars will fall, and the heavens will be in disarray.[145]

Of course, nothing can remain alive in the face of such events and every creature will enter the realm of the dead. However, the situation is no better in that realm either. That which laid the world to waste has not spared the world of *barzakh* and the world of the angels. There also, the tumult of the end of the world has brought death to all.

The Blowing of the Trumpet

The death of the world shall be heralded by a fearsome blast of sound, which is in fact itself the cause of the end of the world. The blast shall be generated by Israfil, one of the greatest angels of God, and it will be of a nature unknown or previously unexperienced. The Qur'an refers to the action of Israfil as the "blowing of the trumpet" (*nafakhat al-ṣūr*), "*And when the trumpet is blown with a single blast, and the earth and the mountains are carried away and crushed with a single crushing; on that day the Great Event shall come to pass; and the heaven shall cleave asunder, and become weak...*"[146] And also, "*The trumpet shall be blown, and all those that are in the heavens and all those that are in the earth shall die, except whom God pleases.*"[147] In this verse, the dwellers of the heavens refers to angels and the dwellers of earth refer to mankind and *jinn*, both in the material world and in *barzakh*. Obviously, this is no ordinary loud sound, because it will affect the corporeal world as well as the world of souls, and beyond that, it shall encompass the angelic realm as well. Even Israfil, who initiated the event at the command of God, will die as a result of the blast.

---

[145] Gospel of Mark, 13:24,25.

[146] Surat al-Hāqqā, 69:13-16.

[147] Surat al-Zumar 39:68.

No creature shall remain sentient in the entire cosmos, except a handful who will remain alive by God's will. Death shall encompass all; every perception shall be silenced, and the world will be taken over by a total stillness and darkness. It shall be as if life never existed at all; indeed, God is needless of everything.

A Protracted Death as a Prelude to Eternal Life

What does this complete death, this total stillness and absence of perception serve? All this is to facilitate the evolution of the universe into a new phase of existence. During this interval all dimensions of the universe - from the earth to the heavens, from the realm of *barzakh* to the deepest realms of the angels - cannot be inhabited by life. The universe is in the all-capable hands of God, Who with infinite love and care prepares, in the absence of all living beings, the ground for their return to a richer life and a more expansive world, so that they can continue on their journey towards Him.

As for how long this lifeless silence, devoid of humans or angels, will last, no one shall exist to measure or appreciate its duration. It is for this reason that when everyone returns to life again, they think that no more than a few hours or days have passed. In truth what has actually occurred during their stasis is an evolution that has lasted longer than the age of creation. Billions of years will pass before the world assumes its final form, ready to be inhabited by man and other creatures for eternity. And during this process, God in His mercy has placed all His creatures in a deep slumber to protect them from the tumultuous and violent changes as the universe transforms and rejuvenates itself.

It can be imagined that at the blast of Israfil's trumpet everyone dies immediately[148] or alternatively, the blast sets into motion the gradual death of different layers of existence. This process, and the time scale associated with it is astonishing. A lengthy narration reported from Imam al-Sadiq (a) can shed some light on it:

"After God causes the inhabitants of the earth to die, He will wait for a duration several times as long as the entire lifetime of humanity and then he will cause the death of the inhabitants of the heavens of this world (the angels and the souls in the first layer of *barzakh*). Then, after a pause several times longer than the lifetime of humanity and the duration between the death of the inhabitants of the world and that of the inhabitants of the first heaven, He will cause the death of inhabitants of the second heaven (the souls in the second layer of *barzakh*). Then after a pause several times longer than the previous two durations He will cause the death of the inhabitants of the third heaven (the third layer of *barzakh*). And this will continue in the same manner for all the heavens until the seventh heaven. After a pause several times longer in duration than the time since creation, He will cause the death of Mika'il. After a pause several times longer again, he will cause Jibra'il to die. In the same manner, he will then cause Israfil to die. Finally, He will cause the angel of death to die, after a duration several times longer than the time from the beginning of creation to the death of Israfil."[149]

These timescales are far beyond our limited capacity to imagine and also give an indication of the exalted ranks of the four grand angels, Mika'il, Jibra'il, Israfil and 'Izra'il.

---

148 As mentioned in some narrations.

149 Majlisī, *Biḥāral-Anwār*, 6:326, quoting Imam al-Sadiq (a).

In any case, after every living creature dies, then after a duration several times longer than what has been mentioned above,[150] the form of the after-world will appear in the corporeal world and the material realm will be able to provide eternal homes for the mature souls of mankind and angels. At this time, God will bring Israfil back to life to once again blow his trumpet. This time however, the blast of Israfil's trumpet will not bring about death; rather it will revive the dead and make them alive once more.

The Fate of the Universe between the Two Blowings of Israfil's Trumpet

During the long period between the two blasts of the trumpet several developments occur. First of all the earth and the solar system are transformed both in their structure and properties, "*On the day when the earth shall be changed into a different earth, as will the heavens.*"[151] The earth will be stretched and expanded[152] and the mountains and valleys will all disappear, "*And they ask you about the mountains. Say: My Lord will carry them away from the roots. Then He shall leave the earth a plain, smooth level. You shall not see therein any crookedness or unevenness.*"[153] The skies will look quite different and probably take on a different hue, "*And when the heaven is rent asunder, and then reddens like red ointment.*"[154] The different dimensions of the universe are either replaced by new systems or their properties altered to facilitate the

[150] Ibid.

[151] Surat Ibrāhīm, 14:48.

[152] Surat al-Inshiqāq, 84:3.

[153] Surat Ṭā Hā 20:105-107.

[154] Surat al-Raḥmān, 55:37. It is not certain whether this redness that appears when the heavens are going through tumultuous change will persist later or not.

extraordinary life of the world of *ākhira*. This new world will also contain water, earth and fire, gold, silver and rubies, etc., but the enhanced properties and potentials of these substances cannot be understood until we personally experience them in that world.

The second major change will be that every atom in the universe will gain the ability to perceive, understand and communicate. The earth will recount the events that it silently witnessed throughout the long and eventful history of mankind, because God has given it a higher level of life, "*That Day it will relate its chronicles, now that God has inspired it.*"[155] People will dispute with the stone and wooden idols that they had carved and then worshipped, but the idols will display aversion to the idolaters, "*If you invoke them they do not hear your call, and even if they could hear they could not grant you (your request); and on the Day of Resurrection they will disown your association of them with God.*"[156] Even man's own limbs are now able to converse with him, and this is referred to as the resurrection of inanimate beings (*ma'ād al-jamādāt*).

Thirdly, the transformation is not confined just to the earth and heavens but encompasses the deepest layers of the system of creation. The seven layers of *barzakh* which are called the seven heavens are replaced with new layers. Three major layers are formed under each of which lie smaller layers. The first layer is Paradise, the second is Hell and the third is called *maḥshar*, the place of gathering. It is here that the inhabitants of the first two layers will initially be gathered before they go to their eternal abode, Paradise or Hell.

---

155 Surat al-Zilzāl, 99:3,4.

156 Surat al-Fāṭir, 35:14.

Fourthly, the hand of God that is hidden today behind the system of causes and effects will become apparent and obvious, and the system of causes and effects will fade from sight behind it. On that day everyone will see and realize that everything is from God and can only be sought from Him. Both His Sovereignty and Authority will be clearly apparent to all, "*Whose is the Kingdom today? To Allah, the One, the Mighty!*"[157] He is the "*Master of the day of Judgement*".[158] Of course, this does not mean that the system of cause and effect is annulled; rather it fades behind the glorious manifestation of the One who initiated and sustains existence. And there will be many other wonders experienced during mankind's journey towards the meeting with God which we will discuss in due course.

The Second Blowing and Resurrection

The second blast or blowing of the trumpet will also be executed by Israfil. However, this is no longer the same Israfil who blew into the trumpet that caused the death of creation, rather he is the Israfil who has been resurrected by God in the realm of the afterlife. With his enhanced form, he grasps the trumpet of life, and as he blows into it, by God's command the breeze of life enters every atom in creation and enlivens every dead being: angels, *jinn*, man and animal.

Now the setting is prepared. All dimensions of *ākhira* have been formed; the place and station of every angel has been determined. As each of them returns to life he finds himself at his station, which is more wondrous and beautiful than previously. What is now seen of the mercy and might of God cannot be compared to what was witnessed before. A new grace flows from God tinging the cosmos with a new

[157] Surat al-Ghāfir, 40:16

[158] Surat al-Fātiḥa, 1:4

hue. Creation has been renewed and a more beautiful and wondrous universe than that which the angels had ever witnessed before reflects the glory of God.

The Return of Man

The return to consciousness for human beings is a surreal experience. They find themselves in the same place where they had been buried and where their body had decomposed, but now their material body has been resurrected and transformed. It does not resemble the *barzakhi* body; rather it appears initially more like the body that they had in the world, except that it is composed of a different material. In amazement, he realizes that now he has two bodies, the imaginal (*barzakhi*) body and a material body; he learns that he can make use of either one or both at the same time, thus simultaneously appreciating the blessings of the material (*mulk*) as well as angelic realms (*malakūt*).

For long moments after waking from his lengthy sleep the feeling of bewilderment and wonder persists, "*They say: Are we indeed restored to our former state in our grave? Even after we were crumbled bones?*"[159] How has he become flesh and bone again? When this new body was fashioned, he had still been asleep and unaware, and he cannot understand where it has appeared from. The body seems different in some way yet even its fingerprints are the same as before, "*Does man think that We shall not reassemble his bones? In fact, We are able to restore his very fingertips!*"[160] "*And on the Day that He shall gather them together, it will seem as if they had not tarried (in* barzakh*) except for an hour of the day, and they will recognize one another.*"[161]

---

[159] Surat al-Nāzi'āt, 79:10-11.

[160] Surat al-Qiyāma, 75:3-4.

[161] Surat Yūnus, 10:45.

They cannot understand how they have once again assumed human form and they can once more appreciate the bounties of the earth, yet at the same time witness the throne of God. Their existence has been enhanced out of all proportion as they arrive in the vicinity of God. They do not realize that this was due to the rain of *qiyāma* that poured down, revitalizing and reshaping every cell of their lifeless former bodies, "When God wills to bring creation back to life, He makes a rain fall for forty days that causes bones to knit together and become clothed in flesh."[162]

They do not yet understand that the earth of *dunyā*, which nurtured and matured seeds planted within it and in which strong trees grew, has now been transformed to the earth of *ākhira*, within which the cells of human beings are nurtured and grow to maturity, transforming them at the same time into more enhanced forms. Consider the verse, *"And We have sent down blessed rain from the skies through which we make grow gardens and crops for harvest. And lofty palm trees with fruit in clusters, a sustenance for My servants. And (through rain) We give life back to dead land, and thus will be the Resurrection also."*[163] The dead will come back to life in the same way, "When the rain falls from the skies at God's command, it will persist for forty days until the waters will rise to twelve cubits. Then God will command the human bodies to begin to grow and they will do so, just as plants do, until their bodies are completely formed."[164]

---

[162] Majlisī, *Biḥār al Anwār*, 7:33, reporting from Imam al-Sadiq (a) |
إِذَا أَرَادَ اللهُ عَزَّ وَجَلَّ أَنْ يَبْعَثَ الْخَلْقَ، أَمْطَرَ السَّمَاءَ أَرْبَعِينَ صَبَاحًا، فَاجْتَمَعَتِ الْأَوْصَالُ وَنَبَتَتِ اللُّحُومُ.

[163] Surat Qāf, 50:9-11.

[164] Al-Ṭabarānī, *al-Ḥadīth al-Ṭiwāl*, p. 96 |
ثُمَّ يَأْمُرُ اللهُ عَزَّ وَجَلَّ السَّمَاءَ أَنْ تُمْطِرَ فَتُمْطِرُ أَرْبَعِينَ يَوْمًا حَتَّى يَكُونَ الْمَاءُ فَوْقَهُمْ اثْنَيْ عَشَرَ ذِرَاعًا، ثُمَّ يَأْمُرُ اللهُ عَزَّ وَجَلَّ الْأَجْسَادَ أَنْ تَنْبُتَ فَتَنْبُتُ كَنَبَاتِ الطَّرَاثِيثِ أَوْ كَنَبَاتِ الْبَقْلِ حَتَّى إِذَا تَكَامَلَتْ أَجْسَادُهُمْ.

The earth of *qiyāma* is so potent that only a few cells of the original are required to perfectly resurrect human bodies, with all their previous features and characteristics. Every human cell contains essential information which is never lost, as is alluded to in a tradition, "The earth consumes every part of the human body except the deepest part of his spinal column, which is a grain smaller than a mustard seed, and from this he will be revived."[165]

The Clay of Human Beings and the Reviving Rain of the Hereafter

How are the cellular remnants of human beings distinguished from other material in the earth and how are their dispersed cells brought together? To answer this, we must remember that the new earth of the Hereafter is different from earth of the *dunyā* of old and has undergone millions of years of fundamental change. Now, its soil and rain follow the rules of *qiyāma*. Amongst the wonders of that Day is that "the bodies of beings who possess a soul will be scattered as dust within the ground like gold amongst common rocks. When the resurrection occurs, it will rain so heavily that it will disturb the ground. Then, just as gold is sifted from soil, human dust will break free from the earth around them and assemble."[166] This means that cells that once possessed life shall eternally maintain their identity and when conditions are favourable, they will easily separate from the other elements around them.

---

[165] Muttaqī Hindī, *Kanz al-ʿUmmāl*, trad. 38964, reporting from the Prophet (s) through Abū Saʿīd al-Khudrī |

يَأْكُلُ التُّرَابُ كُلَّ شَيْءٍ مِنَ الْإِنْسَانِ إِلَّا عَجْبَ ذَنَبِهِ مِثْلَ حَبَّةِ خَرْدَلٍ، مِنْهُ تَنْبُتُونَ.

This theme occurs in many reliable narrations in both Sunnī and Shīʿa collections.

[166] Majlisī, *Biḥār al-Anwār*, 7:38, reporting from Imam al-Sadiq (a).

Thereafter, according to the rules that God has ordained for that Day, "the dispersed cells of every human being will move to the location where his soul is placed and reassemble there."[167] The rain will continue for a long time until this process is complete. "When God wills to resurrect the human beings, he will cause it to rain for forty days during which time their bones will gather, and flesh will form over them."[168] For a clearer explanation of this process, let us look at the reply given by Imam al-Sadiq (a) to a man who denied God and the Hereafter:

An unbeliever asked Imam al-Sadiq (a): "How can individuals be resurrected when their bodies have decayed or been consumed by wild animals and insects, or become part of the soil and made into bricks for building walls?" The Imam (a) replied: "The One Who created them from nothing and fashioned them without a previous mould is capable of bringing them back to existence, just as He did the first time." The man asked for further details. The Imam (a) said, "The souls exist in their own specific locations. The souls of the righteous are in a place of light and spaciousness, while the souls of the corrupt are in a place of darkness and narrowness. At the same time the body disintegrates into the earth from which it originated. Everything that was consumed and excreted by animals and insects is preserved in the ground in the knowledge of God, Who is aware of the size and weight of every cell in the depths of the earth. The cells of sentient beings are like gold nuggets which are distinct from the rocks and soil that surrounds them, or like lumps of butter that become separate from milk.

---

[167] Ibid.

[168] Majlisī, *Biḥār al-Anwār*, 7:33, reporting from Imam al-Sadiq (a) |
إِذَا أَرَادَ اللهُ عَزَّ وَجَلَّ أَنْ يَبْعَثَ الْخَلْقَ، أَمْطَرَ السَّمَاءَ أَرْبَعِينَ صَبَاحًا، فَاجْتَمَعَتِ الْأَوْصَالُ وَنَبَتَتِ اللُّحُومُ.

Thereafter, the cells of each being will come together and with God's permission, proceed towards the place where their soul is located. With the permission of the Fashioner, all the bodies will reassume their former features, and the souls will once again occupy them. In this way the individual is once again complete and self-aware."[169]

Thus, as bodies congregate with their souls, they come out of the ground having resumed their former appearance, just as seeds assume the form of the parent plant. Then when Israfil blows into the trumpet of life, the souls awaken and the individual discovers himself in his new and resurrected body, which he finds to be identical in appearance to his former one. Of course, this is not quite the same body, because it has been formed with new cells.

[169] Majlisī, *Biḥār al-Anwār*, 7:37-38, reporting from Imam al-Sadiq (a) | عَنْ هِشَامِ بْنِ الْحَكَمِ أَنَّهُ قَالَ الزِّنْدِيقُ لِلصَّادِقِ عَلَيْهِ السَّلَامُ: أَنَّى لِلرُّوحِ بِالْبَعْثِ وَالْبَدَنُ قَدْ بَلِيَ وَالْأَعْضَاءُ قَدْ تَفَرَّقَتْ؟ فَعُضْوٌ فِي بَلْدَةٍ تَأْكُلُهَا سِبَاعُهَا، وَعُضْوٌ بِأُخْرَى تُمَزِّقُهُ هَوَامُّهَا، وَعُضْوٌ قَدْ صَارَ تُرَابًا بُنِيَ بِهِ مَعَ الطِّينِ حَائِطٌ؟ قَالَ (ع): إِنَّ الَّذِي أَنْشَأَهُ مِنْ غَيْرِ شَيْءٍ وَصَوَّرَهُ عَلَى غَيْرِ مِثَالٍ كَانَ سَبَقَ إِلَيْهِ، قَادِرٌ أَنْ يُعِيدَهُ كَمَا بَدَأَهُ. قَالَ: أَوْضِحْ لِي ذَلِكَ.

قَالَ (ع): إِنَّ الرُّوحَ مُقِيمَةٌ فِي مَكَانِهَا: رُوحُ الْمُحْسِنِينَ فِي ضِيَاءٍ وَفُسْحَةٍ، وَرُوحُ الْمُسِيءِ فِي ضِيقٍ وَظُلْمَةٍ، وَالْبَدَنُ يَصِيرُ تُرَابًا مِنْهُ خُلِقَ، وَمَا تَقْذِفُ بِهِ السِّبَاعُ وَالْهَوَامُّ مِنْ أَجْوَافِهَا فَمَا أَكَلَتْهُ وَمَزَّقَتْهُ كُلُّ ذَلِكَ فِي التُّرَابِ مَحْفُوظٌ عِنْدَ مَنْ لَا يَعْزُبُ عَنْهُ مِثْقَالُ ذَرَّةٍ فِي ظُلُمَاتِ الْأَرْضِ وَيَعْلَمُ عَدَدَ الْأَشْيَاءِ وَوَزْنَهَا، وَإِنَّ تُرَابَ الرُّوحَانِيِّينَ بِمَنْزِلَةِ الذَّهَبِ فِي التُّرَابِ، فَإِذَا كَانَ حِينُ الْبَعْثِ مَطَرَتِ السَّمَاءُ فَتَرْبُو الْأَرْضُ ثُمَّ تَمْخَضُ مَخْضَ السِّقَاءِ فَيَصِيرُ تُرَابُ الْبَشَرِ كَمَصِيرِ الذَّهَبِ مِنَ التُّرَابِ إِذَا غُسِلَ بِالْمَاءِ وَالزُّبْدِ مِنَ اللَّبَنِ إِذَا مُخِضَ فَيَجْتَمِعُ تُرَابُ كُلِّ قَالَبٍ فَيُنْقَلُ بِإِذْنِ اللهِ تَعَالَى إِلَى حَيْثُ الرُّوحِ، فَتَعُودُ الصُّوَرُ بِإِذْنِ الْمُصَوِّرِ كَهَيْئَتِهَا وَتَلِجُ الرُّوحُ فِيهَا، فَإِذَا قَدْ اسْتَوَى لَا يُنْكِرُ مِنْ نَفْسِهِ شَيْئًا.

CHAPTER 4

THE DAY OF JUDGEMENT

Awakening

In most cases, human bodies will develop and mature within the ground where they were buried, because most of their cellular remnants are in that area. Then will come a time when the ground splits all around and the dead begin to emerge swiftly, "*On the Day when the ground will cleave asunder and mankind shall rush out - that is an easy gathering for Us.*"[170] In other words, the earth discharges its contents, "*And when the earth is spread out, and casts out what it contains and becomes empty.*"[171]

Human beings will emerge one by one from the earth and remain waiting next to their graves. It will take some time for the stupor of their long sleep to dispel. They will be wiping away the mud and grime from their faces as they look around in amazement, unsure about what exactly has happened. They do not know how they have awakened in a new body after just a short nap! There are no signs of the darkness or illumination, narrowness or expansiveness of their life in *barzakh*. As far as they can see, they are back in their former human form; they have come out of the ground and are sitting next to their grave. Their multitudes resemble moths that flutter in a vast and desolate desert, "*The Day on which mankind will be as scattered moths.*"[172]

---

170 Surat Qāf, 50/44.

171 Surat al-Inshiqāq, 84:3,4.

172 Surat al-Qāri'ā, 101:4.

The Structure of the Human Body in the *Ākhira*

The genetic information contained in the scattered cells of an individual play an essential role in the reassembly of his limbs and flesh to create his new body in the *ākhira.* However, it is not the only factor that determines the nature of the *ākhira* body. In this resurrection, the imaginal body also plays a fundamental role, because an individual's features, personality and characteristics are modelled on his *barzakhi* body. And if you recall, that body in turn was largely affected by the actions, disposition and inclinations of the individual when he lived in the *dunyā,* and which had etched themselves in his soul and mingled with his being. As a consequence, these factors act like genes to give rise to the various physical and spiritual qualities of his new and eternal body.

When people see each other in the assembly of *maḥshar*, they notice how the spiritual genetic variances have caused some faces to become illuminated and dignified and others dark and gloomy, "*And on the Day of Judgement you will see that those who lied concerning God will have their faces blackened*"[173] and it will appear that, "*their faces are covered with patches from the depths of the dark night.*"[174]

Some will be blind, and terror will drain their colour, "*On the Day when the (second) trumpet shall be blown, We shall gather the criminals on that day blue (or blind) with terror*"[175] Some will be deaf and unable to hear most sounds. Those who sold their religion in the world and used it only expediently to earn their livelihood will have no flesh on their faces and they

---

[173] Surat al-Zumar, 39:60.

[174] Surat Yūnus, 10:27.

[175] Surat Ṭā Hā, 20:102.

will appear with hideous and skull-like faces. In a tradition we read that, "Those who recite the Qur'an so that they can earn their livelihood from the people thereby will appear on the Day of Judgement with faces that have been stripped of flesh and resemble skulls."[176] Some will be resurrected so tiny that if they tried to walk with the multitudes of people they would be crushed underfoot, "The arrogant will become the size of ants and they will be kicked about by the people until God finishes taking the accounts (*ḥisāb*)."[177]

In summary, everyone's features and forms will alter in strange manners, although people will still be recognizable from their faces. It has been narrated from the Prophet (s) that he said the following about the sinners from his nation:

["Ten groups from my nation will be resurrected apart. God will separate them from the ranks of the Muslims and their features will be transformed. One group will resemble apes and another will resemble pigs; some will undergo a reversal so that their faces and feet will change places and they will be dragged everywhere in this manner; others will be blind, and will be stumbling about in confusion; some will be deaf and dumb and will not understand anything; some will be chewing on their own bloated tongues and blood and pus will ooze from their mouths in a manner that it will fill people with disgust; others will have had their arms and legs cut off, and others will be hanging from branches of fire. A group will be emitting a foul odour much worse than that of rotting corpses, and a group will be clothed in pitch and tar which will be stuck on their bodies."]

---

176 Ṣadūq, *Thawāb al-Aʿmāl*, p. 268, reporting from Imam al-Sadiq (a) | مَنْ قَرَأَ الْقُرْآنَ يَأْكُلُ بِهِ النَّاسَ جَاءَ يَوْمَ الْقِيَامَةِ وَوَجْهُهُ عَظْمٌ لَا لَحْمَ فِيهِ.

177 Kulaynī, *al-Kāfī*, 2:311, reporting from Imam al-Sadiq (a) | إِنَّ الْمُتَكَبِّرِينَ يُجْعَلُونَ فِي صُوَرِ الذَّرِ يَتَوَطَّؤُهُمُ النَّاسُ حَتَّى يَفْرُغَ اللهُ مِنَ الْحِسَابِ.

["As for those who appear as apes, they were the gossipers and slanderers. And those that appear as pigs used to consume from unlawful sources. Those who are being dragged upside-down earned their livelihood from interest and usury and those who are blind were unjust in their judgements and oppressed the people. Those who are deaf and dumb were proud and self-centred. As for those who are chewing on their own tongues, they are the scholars and orators who did not themselves act on what they told others to do. Those that have had their limbs cut off used to harass their neighbours and those that are hanging on gallows of fire are the spies and talebearers who slandered innocent people to rulers. Those who emit a foul stench are the ones who gave in to their base and unlawful sexual desires and also those who did not pay the purifying tax (*zakāt*). As for those who are clothed in burning tar (*qaṭirān*), they used to be conceited and boastful (in dress and conduct)."][178]

Self-realization on the Day of Judgement

Why should people linger in this state and why do they have to undertake such a lengthy journey towards Paradise or Hell? Has man not evolved sufficiently by undergoing the tests of the *dunyā* and the maturation process in *barzakh* that he can now be led directly to his eternal abode, whichever it is?

The answer to this question is clear. Between the material world in which we are physically living at present and the

[178] This tradition is mentioned by many exegetes when discussing the verse, "*The Day when the trumpet shall be blown, and you will all come forth in groups.*" (Surat al-Nabā', 78:18). Some exegetes who have mentioned this tradition are: Zamakhsharī in *al-Kashshāf*, 2:518; Ṭabarsī in *Majma' al-Bayān*, 5:423; Abū al-Futtūḥ al-Rāzī in *Rawḍ al-Jinān*, 5:462; Fakhr al-dīn al-Rāzī in *Mafātiḥ al-Ghayb* 8:433,434; al-Suyūṭī in *al-Durr al-Manthūr*, 6:307; and Fayḍ al-Kāshānī in *al-Ṣāfī*, 5:555.

world of the Names and Attributes of God which can only be perceived in Paradise, there are two other realms. One is the imaginal world or the world of analogies (*'ālam al-mithāl*) and the other is the spiritual world or the world of souls (*'ālam al-nafs*). These two realms are also called *barzakh* and *qiyāma* respectively. Unless he passes through these two worlds, a human being cannot attain the level where he can perceive the realities of the Divine names and attributes. In other words, just as it is not possible to reach the world of *ākhira* without gaining capacity from traversing the world of *barzakh*, reaching the realm of the names and attributes and perceiving the true beauty of God is not possible without the self-realization and insights gained in traversing through the world of *qiyāma*. Perhaps this is the meaning of the narration of the Prophet (s) about the Day of Judgement, "When a believer comes out of his grave, his actions will appear before him in a beautiful form. He will enquire, "Who are you? By God, you appear to be a virtuous person." It will reply, "I am the embodiment of your good actions." It will then illuminate his path and guide him to Paradise. And when a disbeliever comes out of his grave, his actions will appear before him in an abominable form. He will ask, "Who are you? By God, I find you repulsive." It will reply, "I am the embodiment of your actions," then it will carry him to the fire of Hell."[179]

The world of souls does not have any discernible boundaries. As we move above the world of matter there exist greater

---

[179] Muttaqī al-Hindī, *Kanz al-'Ummāl*, tradition 38963 | إِنَّ الْمُؤْمِنَ إِذَا خَرَجَ مِنْ قَبْرِهِ صُوِّرَ لَهُ عَمَلُهُ فِي صُورَةٍ حَسَنَةٍ، فَيَقُولُ لَهُ: مَا أَنْتَ؟ فَوَاللهِ، إِنِّي لَأَرَاكَ امْرَأَ الصِّدْقِ، فَيَقُولُ لَهُ: أَنَا عَمَلُكَ، فَيَكُونُ لَهُ نُورٌ وَقَائِدٌ إِلَى الْجَنَّةِ، وَإِنَّ الْكَافِرَ إِذَا خَرَجَ مِنْ قَبْرِهِ صُوِّرَ لَهُ عَمَلُهُ فِي صُورَةٍ سَيِّئَةٍ وَبِشَارَةٍ سَيِّئَةٍ فَيَقُولُ مَنْ أَنْتَ؟ فَوَاللهِ! إِنِّي لَأَرَاكَ امْرَأَ السُّوءِ، فَيَقُولُ: أَنَا عَمَلُكَ، فَيَنْطَلِقُ بِهِ حَتَّى يَدْخُلَ النَّارَ.

and more potent worlds; in contrast as one descends from higher realms, the worlds get smaller and weaker, "Just like the image in a mirror which is a mere reflection of the features and colour of the face and gives no clue about the true nature of the person." It cannot give an indication of the intelligence, generosity, courage or other qualities of the person standing in front of it. And certainly, it cannot reflect his inner soul, which in any case has no shape or structure. For this reason, the realities of the imaginal world (*barzakh*) cannot be reduced and interpreted in the language of matter; in fact, what the *dunyā* displays of the world of *barzakh* is confined to the capacity and limitations of material concepts. In the same way the realities of the after-world (*qiyāma*) and the realities of the world of souls (*ʿālam al-nafs*) cannot be reflected in the mirror of the *barzakh*, and whatever *barzakh* displays of *qiyāma* is only to the extent of its own capacity and limitations."[180]

To enter the imaginal world, it is necessary to pass through this material world; we have to shed our primitive material bodies to enter into a more expansive world. In the same way, in order to enter the world of souls or *qiyāma*, we have to die in the world of *barzakh* and shed our relatively primitive imaginal bodies in order to perceive that immense world. And in this last world we have to travel within our own souls to find our true purpose. The many stations of *qiyāma* including the resurrection and dispersion (*ḥashr wa nashr*), the accounting (*ḥisāb*), the book (*kitāb*), the witnessing (*shahāda*), the balance (*mīzān*) and the bridge (*ṣirāṭ*) all exist to better acquaint us with ourselves, so that soul may begin to reflect those Divine names and attributes that it has the capacity to – whether these are His attributes of beauty (*jamāl*) or His attributes of majesty (*jalāl*).

[180] Allāma Ḥusainī Tehrānī, *Maʿād Shināsī*, vol. 2. The characteristics of *barzakh*.

And this is the world of the meeting with God (*liqā Allah*). It is a world in which our souls reflect God's attributes like a mirror. In fact, the meeting with God begins from the moment we wake up in the after-world. The Prophet stated, "Mankind is asleep, and when they die, they wake up."[181] When we enter *barzakh* it seems that we have woken up from a deep sleep. Compared to *barzakh* this world is no more than a slumber. In the same way, the world of *barzakh* when compared to that of *qiyāma* is just like sleep compared to wakefulness. When we enter into the world of *qiyāma* from *barzakh* it will seem to us that we have finally woken up. It is for this reason that the imaginal world is called the minor *qiyāma* (*qiyāmat al-ṣughrā*) and the world of souls is called the major *qiyāma* (*qiyāmat al-kubrā*).

Some believe that just as the soul detaches from our material bodies at death so as to be able to witness the wonders of the imaginal world, similarly the soul must also detach from the imaginal body so that it can witness the wonders of *qiyāma*. In other words, the soul must become absolutely immaterial (*mujarrad*) so that it can get to know itself intimately; it is only then that it can meet God and witness the wonders of that realm. However, this view does not appear to be correct because, in the world of *qiyāma*, the material body, the imaginal body and the soul unify into one efficient entity. The difference between the *ākhira* and *dunyā* is that in *qiyāma*, the human being has control over all three realms: material, imaginal and spiritual. His material dimension does not inhibit his imaginal capacity, and his imaginal dimension does not inhibit his spiritual capacity. The human being, in fact needs to be all three simultaneously in order to comprehensively perceive the Divine names and attributes.

---

[181] Majlisī, *Biḥār al-Anwār*, 4:43 narrating from Imam Ali (a) |
النَّاسُ نِيَامٌ، فَإِذَا مَاتُوا انْتَبَهُوا.

Not all human beings can properly exercise their newfound ability when they first enter *qiyāma*. Some time is required for them to get acquainted with this new world, just as when they first arrived in *barzakh*. It is for this reason that it takes them a while to realize what must have happened, "*They shall say: Woe be to us! Who has roused us from our sleeping place? This is what the Merciful Lord promised, and the messenger spoke the truth.*"[182] Can it be that their withered bodies are whole again? How did the ground split asunder and expel them out from their graves? It seems incredible to them, but they soon realize that it is quite real.

In this surreal scene, the joy and hope of the virtuous and the sorrow and despair of the corrupt is beyond description. The believers will raise the slogan, "There is no God but Allah and on Him do we rely!"[183] And they have brought this conviction from their life in *dunyā*. As for the disbelievers, they will be filled with hesitation and confusion, and this will be due to what they were accustomed to in *dunyā*. However, at this point both groups will still be together, scattered amongst a congregation of billions of human beings. People will find their friends and acquaintances around them and approach one another and greet each other warmly. Even distant acquaintances will seek out familiar faces to renew ties; "*And on the Day that He shall gather them together, it will seem as if they had not tarried (in barzakh) except for an hour of the day, and they will recognize one another.*"[184]

However, no-one will have any idea about what to do next or what will happen next. Fear and anxiety will also be visible

---

182 Surat Yā Sīn, 36:52.

183 Muttaqī Hindī, *Kanz al-ʿUmmāl*, trad. 39032 |

شِعَارُ الْمُؤْمِنِينَ يَوْمَ يُبْعَثُونَ مِنْ قُبُورِهِمْ: لَا إِلَهَ إِلَّا اللهُ وَعَلَى اللهِ فَلْيَتَوَكَّلِ الْمُؤْمِنُونَ.

184 Surat Yūnus, 10:45.

on the faces of the waiting crowds. Everyone will be seeking out someone who may know something or could provide information about what is to happen now. They will seek out those people who were knowledgeable about *ākhira* in the *dunyā* and were familiar with its ways, "*In whispers they will consult one another, saying: It can't have been more than ten (days)? But We know better about what they speak, and the best in conduct amongst them will inform them: You have not tarried more than one interval.*"[185] "*And on the Day of Judgement the guilty will swear that they did not tarry but an hour (between the two blowings); they were always deluded thus. But those who were granted knowledge and faith will say, "Indeed you tarried as per God's decree until the Day of Resurrection and this is the Day of Resurrection, but you used not to know!*"[186]

This confusion and waiting will not last very long. However, while they wait, there is more fear than hope except for those whom the angels of mercy come to assist and comfort. These are the same angels who had come to them in the grave and promised to accompany them every step of the way on the Day of Judgement, "*Verily those who profess, "God is our Lord" and then stay steadfast – the angels will descend on them saying, "Do not fear and do not grieve, but receive good news of Paradise, which you were promised. We are your protectors in the world and in the Hereafter.*"[187] As for the rest of the people, the predominant emotion is fear, because everyone sees that they are in God's grasp and are anxious and fearful about the accounting for their deeds and having to explain how they had utilized the Divine blessings that they had received during their life. What is certain is that mankind has to now

185 Surat Ṭā Hā, 20 :103, 104.

186 Surat al-Rūm, 30:55,56.

187 Surat al-Fuṣṣilat, 41:30,31.

prepare itself for this new stage in the journey towards God. This is a journey that began the day they gained life in their mothers' wombs and continued when they were born into the world, and entered a new phase when they died and reached the world of *barzakh* and now, on the Day of Judgement as they stand witnessing the undeniable sovereignty of God, they have reached the most important and hardest part of their travels.

The Day of Gathering (*Ḥashr*) and Assembly (*Jamʿ*)[188]

This is the gathering and assemblage that had always been promised. *Ḥashr* refers to the gathering together of the people and *jamʿ* means assembling them in an orderly fashion. God will gather the dead from every corner of the earth and then assemble them in one place. Young and old, men and women, people of the former times and those from later generations, each will be gathered, "*And We will gather them and not leave any one of them behind.*"[189] Countless multitudes, freshly resurrected, will throng together and be herded towards their specific sections. Gradually, the congestion will increase and it will be difficult to find room to even stand, "The fortunate ones will be those who find a place to stand or even to draw breath."[190] The crush of the masses, the uncertainty about the future and the overpowering and steadily increasing heat will leave everyone thirsty and agitated.

It will seem as if the sun is drawing ever closer to the earth and the heat will become intense. Of course, this is not the

---

188 One of the names of the Day of Judgement is *Yawm al-jamʿ* - see Surat al-Taghābun, 64:9.

189 Surat al-Kahf, 18:47.

190 *Nahj al-Balāgha*, Sermon 102 | فَأَحْسَنُهُمْ حَالًا مَنْ وَجَدَ لِقَدَمَيْهِ مَوْضِعًا، وَلِنَفْسِهِ مُتَّسَعًا.

sun that we know of in our solar system, because with the blowing of the trumpet our own sun will die and its light and heat will be extinguished.

This gathering and assembly will not be for the human race only. The *jinn*, who used to distract human beings in devilish forms, will also be brought forth and they will be spread out within their ranks, "*By your Lord! We shall certainly gather them and the satans.*"[191] And also, "*And on the Day that we gather them all together and say: "O assembly of* Jinns! *You misled many men." And their friends from amongst mankind shall say: "O Lord! We benefitted from each other, but now we have reached the appointed hour which You had appointed for us ...*"[192]

The System and Administrators of the Day of Gathering

The apparent chaos as millions of people streams out of their graves and assemble, unsure about their fate, does not mean that preparations have not been made to efficiently process them. In fact, as groups are revived from their graves, there will be someone waiting to meet them, direct them to their predetermined positions and guide them on the path they must take. Obviously, these huge multitudes of people will not all go in one direction and will not pass through just one door on their way to the meeting with God. Each must traverse a path that he has the capacity for, and which he has willingly selected through his words and deeds and choices during his life in *dunyā*.

It is here that the powerful and imposing administrators of the day of gathering make an appearance. They separate the crowd into different groups. The administrators are angels, whom the Qur'an refers to as "callers" (*dāʿī*) because they

---

[191] Surat Maryam, 19:68.

[192] Surat al-Anʿām, 6:128.

prompt individuals by accessing the depths of their beings and get them to follow them unresistingly towards their positions in the waiting assembly.

The callers are intimately aware of the individual's personality and their total control over him is such that he is powerless to resist their summons. They identify every individual human being no matter where their remains lie and draw them with an unbelievable speed to their allocated positions, "*On that Day they shall follow caller unerringly, and all voices shall be hushed before the all-Merciful so you will not hear anything except muted whispers.*"[193] And mankind will be swiftly drawn to their positions, "*The Day when they will come forth from their graves in haste as if they were rushing to a goal.*"[194] No matter how much we try, we cannot quite imagine the reverberation across the plains of *maḥshar* as the callers summon every resurrected being to assemble. Everyone will be hastened to their own destination and be oblivious to the plight of others. This destination will be terrifying and disheartening for some but pleasant and comforting for others. As the disbelievers and evildoers are drawn to their destinations, they will begin to realize the hardships that lie in store for them; "*The Day when the caller calls them to a painful thing. With eyes downcast, they will stream forth from their graves like locusts dispersing, racing towards the caller. The disbelievers will say: This is a difficult day.*"[195]

And so, they will helplessly hasten towards the caller in fear and dread. The speed with which they are drawn forward will pull their heads back and the knowledge of their fate will cause their eyes to remain unblinking and their hearts

---

193 Surat Ṭā Hā, 20:108.

194 Surat al-Maʿārij, 70:43.

195 Surat al-Qamar, 54:6-8.

to fill with dread, "*And do not think that God is unaware of what the unjust do; He only gives them a respite to a Day on which eyes will be fixed open (in terror). (They will) hasten forward with their heads upraised, their gaze unblinking and their hearts vacant!*"[196]

This sifting and isolating of groups are to allow people with the same qualities to be banded together. The route that each must take, and the duration that they remain at each station, is different for every group. As these groups are formed, blood relationships no longer hold meaning and kinship will now be defined by closeness or remoteness in terms of the dispositions and deeds of human beings, "*And when the (second) trumpet is blown, there shall no longer be ties of kinship amongst them that day, nor shall they ask after one another.*"[197] Individuals who possess similar levels of spiritual purity will be gathered together, even though they will be completely unrelated to one another by familial ties. And those who are at different levels of spiritual purity will be separated from one another, even though they may have been the closest of relatives. And their alienation increases as they go their separate ways, and they no longer care to enquire about each other.

The Beginning of the Journey

It is only after the various groupings are complete that the journey towards God begins anew. As we have mentioned, each group will go its own way. This is not a journey measured in distances; rather, it is a journey into the depths of the soul and psyche, although it is possible that at some stages there may be physical movement also. It is a journey whose course we cannot influence or control. We can only go in the

[196] Surat Ibrāhīm, 14:42,43.

[197] Surat al Mu'minun, 23:101

direction that we had determined while in this world. We will be transported along a path that we had previously charted out for ourselves. This journey may be very long for some, and very brief for others.[198] However, there will be stages and stations that must be crossed by everyone. Imam al-Sadiq (a) has mentioned in regard to the longest stoppage at one of these stations, "Beware! Evaluate your deeds before they are evaluated for you, because *qiyāma* has fifty stations, each of which will be of one thousand of your years in duration." Then he recited the verse, "*A Day whose extent is fifty thousand years.*"[199]

The Meaning of Location in *Ākhira*

In his explanation of movement in *barzakh*, Swedenborg says that proximity and remoteness is defined as being similar and dissimilar in one's inner states. When one says that an individual has become close to someone or something, what we mean is that the inner states of the two have approximated one another, and the converse is true also. Therefore, geographical considerations have no meaning in that realm except as external expressions of inner realities. In order to meet someone, there, all that is required is an intense inner desire to see them, and in no time at all individuals are in each other's presence; the distance between them is of no consequence. The expanse between

[198] Majlisī has mentioned in his explanation of a narration in this regard (*Biḥār al-Anwār*, 7:128) that it is quite plausible that the length of the Day of Judgement may vary due to the differences in the status of the virtuous and the wrongdoers. We will discuss this in greater detail later.

[199] Kulayni, *al-Kāfī*, 8:143 |

قَالَ أَبُو عَبْدُ اللهِ جَعْفَرُ بْنُ مُحَمَّدٍ عَلَيْهِمَا السَّلَامُ: أَلَا، فَحَاسِبُوا أَنْفُسَكُمْ قَبْلَ أَنْ تُحَاسَبُوا، فَإِنَّ فِي الْقِيَامَةِ خَمْسِينَ مَوْقِفًا، كُلُّ مَوْقِفٍ مِثْلُ أَلْفِ سَنَةٍ مِمَّا تَعُدُّونَ، ثُمَّ تَلَا هَذِهِ الْآيَةَ ﴿فِي يَوْمٍ كَانَ مِقْدَارُهُ خَمْسِينَ أَلْفَ سَنَةٍ﴾.

Paradise and Hell operates in the same manner, and all that separates the inhabitants of the two is the great difference in their desires. It is for this reason that when the inner inclinations of people are similar, they assemble around one another and the moment their desires are different, their meeting comes to an end.[200]

We experience a similar phenomenon in this world also, albeit with some differences. For instance, we could be engrossed in the remembrance of God or listening to a speech when our mind suddenly wanders, and we find our thoughts somewhere else. Now imagine what that would mean if we did not have a physical body and were just composed of our soul and mind. The moment we thought of a person or thing, we would be in its presence.

However, in *qiyāma*, the issue of location is much more complex than this, because in that world both the physical as well as the imaginal body are active. The soul uses both these faculties at the same time. This feature poses a major problem in our understanding of the meaning of location in the realm of *ākhira*. When we speak of travel and movement in that world, we must keep in mind that we do not mean physical movement in the sense of this world, nor do we mean a purely spiritual movement in the manner of the wayfaring of mystics; rather, it is a synergy of the two.

A Journey of Fifty Stations

As we have mentioned, this journey consists of fifty stations and every traveller must pass through all of them. For those who have brought a lot of baggage from their life in *dunyā* it can take fifty thousand years. And God refers to this long journey as a single Day, "*The Angels and the Spirit ascend to Him*

[200] Swedenborg, sections 193,194.

in a Day whose extent is fifty thousand years."[201] Yet for others this journey will take no more than an hour. One reason for this is that this journey can either take place in pitch darkness or in bright light, and it is obvious that travelling on a lighted path is quicker and easier. Additionally, if certain truths have not been absorbed into the soul in *dunyā*, then an individual may spend a long time at each of these stations - even a thousand years - so that perhaps these truths may enter his soul and permeate his being. This process is necessary because in order to be admitted to heaven and reside in the proximity of God, every soul must possess a certain wisdom and appreciation of realities.

Travelling in darkness towards the final destination coupled with the lengthy stops at the fifty stations can take the full fifty thousand years, every step of which is filled with fear and anxiety, despair and desperation, and pain and remorse. However, travelling in illuminated surroundings, with light earned in *dunyā* will be much easier. The pace of the traveller will depend on the brightness of his light and the competency of his soul in satisfying the requirements of each station. During this journey, people will be constantly moving according to the brightness of the light they possess in that sector. The brighter their light, the faster they travel in that section, and the closer they get to God. It is quite possible that for some the journey will be easier than praying two units of prayer or may take no more than an hour. In this regard the Prophet (s) said, "I swear by the One who holds my life in His hands, for the believer that Day will be easier than performing one obligatory prayer in the *dunyā*."[202]

---

[201] Surat al-Maʿārij, 70:4.

[202] Fayḍ Kāshānī, *al-Ṣāfī*, 5:225 | وَالَّذِي نَفْسِي بِيَدِهِ إِنَّهُ لَيُخَفَّفُ عَلَى الْمُؤْمِنِ حَتَّى يَكُونَ أَهْوَنَ عَلَيْهِ مِنَ الصَّلَاةِ الْمَكْتُوبَةِ يُصَلِّيهَا فِي الدُّنْيَا.

But for others, it may take hundreds or even thousands of years.[203] It is also possible that some may never reach their destination.

The First Station

It is reported from Imam Ali (a) that, "There are fifty stations on the Day of Judgement, each of which takes one thousand years to pass through. The first station is encountered soon after the individual is resurrected from his grave. He will be detained at this stage for a thousand years - naked, hungry and thirsty."[204] At this station, everyone's position will be assigned by the angels (*dāʿī*) who called them forth. As we have mentioned, people's wait at these stations will be of varying durations, just as their spiritual stations are different. Nakedness, hunger, thirst and a thousand years are for those whose souls cannot be purified except in this manner and within this time frame. Those who do not possess impurities at this stage will not remain hungry or thirsty or naked, nor will they have to wait long. On the other hand, there are also those whose impurities cannot be erased even after a thousand years. These are the most wretched of all, because they will have to proceed to the second station with their souls still corrupt and impurified.

---

[203] Majlisī does not consider it improbable that the duration of waiting on that Day for most disbelievers will be a thousand years and for some disbelievers, up to fifty thousand years, which is the maximum extent of the Day of Judgement. And for some believers it is possible that it lasts no more than an hour. See also, "The difference in the state of the righteous and the wrongdoers on that Day."

[204] Majlisī, *Biḥār al-Anwār*, 7:111 |

إِنَّ فِي الْقِيَامَةِ لَخَمْسِينَ مَوْقِفًا، كُلُّ مَوْقِفٍ أَلْفُ سَنَةٍ، فَأَوَّلُ مَوْقِفٍ خَرَجَ مِنْ قَبْرِهِ، حُبِسُوا أَلْفَ سَنَةٍ عُرَاةً، حُفَاةً، جِيَاعًا، عَطَاشَى.

The First Station and Nakedness

Human beings will arise from their graves naked because their newly formed bodies are as yet unclothed. ʿAisha, the wife of the Prophet (s), reported from him that he said: "People will be gathered on the Day of Judgement naked and barefoot." She then asked, "Will men and women be able to look at one another?" He replied, "The Day will be too grievous for them to bother staring at each other."[205] However, it appears that the shamefulness of nudity will not be visited on everyone; a group will be clothed in a garment of radiant light as soon as they are resurrected. According to some narrations, the first person to be clothed in this manner will be Abraham (a), "The first to be clothed on the Day of Judgement shall be Abraham (a)"[206] However this is not a favour unique to him and the rest of the Prophets (a) and close servants of God (*awliyā*); rather, "The nudity of the believers shall be covered while the nudity of the unbelievers shall be exposed." The clothes will be of "a radiant light beneath which the bodies of the believers shall become hidden."[207]

Hunger and Thirst

The souls of human beings are once more resident in physical bodies, and these material bodies will require food and drink,

---

[205] Muslim, *Ṣaḥīḥ*, 8:156 |

عَنْ عَائِشَةَ قَالَتْ: سَمِعْتُ النَّبِيَّ (صَلَّى اللهُ عَلَيْهِ وَآلِهِ) يَقُولُ: يُحْشَرُ النَّاسُ يَوْمَ الْقِيَامَةِ حُفَاةً عُرَاةً، قُلْتُ: يَا رَسُولَ اللهِ، الرِّجَالُ وَالنِّسَاءُ يَنْظُرُ بَعْضُهُمْ إِلَى بَعْضٍ، فَقَالَ: الْأَمْرُ أَشَدُّ مِنْ أَنْ يَنْظُرَ بَعْضُهُمْ إِلَى بَعْضٍ.

[206] Bukhārī, *Ṣaḥīḥ*, 4:110 |

أَوَّلُ مَنْ يُكْسَى يَوْمَ الْقِيَامَةِ، إِبْرَاهِيمُ.

[207] Majlisī, *Biḥār al-Anwār*, 7:110,111 |

تُسْتَرُ عَوْرَةُ الْمُؤْمِنِ وَتُبْدَى عَوْرَةُ الْكَافِرِينَ، قَالَتْ: يَا أَبَتِ، مَا يَسْتُرُ الْمُؤْمِنِينَ؟ قَالَ: نُورٌ يَتَلَأْلَأُ، لَا يُبْصِرُونَ أَجْسَادَهُمْ مِنَ النُّورِ.

a need that will persist for eternity, whether in Paradise or Hellfire. The question arises as to where the food and water for all these masses of people will come from on the plain of *maḥshar*, and what will they eat and drink to satisfy their hunger. There will be no vegetation in sight and no goods for sale. No gardens or orchards will be available from which food could be harvested. However, to their astonishment, people will soon realize that the very ground of *qiyāma* is edible and tastes like delicious bread that is perfectly able to nourish their bodies. Indeed, the all-Merciful Creator never forgets His creatures. Ample food which is ready to eat and plentiful rivers with wholesome water have been made ready for them even before the resurrected come out of their graves, "People will be resurrected on a plain which resembles bread made from pure wheat. Many rivers will flow through it. They will eat and drink from these until their period of accounting is over."[208] This was God's practice in *dunyā* also, where ready nourishment was prepared in the breast of the mother even before her child was born; and before he developed teeth, the earth was already spread out for him with fruits and grain and edible animals.

However, everyone does not have the same ability to eat. Some will have to endure severe hunger and thirst in proportion to the vileness of their deeds. In this regard, Imam Ali (a) said that "The first station is encountered when the individual is

---

[208] Ṭabarsī, *Kitāb al-Iḥtijāj*, p. 176, reporting from Imam al-Baqir (a). A similar narration is found in *Kitāb al-Maḥāsin* also from Imam al-Baqir (a). In that report it is also mentioned that human beings are in need of food and water in *maḥshar*, and this need will persist even after he enters into the Hellfire, see Majlisī, *Biḥār al-Anwār*, 7:109. A similar report is also found in *Tafsīr al-ʿAyyāshī* with different wordings from Imam al-Baqir (a), see Majlisī, *Biḥār al-Anwār*, 7:111 |

يُحْشَرُ النَّاسُ عَلَى مِثْلِ قُرْصَةِ الْبُرِّ النَّقِيِّ، فِيهَا أَنْهَارٌ مُتَفَجِّرَةٌ، يَأْكُلُونَ وَيَشْرَبُونَ حَتَّى يَفْرُغَ مِنَ الْحِسَابِ.

resurrected from his grave. He will be detained at this stage for a thousand years - naked, hungry and thirsty. However, whoever comes forth from his grave having faith (*īmān*) in God and in His Paradise and Hell, and in the resurrection, in the accounting and the Day of Judgement, and had acknowledged His Prophet (s) and what he brought of God's message, will be free of hunger and thirst. Indeed, God has stated: "*You shall come in different groups*", that is, from your graves to the station. Every group will arrive with its Imam."[209]

The Putrid Perspiration of Sin

The first station is a difficult and exhausting one because it is here that God, the all-Merciful, has decided to cleanse the impurities of those who are able to become pure, and thereafter draw them higher to Himself.

For this reason, He makes people sweat out the evil of their sins through every pore of their beings and thus purify themselves. However, this healing through perspiration is much like recovery from a severe and debilitating illness and causes great pain and discomfort to the wrongdoers; the pain is so severe that, "the sweat chokes their mouth and causes the ground beneath them to shudder." It appears that the sweat pours out from them so forcefully that they are convulsed with pain and rendered unable to speak. In another tradition we read that, "On the Day of Judgement, people will perspire so profusely that their sweat will

---

[209] Majlisī, *Biḥār*, 7:111 |

عَنْ ابْنِ مَسْعُودٍ، قَالَ: كُنْتُ جَالِسًا عِنْدَ أَمِيرِ الْمُؤْمِنِينَ عَلَيْهِ السَّلَامُ، فَقَالَ: إِنَّ فِي يَوْمِ الْقِيَامَةِ لَخَمْسِينَ مَوْقِفًا، كُلُّ مَوْقِفٍ أَلْفُ سَنَةٍ، فَأَوَّلُ مَوْقِفٍ خَرَجَ مِنْ قَبْرِهِ، حُبِسُوا أَلْفَ سَنَةٍ عُرَاةً، حُفَاةً، جِيَاعًا، عَطَاشَى، فَمَنْ خَرَجَ مِنْ قَبْرِهِ مُؤْمِنًا بِرَبِّهِ وَمُؤْمِنًا بِجَنَّتِهِ وَنَارِهِ وَمُؤْمِنًا بِالْبَعْثِ وَالْحِسَابِ وَالْقِيَامَةِ مُقِرًّا بِاللهِ، مُصَدِّقًا بِنَبِيِّهِ صَلَّى اللهُ عَلَيْهِ وَآلِهِ، وَبِمَا جَاءَ مِنْ عِنْدِ اللهِ عَزَّ وَجَلَّ - نَجَا مِنَ الْجُوعِ وَالْعَطَشِ. قَالَ اللهُ تَعَالَى: ﴿فَتَأْتُونَ أَفْوَاجًا﴾ مِنَ الْقُبُورِ إِلَى الْمَوْقِفِ أُمَمًا، كُلُّ أُمَّةٍ مَعَ إِمَامِهِمْ

penetrate seventy cubits into the ground and create deep pools that will cover their mouths and reach their ears.[210]

Naturally, this hardship and perspiration will not be the same for everyone, because it is due to a spiritual fever and serves to remove the sicknesses of the soul. Those whose souls are already sound do not experience this, but those who are sick go through this gruelling sweating in proportion to the pollution of their soul, "Everyone will perspire to the extent of his sins."[211]

In a narration we read that, "On the Day of Judgement the sun will come so close to human beings that it will seem to be only a mile above them. As a result, people will perspire in proportion to their misdeeds. Some will perspire so heavily that their sweat will pool at their feet, for others it will reach their knees, while for some it will reach their waists, and for others it will cover their mouths [preventing them from speaking].[212]

This fever will become so severe for some that they will pray to God to be released from it, even if it means going towards

---

[210] Muttaqī al-Hindi, *Kanz al-ʿUmmāl*, tradition 38923 |

يَعْرَقُ النَّاسُ يَوْمَ الْقِيَامَةِ حَتَّى يَذْهَبَ عَرَقُهُمْ فِي الْأَرْضِ سَبْعِينَ ذِرَاعًا، وَيُلْجِمُهُمْ حَتَّى يَبْلُغَ آذَانَهُمْ.

[211] Muttaqī al-Hindi, *Kanz al-ʿUmmāl*, tradition 38965 |

يَعْرَقُونَ مِنْهَا عَلَى قَدْرِ خَطَايَاهُمْ.

[212] Muttaqī al-Hindi, *Kanz al-ʿUmmāl*, tradition 38921, quoting from *Ṣaḥīḥ* of Muslim. Of course, we cannot tell if this is the exact case, because what we know about this from both Sunnī and Shīʿī sources is that the perspiration is so profuse that it does not allow the individual to open his mouth to speak. Reports of this type appear more numerously in Sunnī sources |

تُدْنَى الشَّمْسُ يَوْمَ الْقِيَامَةِ مِنَ الْخَلْقِ، حَتَّى تَكُونَ مِنْهُمْ كَمِقْدَارِ مَيْلٍ، فَيَكُونُ النَّاسُ عَلَى قَدْرِ أَعْمَالِهِمْ فِي الْعَرَقِ، فَمِنْهُمْ مَنْ يَكُونُ إِلَى كَعْبَيْهِ، وَمِنْهُمْ مَنْ يَكُونُ إِلَى رُكْبَتَيْهِ، وَمِنْهُمْ مَنْ يَكُونُ إِلَى حَقْوَيْهِ وَمِنْهُمْ مَنْ يُلْجِمُهُ الْعَرَقُ إِلْجَامًا.

Hell, "On the Day of Judgement extreme perspiration will overcome the disbeliever to the extent that he will plead: My Lord, release me, release me, even if it is to the Hellfire."[213] Or, "When their perspiration engulfs them, the disbelievers will say: If only God would make a judgement about our fate, even if it is to go to the Hellfire."[214]

However, in His infinite mercy God does not answer their plea swiftly because these creatures have not yet understood two things; first, that they do not have a clear idea of what Hell is actually like, because if they did, they would never have asked Him to cast them into it. Secondly, they do not recognize the blessing of this spiritual fever which is designed to cleanse the worst of the pollution from their souls. And God is too merciful and forbearing to accept the ignorant supplication of His feeble and simple servants.

The Meeting with God

The stressful experience at the first station and the severe perspiration that cleanses the pollution of sin prepare the individual for the moment of the grand meeting, "*O Man! You are continually striving towards your Lord with a great exertion and then you will meet Him.*"[215]

Now at the end of the first stage and station there is a momentous event in this strenuous yet wondrous journey; the Lord of the universe becomes apparent to His creatures. They have crossed a long and difficult road to reach this point and now possess the capacity and readiness for this

---

[213] Muttaqī al-Hindi, *Kanz al-ʿUmmāl*, tradition 38925 |

الْكَافِرُ يُلْجِمُهُ الْعَرَقُ يَوْمَ الْقِيَامَةِ حَتَّى يَقُولَ: رَبِّ أَرِحْنِي، أَرِحْنِي وَلَوْ فِي النَّارِ.

[214] Majlisī, *Biḥār al-Anwār*, 8:45 |

يَقِفُونَ حَتَّى يُلْجِمَهُمُ الْعَرَقُ، فَيَقُولُونَ: لَيْتَ اللهَ يَحْكُمُ بَيْنَنَا وَلَوْ إِلَى النَّارِ.

[215] Surat al-Inshiqāq, 84:6.

crucial meeting. Now this mixture of a drop of water and a handful of clay has matured to a point that he can witness the ultimate unveiling of God. The promised moment has arrived, and humanity has reached at the appointed time and at the prearranged place in the presence of the Almighty.

The entire mankind is now ready for this meeting. Their Lord has brought them here. He has endowed them with the necessary qualities and maturity to enable them to reach this far so that they can meet Him. However, do not imagine that this a meeting like those between physical bodies; or that the coming forth of God in the plains of *maḥshar* is like the appearance of a physical person at a particular location. In fact, this meeting is actually the elevation of the perception of the human being on the one hand and the revelation of God's presence on the other - and this is what is meant by the coming of God. This meeting refers to cognizance of the infinite might, power, knowledge and life of God; in other words, a realization of truths that we were only superficially made aware of in *dunyā*.

Even here there is a difference between those who have come to this meeting through God's attributes of Beauty (*ṣifāt al-jamāliyya*) and were drawn towards Him thereafter, and those who have had their veils removed through His attributes of Majesty (*ṣifāt al-jalāliyya*) and have turned towards Him thereafter. For the first group, the meeting is with the Beloved; it fills them with delight, hope and happiness. For the second group, the meeting is that of strangers; all their life they had only shown God hostility and now they remain helpless and defeated in His presence.

The Qur'an describes the coming of God at this time as resplendent and awe-inspiring, "*Nay! When the earth has been levelled - pounded and crushed. And your Lord comes, accompanied by angels arrayed in rows. And Hell is brought near on that Day. On that Day man will become mindful, but what good will his remembrance be?"*[216] And, "*On the Day when Spirit and the angels will stand in rows; no-one will speak except he who is allowed to by the Merciful Lord, and he will say what is right. That is the Day of reality, so whoever wants, let him turn back to his Lord."*[217]

With the coming of God, the light of Reality permeates everywhere, and the hidden and manifest qualities of everyone become visible. Books of deeds are opened, and the accounts are examined; "*And the land shall be illuminated by God's light, and the book (of deeds) shall be opened, and the prophets and the witnesses shall be brought forward, and a just decision will be pronounced for everyone. And they will not be wronged at all.*"[218] Now mankind will traverse the next stations in the presence of God.

All Fifty Stations are not Known

Although we have mentioned that human beings will have to cross fifty stations and stages, it does not mean that we are aware of the nature of all of them in detail. Those who know of the unseen have only given us information about some stages and have not mentioned the rest. For this reason, in the pages that follow we cannot say precisely where each station is located along the journey or list each and every one of them. What will be possible is to describe some of the stations about which we have information.

---

[216] Surat al-Fajr, 89:21-23.

[217] Surat al-Nabā', 78:38-39.

[218] Surat al-Zumar, 39/69.

The Next Station: The Opening of Books

We have previously discussed how Rūmān inserts their Book of deeds into the breast of every human being during their first night in the grave. At the time he declared that this book shall remain closed within them until the Day of Judgement when God will resurrect the dead.

Now that Day has arrived, and God is ready for the accounting; it is time for the books of deeds to be opened for examination. At this time the books that had been embedded into the human beings are opened, in the sense that an individual's deeds and conduct assume their *qiyāmati* forms. In fact, every act that we do assumes simultaneously a form in the material (*dunyā*), imaginal (*barzakh*) and spiritual (*qiyāma*) worlds. The material form is the one that is visible to all in this world, but the imaginal and spiritual forms remain behind the curtain of *barzakh* and *qiyāma*, and only become visible when each of these curtains is drawn aside.[219] For example, backbiting or lying or slander has a form in this world, in *barzakh* and in *qiyāma*. Similarly, performing the ritual prayers, supplicating and reciting from the Qur'an have their forms in all three worlds. Imam al-Baqir (a) said to Saʿd al-Khaffāf, "O Saʿd! Learn the Qur'an, because on the Day of Judgement it will come forth in a form more beautiful than any that the entire creation has ever beheld. On that day mankind will be arrayed in a hundred and twenty thousand rows, eighty thousands of which will comprise the nation of Muhammad (s) and forty thousand will be from the rest of the nations."[220]

---

219 Ḥusaini Tehrānī, *Maʿād Shināsī*, 4:26.

220 Kulaynī, *al-Kāfī*, 2:596 |

يَا سَعْدُ! تَعَلَّمُوا الْقُرْآنَ، فَإِنَّ الْقُرْآنَ يَأْتِي يَوْمَ الْقِيَامَةِ فِي أَحْسَنِ صُورَةٍ نَظَرَ إِلَيْهَا الْخَلْقُ، وَالنَّاسُ صُفُوفٌ،

As an individual's book is opened, the *qiyāmati* forms of his deeds immediately become manifest, revealing things that were hidden until now and could not even be imagined, "*And the evil of what they did will appear to them, and they will be encompassed by what they used to mock!*"[221]

The Station of Actions being Displayed before God (*'Arḍ*)

The opening of books has another aspect also and that is that the curtain in front of people's eyes fall away; they see clearly that their actions are in the sight of God as if they are being displayed and arrayed before Him. For this reason, the station where the books of deeds are opened can also be called the station where the deeds are displayed. Consequently, this is one of the most difficult stations on the Day of *qiyāma*, "*On this Day you will be exposed and no secret of yours shall remain hidden.*"[222] At this station, heads will hang down in embarrassment and breasts will be constricted in shame; "*If you could only but see when the guilty will hang their heads before their Lord, (saying): Our Lord! We have seen and we have heard, so send us back (to the world) and we will do good; we are now certain.*"[223] It has been reported that whenever Imam al-Hasan (a) would think of this station, he would sigh deeply and fall unconscious.[224]

This station will take a long time to pass through. There will be people who will initially try to justify their deeds by

---

عِشْرُونَ وَمِائَةُ أَلْفِ صَفٍّ: ثَمَانُونَ أَلْفَ صَفٍّ أُمَّةُ مُحَمَّدٍ صَلَّى اللهُ عَلَيْهِ وَآلِهِ وَسَلَّمَ، وَأَرْبَعُونَ أَلْفَ صَفٍّ مِنْ سَائِرِ الأُمَمِ.

[221] Surat al-Jāthiya, 45:33.

[222] Surat al-Ḥāqqa, 69:18.

[223] Surat al-Sajda, 32:12.

[224] Ṣaduq, *al-Āmālī,* p. 244 | إِنَّ الْحَسَنَ (ع) ذَكَرَ الْعَرْضَ عَلَى اللهِ تَعَالَى ذِكْرُهُ شَهَقَ شَهْقَةً يُغْشَى عَلَيْهِ مِنْهَا.

disputing and arguing and some will try to outright deny their acts; but this will not get them very far, so then they will try to make excuses for their deeds. It has been reported from the Prophet (s) that: "On the Day of Judgement, when mankind will be presented, they will go through three phases. Initially they will argue and then they will make excuses. The third phase is when the scroll of deeds will be finally returned to their owners, for some in the right hand and for others, in their left."[225] At this station God allows people to speak so that they can say whatever they wish in their defence, "*On the Day when every person will come disputing in their own defence, and every soul shall be recompensed (justly) for what it did, and they will not be wronged.*"[226]

It is only after this lengthy wrangling and defence that their scroll of deeds will be presented to everyone. That is, only after everyone is completely satisfied that what they have received is correct and anything else is false, "*On the Day when He will call to them saying: "Where are "my partners" whom you used to assert?" And We will bring forth from every nation a witness and We shall say: "Produce your proof." Then they shall know that the Truth is with God (alone) and the lies which they had invented shall fail them.*"[227] Some examples of the arguments that will be presented by people are mentioned in the Qur'an, and we recount them below.

[225] Muttaqī al-Hindi, *Kanz al-'Ummāl*, tradition 38937 |

يُعْرَضُ النَّاسُ يَوْمَ الْقِيَامَةِ ثَلَاثَ عَرْضَاتٍ: فَأَمَّا عَرْضَتَانِ فَجِدَالٌ وَمَعَاذِيرُ، وَأَمَّا الثَّالِثَةُ فَعِنْدَ ذَلِكَ تَطِيرُ الصُّحُفُ فِي الْأَيْدِي فَآخِذٌ بِيَمِينِهِ وَآخِذٌ بِشِمَالِهِ.

[226] Surat al-Naḥl, 16:111.

[227] Surat al-Qaṣaṣ, 28:74,75.

Arguing with God

"*On the Day when We gather them all together - then We will say to those who ascribed partners in worship (with Us): "Remain in your place, you and your 'partners' (whom you worshipped)!" Then We will lift the veil between them, and their 'partners' will say, "It was not us that you worshipped. And God is sufficient as a witness between us, and you that we were unaware of your worship (of us)." Every soul shall be put on trial there for what it sent forth previously; and they will be returned to God, their rightful Lord. And their false gods will abandon them.*"[228] Here, the lifting of the veil between the idolaters and their false idols refers to the lifting of the barrier that prevented dialogue between them in the *dunyā*. Now, in this new world, they can communicate with each other. "*When those who ascribed partners with God see the 'partners', they will say, "Our Lord! Here are the partners we invoked besides You." But they will throw their words back at them saying, "Indeed, you are liars!" And they will offer their submission to God that Day; and all their idols will abandon them.*"[229]

"*And on the Day when He shall gather them all, and that which they worship besides God, and ask, "Was it you who misled these servants of Mine, or did they stray from the path themselves?" They will say, "Glory be to You! It was not befitting for us that we should take any guardians besides You; however, You gave them and their fathers respite until they forgot the remembrance and were ruined." So, they will reject your lies and you cannot avert (punishment) nor get help. And whosoever among you commits injustice (worships idols), We will make him taste a grievous chastisement.*"[230]

---

[228] Surat Yūnus, 10:28-30.

[229] Surat al-Naḥl, 16:86-87.

[230] Surat al-Furqān, 25:17-19.

Everyone Tries to Place the Burden of their Sins on Someone Else

"*And those who disbelieve say, "We will never believe in this Qur'an, or the scriptures sent before it." But if you could see when the wrongdoers are made to stand before their Lord, how they will blame one another! Those who were weak shall say to those who were arrogant (in authority), "Had it not been for you, we would have been believers." The arrogant will reply to the weak, "Did we keep you from the guidance once it had come to you? No! You were the transgressors." But the weak will respond to the arrogant, "Rather it was your plotting night and day when you ordered us to disbelieve in God and to set up equals to Him." But they are secretly filled with regret when they see the punishment; We shall place iron collars around the necks of those who disbelieved - shall they not receive punishment except for what they did?*"[231]

"*His companion (Shayṭān) shall say, "Our Lord! I did not make him transgress; rather, he himself was far astray. God will say, "Do not dispute before Me. I had already warned you from before. My word will not change, and I am not in the least unjust to My servants.*"[232]

Followers will Plead for Help from their Masters

"*And they will all assemble before God. The weak will say to the arrogant (their authorities), "Indeed, we were your followers, so can you avert from us some of God's chastisement?" They would say, "If we had received Divine guidance, we would have certainly guided you. It makes no difference now whether we rail against the punishment or bear it with patience - we have no place to escape to." And when the matter has been decided, Shayṭān shall say, "Indeed, God made you a true promise. I also made a promise, but I*

[231] Surat Saba', 34:31-33.

[232] Surat Qāf, 50:27-29.

betrayed you. However, I never had power over you; I merely invited you and you responded. So do not blame me, blame yourselves. I cannot come to your aid, just as you cannot come to mine."[233]

The Sinners will Disown Each Other

"On the Day of Judgement some of you will disown others and some of you will curse others; but your abode will be Hellfire, and no one will assist you."[234]

"And whoever turns away from the remembrance of the all-Merciful God, We appoint from him a shayṭān, who will become his constant companion. And they (the satans) constantly divert them from God's path, yet they (people) imagine that they are being guided aright! Until he comes before Us, then he says to his companion, "I wish you were as distant from me as the east is from the west - how evil a companion you are!"[235]

False Oaths in God's Presence

Those to whom lying had become second nature cannot stop themselves from doing so even in God's presence; *"The Day we gather them all together we shall say to the polytheists, "So where are the associates whom you asserted?" They will have no excuses left but to say, "By Allah! Our Lord, we were never polytheists." See how they lie against their own interests! But that which they forge will disappear from their sight."*[236]

"On the Day when God resurrects them all, they will swear to Him as they swear to you, and they will imagine that they have some standing. Indeed, they are liars!"[237]

[233] Surat Ibrāhīm, 14:21-22.

[234] Surat al-ʿAnkabūt, 29:25.

[235] Surat al-Zukhruf, 43:36-38.

[236] Surat al-Anʿām, 6:22-24.

[237] Surat al-Mujādila, 58:18.

The Next Station: The Testimony of the Witnesses

Some individuals are accustomed to denial of responsibility and weaving lies; and they even try to use these traits here to justify their conduct. However, in order to make them acknowledge and confront the truth when their books are opened for review and the *qiyāmati* face of their deeds is exposed, well-informed witnesses (*shuhadā*) are brought forward.

Of course, God is aware of the inner reality of all deeds, so the testimonies of the witnesses in the court of God are not for His information; rather, they are to make individuals aware of the real meaning of their deeds. Therefore, like every other station on the Day of Judgement, this station also serves to cleanse the soul and thus allow it to reach a higher level of existence; "*And the book (of deeds) shall be opened, and the prophets and the witnesses shall be brought forward, and a just decision will be pronounced for everyone. And they will not be wronged at all. And everyone shall be paid in full for his deeds; and He is most knowing of whatever they do.*"[238]

At this juncture, "*Who is more unjust than the one who invents a lie against God? They will be presented before their Lord and the witnesses will testify, "These are the ones who lied against their Lord. No doubt God's mercy is far from the unjust.*"[239]

"*On the Day when God will say, "O Jesus' son of Mary! Did you say to the people: Take me and my mother as two deities besides Allah?" He will say, "Glory be to You! It was not befitting for me to say that to which I had no right. If I had said such a thing, then You would have known it. You know what is in my inner self, but I do not know what is in Yours. Indeed, You are the ultimate Knower of secrets. I*

[238] Surat al-Zumar, 39:69-70.

[239] Surat Hūd, 11:18

only told them what You commanded me (to say): Worship God, my Lord and your Lord. And I was a witness over them as long as I was among them. But when You took me, You were the Watcher over them. Indeed, You are a witness over all things."[240]

When the witnesses come forth and testimonies are presented, all excuses become redundant and nothing remains for the deniers except admission and regret, "*What will their state be when We bring forth a witness from every nation and We bring you (O Muhammad) as a witness against them? On that Day the disbelievers and those who disobeyed the messenger will wish that the earth would swallow them. And they will not be able to conceal any event from God."*[241]

These testimonies will not be just verbal; rather, in addition the deeds of people and entire nations will be made a benchmark for others, according to their own capacities. In this regard, Jesus (a) said to the Jewish scholars, "On the Day of Judgement, the people of Nineveh shall rise to condemn you, because when they heard the admonition of Jonas (a) they repented, while today a man greater than Jonas (a) stands before you, but you pay him no heed. And the Queen of Sheba will also come forward that Day and condemn you because she travelled a great distance to the land of Solomon (a) to hear his words, while today a greater personality than Solomon (a) stands before you, but you ignore his words.[242]

The Next Station: The Distribution of Books

It is only after this presentation and argumentation and the testimony of the witnesses that the books that were opened

---

240 Surat al-Mā'ida, 5:116-118.

241 Surat al-Nisā', 4:41-42.

242 Gospel of Matthew, 12:41,42. cf. Gospel of Luke 11:34,35, with slightly different wording.

to reveal the records of people's actions shall now be returned and reattached to their owners. Just as we indicated earlier, these books, which are already merged with the soul of every individual, also have a copy in the higher realm. This copy is its spiritual or *qiyāmati* form. In the Hereafter, goodness and evil are not mixed with each other; so, the books of deeds of the righteous are stored in one place and those of the wrongdoers are stored in another, "*Indeed, the books of the evildoers are stored in Sijjīn. And what do you think Sijjīn is? It is a written register. Woe on that Day to the deniers - those who denied the Day of Judgement...Indeed, the books of the righteous are placed in 'Illiyīn. And what do you think 'Illiyīn is? It is written register that is witnessed by the close servants (muqarrabūn) of God.*"[243] These books, some of which are stored in *sijjīn* and others in *'illiyyīn*, are nevertheless accurate copies of the same books that have been embedded into the souls of their owners. To be more exact, they are not the same books but are their images that exist in *qiyāma* and the spiritual realm; they are its opened visages displayed in these locations.

The books had remained closed for a long time, but now the time has come to attach the copy of it to its owner. At this time the individual is able to clearly see the *qiyāmati* form of his deeds, which have now been fully revealed; "*And We have fastened every man's action to his neck, and on the Day of Judgement We shall produce for him an account which he will find wide open.*"[244]

The meaning of the book being wide open is that the spiritual forms which were confined to *sijjīn* or *'illiyyīn* are now attached to the individual, and they coincide with the book that he already has embedded within him. Or alternatively,

[243] Surat al-Muṭaffiffīn, 83:7-11, 18-21.

[244] Surat al-Isrā', 17:13.

the records of an individual's deeds that are stored in *sijjīn* or *'illiyyīn* are transported and attached to their owners and give deeper layers of meaning to the information to the book of deeds that is already embedded in his soul. And this is what is referred to as the distribution of records or "*tatāyur al-kutub*". These records fly towards their owners, not like the flying of birds but rather like the attachment of a branches to a root. It can also be said that the individual himself is drawn towards his record, "*Every nation will be called to its record (and told), 'Today you will be recompensed for what you used to do. This is Our book; it speaks about you with truth. We were constantly recording everything that you did.*'"[245] That is, a copy of everything that was recorded in the lower realm was simultaneously made in the higher realm also. This then is the Book of every human being with God in the higher realm, and which will now be presented to them. For this reason, He does not say, "This is your book", rather, he says, "This is Our book - which speaks about you with truth". It is a copy of your records that We hold. Whatever was recorded of your deeds, its corollary was also recorded here in a manner congruous to this world, and is now presented to you, or you are brought to it.

Receiving the Book in the Right or Left Hand

Right and left are the two aspects mentioned in the discussion about receiving the books of deeds, but we do not quite know what this means in the world of souls and *qiyāma*. What is known is that the scrolls of records that exist in *'illiyyīn* will be received from the right while those from *sijjīn* will be placed on the backs or the left. As we have mentioned, the handing of these records to individuals means the attachment of their *qiyāmati* forms to their souls. This act

[245] Surat al-Jāthiya, 45:28,29.

is necessary for a new and unprecedented evolution of the human being. In truth, it is here that man finally reaches the maturity that is required in the world of *qiyāma*, "*O Man! You are continually striving towards your Lord with a great exertion and then you will meet Him. Then as for he who is given his record in his right hand, he will soon be judged with an easy accounting and he will return to his people joyful. But as for he who is given his record on his back, he shall soon cry out for his destruction and be entered into a blazing fire.*"[246]

Here, there are two points worthy of consideration, which have been alluded to in the verse above. First, it appears that people do not have the capacity to receive their *qiyāmati* records before their maturity and readiness to meet God; they gain that capacity only after their meeting with Him, and only subsequently can their accounting happen. A second point, and one that has been mentioned in Surat al-Isra', is that only those who receive their records in the right hand are able to appreciate its status and understand (or read) its contents, which are the *qiyāmati* forms of their deeds. As for those whose records have come from *sijjīn* and are received in the left hand, they will be bewildered and unable to read its contents, "*On the Day when We shall summon everyone with their Imam. Then those who are given their book in the right hand will read their records, and the least injustice will not be done to them. But whoever was blind in this world, shall be blind in the Hereafter and most astray from the Path.*"[247] In fact, the last verse rephrases the receiving of the records in the left hand by saying that those individuals are spiritually blind. Perhaps this is why Ibn ʿArabi mentions in his *tafsīr* that "right" denotes the aspect of intellect and understanding, and "left"

---

[246] Surat al-Inshiqāq, 84:6-12.

[247] Surat al-Isrā', 17:71,72.

denotes the aspect of caprice and desire which brings about ignorance and confusion.[248]

The Station of Accounting

After the presentation in front of God and the testimonies of the witness and the distribution of the books of deeds, the moment of accounting arrives. Interestingly, just as in this world where every human being enjoys a personal connection to God at the same time, in *qiyāma* also the entire creation is judged simultaneously yet personal attention is given to all. No one act of God stops Him from other acts; listening to one supplicant does not stop Him from hearing another.[249] The second point is that the Qur'anic verses suggest that after the *qiyāmati* forms of deeds have attached themselves to an individual (or he has become aware of them when he was handed his book), the accounting does not start immediately. It seems that people are left on their own for some time so that they become better acquainted with themselves and realize their true station. It is only then that they are summoned for accounting. This is the meaning of the phrase "soon" in the verses of Surat al-Inshiqāq: "*Then as for he who is given his record in his right hand, he will* ***soon*** *be judged with an easy accounting, and he will return to his people joyful. But as for he who is given his record on his back, he shall* ***soon*** *cry out for his destruction and be entered into a blazing fire.*"[250] In addition to indicating that there is an interval between receiving the book of deeds and coming to the station of accounting (*ḥisāb*), the verse also indicates that people will come to it individually. Everyone will give account separately

[248] *Tafsīr ibn ʿArabī*, 1:383,384.

[249] Sh Abbas Qummi, *Mafātih al-Jinān, Duʿā Jawshan al-Kabīr* |
يَا مَنْ لَا يَشْغَلُهُ سَمْعٌ عَنْ سَمْعٍ، يَا مَنْ لَا يَمْنَعُهُ فِعْلٌ عَنْ فِعْلٍ، يَا مَنْ لَا يُلْهِيهِ قَوْلٌ عَنْ قَوْلٍ.

[250] Surat al-Inshiqāq, 84:7-12.

and depending on the outcome, "*will return to his people joyful*" or "*cry out for his destruction*". However, this does not mean that an individual has to proceed to a particular place in order to account for his deeds in front of God as we do in this world when we present ourselves to attend a meeting; rather it means that everyone finds himself alone in front of God and he does not see anyone else during his accounting – as if he has left everyone else and moved away, "*Leave Me alone with the one I have created; I gave him resources in abundance and sons by his side, and I made his life comfortable...*"[251]

But what is the actual meaning of accounting (*ḥisāb*)? In truth, it means that at this station, the personality of an individual assumes its final form. That which is possible to overlook and forgive is forgiven and that which is acceptable from his good acts is accepted; additions and erasures are made, and in this way his final form is shaped. During *ḥisāb* that which is most precious and necessary is God's pardon. The experience at every subsequent station depends greatly on what happens at this station. It was for this station that Abraham (a) pleaded for God's forgiveness, asking, "*Our Lord! Forgive me and my parents and the believers on the Day that the Accounting will take place.*"[252]

A believer will leave this station full of joy and satisfaction because the *qiyāmati* forms of his good deeds will have multiplied manifold and attached themselves to him, while his wrongdoing will have been eliminated and departed from him. In fact, his existence will have grown considerably at this station. He becomes so much bigger and beautiful that he would look at himself with wonderment and want others to admire his beauty, "*So as for he who receives his record of*

[251] Surat al-Muddaththir, 74:11-15.

[252] Surat Ibrāhīm, 14:41.

deeds in his right hand, he will say, 'Take and read my book! Indeed, I knew that I would have to meet my reckoning (and used to prepare for it).'"[253]

For the righteous believer this is an easy station to cross, because during the accounting God is lenient and does not bring up every single misconduct; due to the person's essentially good nature many issues are passed over and forgiven without mention.

However, for the wrongdoers this station is extremely difficult because his evil does not separate from him and consequently his every deed is subject to critical scrutiny and account. In other words, he undergoes a terrible reckoning (*sū' al-ḥisāb*). Imam al-Sadiq (a) was asked about the meaning of "*sū' al-ḥisāb*" and he said, "It means the minute scrutiny and detailed examination of every single deed. Their evil acts are counted against them while their good acts are not accepted from them."[254] In other words, detailed examination will reveal that the good deeds were not good after all, and they will not count in his favour; as for the wrong deeds, since it is clear that they were all evil, they shall not be forgiven and will all count against him.

The Expiation (*Takfīr*) and Annulment (*Iḥbāt*) of Deeds

Despite the fact that the destiny of the individual is nearly decided at this advanced stage in his journey into the depths of *qiyāma*, the station of accounting has a great influence in shaping his ultimate personality. Here, the good souls are able to erase any bad acts that they have committed by the

---

253 Surat al-Ḥāqqa, 69:19, 20.

254 Ḥurr al-Āmilī, *Wasā'il al-Shī'a*, 18:350 |
عَنْ هِشَامِ بْنِ سَالِمٍ، عَنْ أَبِي عَبْدِ اللهِ عَلَيْهِ السَّلَامُ فِي قَوْلِهِ: ﴿وَيَخَافُونَ سُوءَ الْحِسَابِ﴾، قَالَ: الِاسْتِقْصَاءُ وَالْمُدَاقَّةُ، وَقَالَ: تُحْسَبُ عَلَيْهِمُ السَّيِّئَاتُ، وَلَا تُحْسَبُ لَهُمُ الْحَسَنَاتُ.

blessing of their Lord. "*Indeed, good deeds take away evil deeds; this is a reminder for the mindful.*"[255] This process is called *takfīr*, which means to cover up, to expiate or to do away with, "*And (as for) those who believe and do good, We shall most certainly do away with their evil deeds and We will most certainly rewards them according to the best of what they did.*"[256] This is because the soul has formed a virtuous disposition by continually doing good and avoiding evil. As a consequence, the small blemishes of sin are washed away from it because good and evil cannot subsist together in that realm. God says, "*If you shun the great sins from which you are forbidden, We will do away with your small sins and cause you to enter an honourable place.*"[257]

On the other hand, evil individuals cannot hold on to any good acts that they may have committed because of the corrupt nature of their soul; any goodness is annihilated by the rule of God that evil, and goodness cannot exist beside each other. This is called *iḥbāt*, which means annulment, "*The parable of those who disbelieve in their Lord: their actions are like ashes on which the wind blows hard on a stormy day; they shall not have power over anything out of what they have earned; this is a great error.*"[258] And, "*We shall attend to their deeds and turn them into scattered dust.*"[259]

The Station of the Balance (*Mīzān*): The Weighing Scales of Justice

When the accounting of human beings is over, and every human being has assumed his final persona and character,

[255] Surat Hūd, 11:114.

[256] Surat al-ʿAnkabūt, 29:7.

[257] Surat al-Nisāʾ, 4:31.

[258] Surat Ibrāhīm, 14:18.

[259] Surat al-Furqān, 25:23.

it is time to assess his true worth and value. This is done through the weighing of his deeds. It must be kept in mind that the weighing of deeds is different from the accounting. The latter is for counting the amount of good and evil deeds; the scales of *mīzān*, however, are to determine the extent of goodness or evil of the deeds.

Mīzān means an instrument for measuring things. Obviously, different things require different measurement devices. For example, weights require scales and a counterweight, time requires a watch, lengths require a ruler, thoughts require logic, poems require metre and rhyme, etc. In short, the weighing scale of everything has a criterion against which the quantity or quality of the thing is evaluated. The *mīzān* on the Day of Judgement similarly has a criterion against which the value of the deeds (*aʿmāl*), morals (*akhlāq*) and beliefs (*aqā'id*) of an individual will be evaluated; and this scale will measure in units of truth (*ḥaq*), "*And the weight (of deeds) that Day shall be the truth (ḥaq); then as for those whose scales are heavy, they are the successful ones. And as for those whose scales are light, they are the ones who have damaged their souls due to their transgressions.*"[260] In other words, the closer and more coincident with *ḥaq* that the deeds of an individual are, the heavier the scales of his deeds shall be; and consequently his station shall be more elevated and noble as well.

The wondrous feature of the *mīzān* is that it is able to register the amount of sincerity and truth contained within an individual's deeds. According to some narrations, these scales are the Prophets (a) and their successors, whose deeds, morals and teachings serve as the measure of sincerity and truth of the deeds of people.[261] Others believe

---

[260] Surat al-Aʿrāf, 7:8,9.

[261] Ṣadūq, *Maʿānī al-Akhbār*, p. 13 |

that since the word scales (*mawāzīn*) has been used in the verse in plural, therefore there exists a separate weight for every deed. The verse mentions that whoever's **scales** are heavy is successful and whoever's **scales** are light is the loser. *Mawāzīn* here could mean both scales as well as the weighed deeds themselves. According to the first meaning it may be that more than one *mīzān* exists, or that there is one for every type of deed. Therefore, everyone will have several *mīzāns* set up to measure the units of *ḥaq* (truth) contained in each action; for example, the *ḥaq* in *ṣalāt*, *ḥaq* in the fast, *ḥaq* in *zakāt*, *ḥaq* in chastity, and so on. It may be that *ṣalāt* is weighed in a scale using one criterion and *zakāt* using another and chastity in yet another scale; just as the qualities of an object may require one instrument to measure its dimensions, another to measure its weight and a third to measure its temperature.

From the foregoing, we also conclude that the balance will only be set up for those who have deeds that can be weighed. Those who have no good acts, or whose good deeds have been annulled and invalidated, have nothing that needs to be weighed, "*They are the ones who deny the signs of their Lord and His meeting, so their deeds become null; and therefore We will not set up a balance for them on the Day of Judgement.*"[262]

The Station of the Path (*Ṣirāṭ*)

After the good and evil actions of human beings are accounted (*ḥisāb*) and then the worth of the deeds of the righteous are weighed at the balance (*mīzān*), they now proceed to their final destination, which is Paradise in the proximity of God.

عَنْ هِشَامِ بْنِ سَالِمٍ قَالَ: سَأَلْتُ أَبَا عَبْدِ اللهِ عَلَيْهِ السَّلَامُ عَنْ قَوْلِ اللهِ عَزَّ وَجَلَّ: ﴿وَنَضَعُ الْمَوَازِينَ الْقِسْطَ لِيَوْمِ الْقِيَامَةِ فَلَا تُظْلَمُ نَفْسٌ شَيْئًا﴾ قَالَ: هُمُ الْأَنْبِيَاءُ وَالْأَوْصِيَاءُ عَلَيْهِمُ السَّلَامُ.

262 Surat al-Kahf, 18:105.

Here each will reside in a particular level according to the worth of his deeds.

However, the weight of deeds for most people is not enough for them to acquire the proper preparedness for entry into Paradise and utilizing its blessings. They do not yet possess the capability to perceive its deeper secrets. If matters were to end here, most people would not be able to find the way to Paradise and proceed towards the ultimate cognizance of their Lord. It is here that God, out of His limitless grace, has prepared a path that will compensate for the shortcomings that still remain and will provide salvation for those who hope for salvation. This path is called the *ṣirāṭ*.

Entry into Paradise requires every human virtue to reach perfection and every trace of pollution to be eradicated. Virtues are those qualities that God had enjoined, and pollution comes from those things that God had forbidden. And people must reach this perfection by passing across the *ṣirāṭ*. In truth that *ṣirāṭ* is no other than the inner aspect of the straight path (*ṣirāṭ al-mustaqīm*) that has been outlined for us in this *dunyā* and which is an accumulation of all virtues. If an individual has perfected these virtues in his soul during his life in *dunyā*, and kept away corruptness from his soul, he will easily pass across the *ṣirāṭ* and will not hesitate along it. However, if his soul has not gained these virtues in *dunyā*, and it is not yet purified fully, his crossing will be a long and arduous one. He will remain at the station of each virtue for as long as it takes for that virtue to enter his soul and become perfect; and he will be stopped at the station of each vice until that vice is completely eliminated from his soul.

These stations, all of which are difficult to cross, exist along the *ṣirāṭ* and present a severe ordeal for souls. This is in the case where souls possess the ability to receive virtues and eliminate vices in the first place; otherwise, they will never cross the *ṣirāṭ* safely, and will be transferred to Hellfire along the way. And this is the meaning of verse, "*And indeed, We know best those who deserve most to be burned therein.*"[263]

That is, those souls whose pollution cannot be purified except in the burnishing fires of Hell.

According to what has been mentioned above, the speed at which people will cross over the *ṣirāṭ* will vary considerably. Those who lived in the Paradise of *barzakh* in that imaginal world were free from every pollution and adorned with all virtues and consequently they will have no impediment on the *ṣirāṭ* and will cross it at the speed of lightning. Those who were in the Hell of *barzakh* had souls that could not be purified or accept any virtues and they will not be able to cross the *ṣirāṭ* and for them there is another path that leads them directly to the Hellfire. In fact, for them there is no point in travelling on the path that perfects virtues and eliminates impurities, "*Indeed, those who disbelieve and do wrong – God will never forgive them, nor guide them to a path; except the path of Hell, to abide therein forever.*"[264] About them the angels receive the command, "*Gather the wrongdoers and their companions and the idols that they worshipped instead of God, and lead them to the path of Hellfire.*"[265] And the *ṣirāṭ* to Hellfire is different from the *ṣirāṭ* that stretches over Hell and leads to Paradise.

As for the people of the middle rank, they will spend varying amounts of time on the *ṣirāṭ* depending on the purity of their souls and their ability to accept virtue and expel evil. It is for this group that we find the following description of

263 Surat Maryam, 19:70.

264 Surat al-Nisā', 4:168, 169.

265 Surat al-Ṣāffāt, 37:22, 23

the *ṣirāṭ* in a narration, "It is a path that is thinner than a hair and sharper than a sword; some will cross over it at the speed of lightning, while others at the speed of a galloping horse. And others will cross it at walking pace, while others will do so crawling. And there will be some who will cross while hanging suspended from it with the flames of Hell scorching them."[266] Just as the speed on the *ṣirāṭ* varies between individuals, so does the level of difficulty or ease of the crossing. It has been reported from the Prophet (s) that, "People will cross over a bridge that stretches over Hell, but the path will be strewn with iron thorns and quills that will impede them from the right and the left. Angels shall be standing on both sides of the path, saying, 'O Lord! Let them pass safely." And from amongst the people there will be those who pass by like lightning, and others who pass like the wind, and yet others who pass through as if riding on horses; some will run, and some will walk and some will walk on all fours and some will crawl on their bellies."[267]

Obviously, these words are not to be understood literally; rather, they are metaphors which indicate the mental and spiritual hurdles that people will encounter on the path to Paradise and due to which they will be exposed to the danger of falling from the path or experience lengthy delays on it. It

---

[266] Tafsīr al-Qummī, 1:29 |
هُوَ أَدَقُّ مِنَ الشَّعْرِ، وَأَحَدُّ مِنَ السَّيْفِ، فَمِنْهُمْ مَنْ يَمُرُّ عَلَيْهِ مِثْلَ الْبَرْقِ، وَمِنْهُمْ مَنْ يَمُرُّ عَلَيْهِ مِثْلَ عَدْوِ الْفَرَسِ، وَمِنْهُمْ مَنْ يَمُرُّ عَلَيْهِ مَاشِيًا، وَمِنْهُمْ مَنْ يَمُرُّ عَلَيْهِ حَبْوًا، وَمِنْهُمْ مَنْ يَمُرُّ عَلَيْهِ مُتَعَلِّقًا فَتَأْخُذُ النَّارُ مِنْهُ شَيْئًا وَتَتْرُكُ مِنْهُ شَيْئًا

[267] Muttaqī Hindī, *Kanz al-'Ummāl*, trad. 39039 |
يَمُرُّ النَّاسُ عَلَى جِسْرِ جَهَنَّمَ، وَعَلَيْهِ حَسَكٌ وَكَلَالِيبُ وَخَطَاطِيفُ، تَخْطِفُ النَّاسَ يَمِينًا وَشِمَالًا، وَبِجَنْبَتَيْهِ مَلَائِكَةٌ يَقُولُونَ: اللَّهُمَّ سَلِّمْ سَلِّمْ، فَمِنَ النَّاسِ مَنْ يَمُرُّ مِثْلَ الْبَرْقِ، وَمِنْهُمْ مَنْ يَمُرُّ مِثْلَ الرِّيحِ، وَمِنْهُمْ مَنْ يَمُرُّ مِثْلَ الْفَرَسِ، وَمِنْهُمْ مَنْ يَسْعَى سَعْيًا، وَمِنْهُمْ مَنْ يَمْشِي مَشْيًا، وَمِنْهُمْ مَنْ يَحْبُو حَبْوًا، وَمِنْهُمْ مَنْ يَزْحَفُ زَحْفًا.

is interesting to note that this narration indicates that God has instructed angels to assist people along the *ṣirāṭ* and this assistance is spiritual in nature. In other narrations we read the Prophet (s) himself will stand on the *ṣirāṭ* and pray for the safety of those who are crossing it.[268]

In any case, this narrow and backbreaking path will contain several wondrous and awe-inspiring stations.[269] Those who require their virtues to be perfected or any residual pollution to be removed must pass through them. Imam Ali (a) said to his companions, "Be aware that in front of you is a difficult pass with daunting and formidable stations; you have no choice but to enter the pass and stop at the stations."[270] On this arduous path, "those who are lightly burdened will be in a better condition than those who are heavily laden."[271]

The word "*'aqaba*" or twisting pass that has been used here denotes a narrow and winding path that is usually found on a mountain precipice, one that someone can easily fall down from. On the *ṣirāṭ* though, the path is not strewn with obstacles made of earth and rocks and hills and valleys; rather they are externally created out of the twisted maze originating from the human's psyche and from the nature of his beliefs and actions.

Failure at any of these stations results in a fall from the path and the person tumbles into the Hellfire. And to come out of the desolate depths of Hell once you have fallen into it is

---

268 Muslim, *Ṣaḥīḥ*, 1:130 |

وَنَبِيُّكُمْ قَائِمٌ عَلَى الصِّرَاطِ يَقُولُ: رَبِّ، سَلِّمْ سَلِّمْ.

269 Ṣadūq, *al-I'tiqādāt* as quoted by Majlisī, *Biḥār al-Anwār*, 7:129. According to the explanation by Sh Ṣadūq, the phrase "*al-'aqabāt al-maḥshar*" (the arduous passages of the Day of gathering) denotes locations on the *ṣirāṭ*.

270 *Nahj al-Balāgha*, sermon 204.

271 *Nahj al-Balāgha*, letter 31.

even harder than crossing the *ṣirāṭ* towards Paradise and the vicinity of God.

Each of the hurdles on the path symbolizes a particular virtue or vice which the individual must either perfect or eliminate from his soul.

In his exposition about the obstacles that are located on this path, Saduq says, "Each of these obstacles has a name that conforms to an obligatory or a forbidden act. Whenever an individual arrives at a station which is related to an obligation, and if he has a shortcoming in that regard, he is detained and asked about God's right for that obligatory act. If he is able to come out of the station due to his righteous acts, or if he receives God's mercy, he is allowed to proceed. In this way he travels from one station to the next, and is detained whenever he has a shortcoming related to a station and questioned about his shortcoming. In the end, if he manages to cross safely past all these stations, he is taken to Paradise where he will live for eternity. He will have earned good fortune that will never diminish, and he will abide in the proximity of God in the vicinity of God Prophets (A) and proofs on earth (*nabiyyīn*) and the veracious (*ṣiddiqīn*) and the witnesses (*shuhadā*) and the righteous (*ṣāliḥīn*). However, if one is detained for questioning at a station and has no good deeds by which to satisfy the requirements for passage and is unable also to receive God's mercy either, his feet will slip at that pass, and he will fall into Hell.... All these stations are dotted along the *ṣirāṭ*. One of these is the station of Divinely-appointed authority (*wilāya*) and all of mankind[272] shall have to stop at it and be questioned about their allegiance to the Commander of the faithful, Ali ibn Abi Talib and the Imams who came after him – may God's peace be on them all. And

272 By "mankind", Ṣadūq is referring to the believers.

everyone who has accorded to them their rights shall receive salvation and be allowed to cross; and everyone who denied them their rights shall be barred and will fall. And it is to this moment that God refers when He said, "*Stop them, for they must be questioned.*"[273] And amongst the most important stations is the watchtower (*mirṣād*), about which God says, "*And your Lord shall be waiting at mirṣād*",[274] because He has sworn by His Might and Honour not to let any transgressor to cross by Him. And the name of one of these stations is womb (*raḥim*),[275] another is trust (*amāna*), and yet another is prayer (*ṣalāt*). And there are stations named after every obligatory act, and every command and prohibition, at each of which people will be detained for questioning."

Mufīd explains further, "There are multiple stations named after the obligatory acts at which individuals will be stopped and interrogated about that particular act. However, this does not mean that the individuals must actually travel across real mountain passes; rather, the stations refer to the acts themselves which have been likened to the mountain passes. In actual fact, the difficulties that individuals go through to compensate for the shortfalls have been described as climbing and traversing steep paths, because these provide a severe and exhausting trial. God says, "*But he has not yet attempted the uphill path (ʿaqaba). And what do you think that uphill path is? It is the freeing of a slave, and feeding on a day of severe hunger to the orphan who is kin, or a needy person in misery.*"[276] In this verse, God has likened the responsibilities that he has assigned to mankind to uphill mountain tracks,

---

[273] Surat al-Ṣāffāt, 37:24.

[274] Surat al-Fajr, 89:14.

[275] Referring to the sanctity of consanguine ties, no matter how distant

[276] Surat al-Balad, 90:11-16.

because these responsibilities are very difficult to fulfil, just as it is difficult to negotiate steep mountains. Imam Ali (a) says, "Ahead of you there is a steep path that is difficult to traverse, and stations that are daunting; you have no choice but to travel on that path and stop at the stations. So, you will either achieve salvation by God's mercy, or be overtaken by a terrible fate from which there is no escape." And what he means is that man must act now in order to free himself from the difficulties of having to climb the uphill paths located on the *ṣirāṭ*. And it is not what simple minds conjecture – that on the Day of Judgement there will be steep mountains which mankind must cross over mounted or on foot, and that these physical mountains are representative of *ṣalāt*, *zakat*, fasting, *ḥaj* or other acts of worship; and consequently, if there was a shortcoming in his worship of God then the ascent of these mountains becomes difficult. In fact, the goal of *qiyāma* is the examination of man's actions and to allocate reward or punishment accordingly and this does not require steep paths over physical mountains which people must climb, with ease or difficulty. Furthermore, we have not received any concise description of the particulars of the *ṣirāṭ* upon which we can base a reliable account."

Actually, whatever happens on the *ṣirāṭ* is designed to complete any shortfall in the net result of man's worship and his efforts at self-purification that he was supposed to achieve in the *dunyā*. And since the philosophy and purpose of worship and self-purification in the *dunyā* is to gain cognizance (*maʿrifa*) of God, it can be said that the *ṣirāṭ* is the path in *ākhira* that completes the journey towards the *maʿrifa* of God which was begun in the *dunyā*. Ibn ʿUmar reports that he asked Imam al-Sadiq (a) about the *ṣirāṭ*, and he replied, "The *ṣirāṭ* is a path towards the cognizance of God, most High."[277] Therefore, it can be said that the *ṣirāṭ* of the Hereafter serves the same purpose as the *ṣirāṭ al-mustaqīm* of this world and perfects it. Fayd Kashani, the famous exegete and traditionist of the 11th/18th century says in this regard, "The *ṣirāṭ al-mustaqīm* is a projection of the guidance that a person in this world finds in his heart and through the obedience of the Imam. In its essence it is thinner than a hair and sharper than a sword edge; darkness prevents people from locating it, and consequently no-one finds his way to it except if God grants him a light by which he separates from the rest of the people. And everyone walk on the path according to the amount of light he possesses. It has been reported from Imam al-Sadiq (a) that, "Both the straight path (*ṣirāṭ al-mustaqīm*) that leads to all virtues, and the bridge (*ṣirāṭ*) situated between Paradise and Hell, are defined in the form of the human being." The meaning of this tradition is that the path and the one who travels across it are one and the same.

In fact, when an individual travels on the *ṣirāṭ*, every step he takes is according to the light of the unique cognizance he possesses. On the other hand, one can also say that his cognizance stems from the path he takes, in the meaning that his *ma'rifa* of God is formed from the result of his actions, which are themselves dependent on the cognizance he possessed previously. And in this way, he crosses stages until he reaches God, and to God is the final destination."[278]

This interpretation - that the *ṣirāṭ* is for cleansing and purifying the soul and completing the process that man left unfinished during his earthly life – is frequently mentioned in the traditions. It has been narrated from the Prophet (s)

---

[277] Ṣadūq, *Ma'ānī al-Akhbār*, p. 32, trad. 1.

[278] Fayḍ al-Kāshānī, *Tafsīr al-Ṣāfī*, 1:86.

that, "As people will gain salvation from the Hellfire, they will be detained on a bridge that stretches between Paradise and Hell; there, the corruption that still persists from their deeds in the world will be removed from them, and only once they are purified and cleansed will they be granted permission to enter Paradise. I swear by the One in whose hands my life is! Each of them will know his own location in Paradise more clearly than he knew the address of his home in the *dunyā*."[279]

The Path to Paradise and the Path to Hell

From the explanation above it becomes clear that not everyone will travel on the *ṣirāṭ* that leads to Paradise; as we have said, this road is only for those who have virtues that are incomplete or need perfecting. Therefore, it can be surmised that there will be two paths on that Day; one path that leads directly to Hell and those who travel on it are stripped of all hope, and another that leads to Paradise. This latter path is suspended over Hell, and Paradise can only be reached by successfully getting across it.

In the first case though, the angels are directed to, "*gather the wrongdoers and their companions and what they used to worship besides God and lead them on the path to Hell.*"[280] It is evident that this path is distinct from the one that passes over Hell and leads to Paradise.

As for the second path, it has been reported from the Prophet (s) that he said, "Hell encompasses the *dunyā* while Paradise

[279] Muttaqī Hindī, *Kanz al-ʿUmmāl*, trad. 38978 |

إِذَا خَلَصَ الْمُؤْمِنُونَ مِنَ النَّارِ حُبِسُوا بِقَنْطَرَةٍ بَيْنَ الْجَنَّةِ وَالنَّارِ، فَيَتَقَاصُّونَ مَظَالِمَ كَانَتْ بَيْنَهُمْ فِي الدُّنْيَا حَتَّى إِذَا نُقُّوا وَهُذِّبُوا، أُذِنَ لَهُمْ بِدُخُولِ الْجَنَّةِ، فَوَالَّذِي نَفْسُ مُحَمَّدٍ بِيَدِهِ، لَأَحَدُهُمْ بِمَسْكَنِهِ فِي الْجَنَّةِ أَدَلُّ بِمَسْكَنِهِ كَانَ فِي دَارِ الدُّنْيَا.

[280] Surat al-Ṣāffāt, 37:22,23.

lies beyond it. For this reason, the only way to Paradise is the path that crosses over Hell."[281] Only those who have a chance of salvation will be allowed on this path, although many of them will be unable to cross all the way to its end and will fall into Hell along the way.

The Darkness of the Path and the Light Possessed by the Travellers

The *ṣirāṭ* is a path shrouded in darkness and those who travel across it need light to illuminate their way. It is just like an unlit road in the wilderness at night, which cannot be safely crossed without light. According to traditions, it is "a dark path on which everyone can only see what is illuminated by his own light."[282] But this darkness and light has no relationship with night and day or the rising and setting of the sun; rather, the darkness is the inner reality of the *dunyā* in which man lived and which had completely captivated his eyes, heart and soul. It is a darkness that can only be dispelledby an inner light that some people had possessed in the *dunyā*. Imam al-Sadiq (a) said, "On the Day of Judgement, God shall gather all the generations of mankind on one plain. Thereafter, an intense darkness will descend on them in a manner that they will cry out to their Lord to take it away. At this time a group will advance with light shining in front of them, illuminating the whole land of *qiyāma*."[283]

---

281 Muttaqī Hindī, *Kanz al-ʿUmmāl*, trad. 39028 |

جَهَنَّمُ تُحِيطُ بِالدُّنْيَا، وَالْجَنَّةُ مِنْ وَرَائِهَا، فَلِذَلِكَ صَارَ الصِّرَاطُ عَلَى جَهَنَّمَ طَرِيقًا إِلَى الْجَنَّةِ.

282 Fayḍ Kāshānī, *al-Ṣāfī*, 1:85 |

أَنَّهُ مُظْلِمٌ، يَسْعَى النَّاسُ عَلَيْهِ عَلَى قَدْرِ أَنْوَارِهِمْ

283 Majlisī, *Biḥār al-Anwār*, 8:36, quoting from the *Āmālī* of Ṣadūq |

عَنْ أَبِي عَبْدِ اللهِ الصَّادِقِ عَلَيْهِ السَّلَامُ ، قَالَ: إِذَا كَانَ يَوْمُ الْقِيَامَةِ جَمَعَ اللهُ الْأَوَّلِينَ وَالْآخِرِينَ فِي صَعِيدٍ وَاحِدٍ، فَتَغْشَاهُمْ ظُلْمَةٌ شَدِيدَةٌ، فَيَضِجُّونَ إِلَى رَبِّهِمْ، وَيَقُولُونَ: يَا رَبِّ اكْشِفْ عَنَّا هَذِهِ الظُّلْمَةَ، قَالَ:

This light is the illumination placed by God in the hearts of His servants in *dunyā* which connected them to Him and, like a bright beacon, constantly moved them to remember and adore Him. It is interesting that there are some people on the *ṣirāṭ* who are totally covered in darkness, and when they see their companions striding forward briskly with hopeful faces, they say to them, "Walk a little slower so that we can benefit from your light also." But in this place, their request is as futile as the desire for a dead person to return to his former life. And those who have light look at them in bemusement, while the angels inform them that, "You need to return to the *dunyā* and bring your light from there."

Here, the light that illuminates the way must come forth from the inside of an individual, and so the light of one person cannot assist anyone else. And this inner light can only be earned in the *dunyā* and not here. Everything that is of worth in this place has been brought from *dunyā* and God out of His grace, expands it for them. And those desperate souls who now realize that they possess nothing of use here and who find themselves helpless in the cover of total darkness, find it hard to accept the awful truth of their predicament.

The Day of Separation (*Yawm al-Faṣl*)

The nature of the darkness and the dilemma of those who have no light is so severe that those who have light are moved to try to assist them, but gradually a barrier forms between the two groups; one side of it is filled with illumination and God's mercy, while the other is engulfed in darkness and chastisement. The wrongdoers call out in terror and desperation to their righteous companions for help crying, "But were we not always together? Were we not friends

فَيُقْبِلُ قَوْمٌ يَمْشِي النُّورُ بَيْنَ أَيْدِيهِمْ قَدْ أَضَاءَ أَرْضَ الْقِيَامَةِ.

and neighbours of one another? Did we not live together? Wasn't our God and Prophet the same? Why then do you abandon us now, and withhold assistance?" As for those who possess light, they can no longer do anything to assist their former companions because they have entered into a new realm. They reply that it is true that we were together once, but unfortunately you kept deluding yourselves, and you exchanged your faith for doubt, and your long dreams led you astray until the time for your death arrived, and the deceitful Satan successfully misled you. And now, you have been left with the disbelievers to live with your souls covered in darkness, because light is not available at any price, "*On the Day when you will see the believing men and the believing women with their lights running before them on their right; (they will be told) Your good tidings today are of gardens from beneath which rivers flow, and wherein you will live forever – this indeed, is a great success. On the Day when the hypocrite men and the hypocrite women will say to the believers, "Wait for us so that we may borrow from your light!" It will be announced, "Go back to seek light." And a wall will come down between them; it will have a door. Inside it will be mercy, while outside will rage punishment. They will cry out, "Were we not with you?!" They will reply, "Yes indeed, but you used to give in to temptations, and looked forward to our misfortune, and constantly doubted, and vain desires deluded you until the command of God came - and the arch-deceiver deceived you about God." So today no ransom can free you or those who disbelieved. The fire shall be your abode, it is the most fitting place for you. What an evil refuge it is.*"[284]

From the foregoing, which is mentioned in Surat al-Ḥadīd, it becomes evident that in *maḥshar* and even on the bridge of *ṣirāṭ*, people will still be with their communities and

[284] Surat al-Ḥadīd, 57:12-15.

able to communicate with their friends and acquaintances, although this proximity will not ultimately be of benefit to the wrongdoers.

We spoke of a wall, one which separates the world of illumination from that of darkness on the *ṣirāṭ*. Of course, this is not a wall of bricks and mortar; rather, it is more similar to the barrier of *barzakh* that separated the world of the living from the world of the dead in the *dunyā*. *Barzakh* divided the world into two dimensions and placed everyone in their own unique positions. In those two dimensions of the *dunyā*, life, time, perception, and the human journey towards perfection were different for everyone. Now on the Day of Judgement, the world of *ākhira* is also divided into two dimensions; one is full of light and the other is in pitch darkness. The dimension that has light points towards God and is illuminated by His mercy and leads towards Paradise. The dimension that is in darkness is distant from God and His mercy and its pathways lead to Hellfire, "Within it is mercy because it is in the vicinity of Paradise and outside its punishment rages because it is in the vicinity of Hellfire."[285]

In fact, these two dimensions represent the two aspects of the life in *dunyā* whose reality now manifests itself; human beings made use of both the hidden aspect of *dunyā* which was directed towards God and consisted of faith in Him, and its apparent aspect which faced away from God and was devoid of His mercy; "*Inside it will be mercy, while outside will rage punishment.*"[286] Indeed, the world of *ākhira* is a place where the people will realize the true meaning of their deeds

[285] Fayḍ Kashānī, *al-Ṣāfī*, 5:134 |

بَاطِنُهُ فِيهِ الرَّحْمَةُ، لِأَنَّهُ يَلِي الْجَنَّةَ، وَظَاهِرُهُ مِنْ قِبَلِهِ مِنْ جِهَتِهِ الْعَذَابُ، لِأَنَّهُ يَلِي النَّارَ.

[286] Surat al-Ḥadīd, 57:13.

because, "*On the Day of Judgement God will inform them of what they did.*"[287]

However, this wall also has a door, "*And a wall will come down between them; it will have a door.*"[288] Once again, this is not the kind of door that is found in the walls in *dunyā*, rather, it denotes a window or portal through which the inhabitants of the two dimensions can see each other and be informed of one another's situation.

In the realm of *dunyā* there was a wall between the living and the dead who lived in *barzakh* which prevented the living from seeing those in *barzakh*, although the converse was possible – and the inhabitants of *barzakh* could occasionally receive information about the living. However, in the Hereafter, this wall allows communication from both sides. In *dunyā* the living could enter the realm of *barzakh* at death, and here also, it is conceivable that those living in darkness – after passing through severe difficulties and being cleansed of their inner arrogance – may well be allowed to enter the realm of illumination. Conversely, those who are in the realm of light may falter in their difficult uphill journey towards perfection and fall into the darkness. It is for this reason that they constantly ask, "*O Lord! Perfect for us our light and forgive us our sins; Indeed, You are able to do all things.*"[289]

Strong and Weak Lights and the Pace of Progress

In the illuminated dimension, the amount of light possessed by people varies according to the level of their deeds, faith and purity. According to a tradition from Imam al-Sadiq (a),

---

287 Surat al-Mujādila, 67:7.

288 Surat al-Ḥadīd, 57:13.

289 Surat al-Taḥrīm, 66:8.

"On the Day of Judgement light will be distributed amongst mankind according to the levels of their faith."[290]

The light radiated by some individuals will be so intense that their path will be illuminated endlessly in front of them, but others will possess a light so weak that they will just about see beyond their toes. It has been narrated from the Prophet (s) that, "Each will be given a light to the extent of his deeds... some will receive a light that will radiate in front of them like a mountain, while others will receive even more. Some will receive a light the size of a palm-tree that will be placed on their right-hand side while others will receive less...and it will vary in this manner, until the one who possesses the least amount of light which will just illuminate the toes of his feet. And the light will go on and off. When he will have light he will walk forward, and when it is extinguished he will wait...At that time they will be told to advance at a pace according to their measure of light; so the speed of some will be like lightning, others like the blink of an eye, others like the wind and some will be running, swiftly or slowly... The rate of everyone's progress will be proportionate to the worth of their deeds. In time even the one whose light only illuminates his toes will cross over, but his progress will be tortuous as he crosses inch by inch with the fire burning at him from below."[291] It has also been reported that, "The light

---

290 *Tafsīr* Ali ibn Ibrahim al-Qummī, 2:351 |

قَوْلُهُ تَعَالَى: ﴿يَوْمَ تَرَى الْمُؤْمِنِينَ وَالْمُؤْمِنَاتِ يَسْعَى نُورُهُمْ بَيْنَ أَيْدِيهِمْ وَبِأَيْمَانِهِمْ﴾، قَالَ الصَّادِقُ عَلَيْهِ السَّلَامُ: يُقَسَّمُ النُّورُ بَيْنَ النَّاسِ يَوْمَ الْقِيَامَةِ عَلَى قَدْرِ إِيمَانِهِمْ.

291 Ṣuyūtī, al-Durr *al-Manthūr*, 6:256 |

فَيُعْطَوْنَ نُورَهُمْ عَلَى قَدْرِ أَعْمَالِهِمْ، فَمِنْهُمْ مَنْ يُعْطَى نُورَهُ مِثْلَ الْجَبَلِ بَيْنَ يَدَيْهِ، وَمِنْهُمْ مَنْ يُعْطَى نُورَهُ فَوْقَ ذَلِكَ، وَمِنْهُمْ مَنْ يُعْطَى نُورَهُ مِثْلَ النَّخْلَةِ بِيَمِينِهِ، وَمِنْهُمْ مَنْ يُعْطَى دُونَ ذَلِكَ بِيَمِينِهِ، حَتَّى يَكُونَ آخِرَ مَنْ يُعْطَى نُورَهُ عَلَى إِبْهَامِ قَدَمِهِ، يُضِيءُ مَرَّةً وَيُطْفِئُ مَرَّةً، وَإِذَا أَضَاءَ قَدَّمَ قَدَمَهُ، وَإِذَا طَفِئَ قَامَ. قَالَ فَيَمُرُّ وَيَمُرُّونَ عَلَى الصِّرَاطِ، وَالصِّرَاطُ كَحَدِّ السَّيْفِ، دَحْضٌ، مَزَلَّةٌ. فَيُقَالُ لَهُمْ، اِمْضُوا عَلَى قَدْرِ نُورِكُمْ،

of the believer will illuminate for him a distance between Sana'a and Aden, and for others it will be lesser to the point that their light will illuminate no more than the space ahead of the feet."[292] In any case, the journey towards God's mercy and entry into Paradise is only possible with the aid of this light, and those who are in darkness can only stumble towards God's wrath.

Travelling on the *ṣirāṭ* in darkness is a long and dangerous journey, fraught with fear and anxiety at every turn. However, the ease of the journey in the dimension that is illuminated with the aid of the light that was earned during the life in *dunyā* depends on the amount and strength of the light that one possesses. Those whose light is greater move quicker across the *ṣirāṭ* and approach Paradise swiftly. In the dimension of darkness though, the closer people get to God, the more their pain increases as a result of the adverse reaction of their corruptness to the pure environment they are trying to approach. During this journey, they come to places and stations where people who used to collaborate in wrongdoing, evil and treachery attempt to avoid one another to the extent that, "*that Day man shall flee from his brother and his mother and his father and his spouse and his children*",[293] and he will curse his friends and accomplices.[294]

كَانْقِضَاضِ الْكَوْكَبِ، وَمِنْهُمْ مَنْ يَمُرُّ كَالطَّرْفِ، وَمِنْهُمْ مَنْ يَمُرُّ كَالرِّيحِ، وَمِنْهُمْ مَنْ يَمُرُّ كَشَدِّ الرَّجْلِ وَيَرْمُلُ رَمْلًا، يَمُرُّونَ عَلَى قَدْرِ أَعْمَالِهِمْ حَتَّى يَمُرَّ الَّذِي نُورُهُ عَلَى إِبْهَامِ قَدَمِهِ، يَجُرُّ يَدًا وَيُعَلِّقُ يَدًا، وَيَجُرُّ رِجْلًا وَيُعَلِّقُ رِجْلًا، وَتُصِيبُ جَوَانِبَهُ النَّارُ.

[292] Majlisī, *Biḥār al-Anwār*, 7:165 |
قَالَ قُتَادَةُ: إِنَّ الْمُؤْمِنَ يُضِيءُ لَهُ نُورُهُ كَمَا بَيْنَ عَدَنٍ وَصَنْعَاءَ وَدُونَ ذَلِكَ، حَتَّى أَنَّ مِنَ الْمُؤْمِنِينَ مَنْ لَا يُضِيءُ لَهُ نُورُهُ إِلَّا مَوْضِعَ قَدَمَيْهِ.

[293] Surat al-ʿAbasā, 80:34-36.

[294] Majlisī, *Biḥār al-Anwār*, 7:314 |
وَيَلْعَنُ أَهْلُ الْمَعَاصِي بَعْضُهُمْ بَعْضًا، الَّذِينَ بَدَتْ مِنْهُمُ الْمَعَاصِي فِي دَارِ الدُّنْيَا وَتَعَاوَنُوا عَلَى الظُّلْمِ

His heart will be overwhelmed with regret when he sees the consequences of his deeds. He will weep for a long time in shame and remorse, in a manner that cannot even be conceived by measures of this *dunyā*. However, this remorse will not bring a change in his character and those tears will do nothing to cleanse his being. A time will come when he even sheds tears of blood, but this will not purify his character either. Soon these people realize that here things are not as simple as they were in *dunyā*, and a character that has been disfigured cannot be easily reformed. That too, in utter darkness and in a situation that drains all hope.

However, in the realm of light, getting closer brings about a greater eagerness and happiness and hope. Here no one runs away from anybody, and no one curses anyone. Rather, everyone is kind to one another, seeking God's forgiveness and mercy for all, "They converse with each other and pray for the forgiveness of everyone. These are the Prophets (a) and their sincere followers, who used to encourage each other to goodness in their life in *dunyā*."[295] They ask God to perfect everyone's light and to forgive them out of His unending mercy and make them reach their goal. And God does not disgrace or abandon them; "*On the Day when God will not disgrace the Prophet and those who believed with him. Their light will run before them and on their right sides. They will say, "O*

وَالْعُدْوَانِ فِي دَارِ الدُّنْيَا، وَالْمُسْتَكْبِرُونَ مِنْهُمْ وَالْمُسْتَضْعَفُونَ يَلْعَنُ بَعْضُهُمْ بَعْضًا وَيُكَفِّرُ بَعْضُهُمْ بَعْضًا، ثُمَّ يُجْمَعُونَ فِي مَوْطِنٍ يَفِرُّ بَعْضُهُمْ مِنْ بَعْضٍ، وَذَلِكَ قَوْلُهُ: ﴿يَوْمَ يَفِرُّ الْمَرْءُ مِنْ أَخِيهِ وَأُمِّهِ وَأَبِيهِ وَصَاحِبَتِهِ وَبَنِيهِ﴾ ﴿إِذَا تَعَاوَنُوا عَلَى الظُّلْمِ وَالْعُدْوَانِ فِي دَارِ الدُّنْيَا﴾ ﴿لِكُلِّ امْرِئٍ مِنْهُمْ يَوْمَئِذٍ شَأْنٌ يُغْنِيهِ﴾ ثُمَّ يُجْمَعُونَ فِي مَوْطِنٍ يَبْكُونَ فِيهِ فَلَوْ أَنَّ تِلْكَ الْأَصْوَاتَ بَدَتْ لِأَهْلِ الدُّنْيَا لَأَذْهَلَتْ جَمِيعَ الْخَلَائِقِ عَنْ مَعَائِشِهِمْ، وَصَدَعَتِ الْجِبَالُ إِلَّا مَا شَاءَ اللهُ، فَلَا يَزَالُونَ يَبْكُونَ حَتَّى يَبْكُون الدَّمَ.

[295] Ibid |

فَيُكَلِّمُ بَعْضُهُمْ بَعْضًا، وَيَسْتَغْفِرُ بَعْضُهُمْ لِبَعْضٍ، أُولَئِكَ الَّذِينَ بَدَتْ مِنْهُمُ الطَّاعَةُ مِنَ الرُّسُلِ وَالْأَتْبَاعِ وَتَعَاوَنُوا عَلَى الْبِرِّ وَالتَّقْوَى فِي دَارِ الدُّنْيَا.

Lord! Perfect our light for us and forgive us! Indeed, You have power of everything."[296]

Intercession (*Shafāʿa*) – an Increase in Kindness and Mercy

The sinners have not been abandoned entirely and as much of God's limitless mercy as their souls and beings will permit to enter is still available to them from different sources. This mercy becomes available after their entry onto the *ṣirāṭ* in the form of intercession or *shafāʿa*.

It has already been mentioned that there are two *ṣirāṭs*; one is the path to Hell which is reserved for those who do not have anything that can be perfected for them and have not brought with themselves the character and deeds that would allow them to be receptive of God's mercy. They will go directly to Hell and intercession will have no effect on them. The other path is the one that leads to Paradise. This is the well-known *ṣirāṭ* which exists to perfect people's merits and expel their impurities. Intercession is of use to those who are already on the *ṣirāṭ* but for whom the journey is intensely difficult and exhausting, or those who have fallen off it into Hell.

The word *shafāʿa* is derived from the root *sh-fa-ʿa*, meaning something that is paired or coupled with something else. It refers to the attachment to a thing or person in order to gain assistance to reach one's desire and goal, a desire and goal that cannot be otherwise achieved. In *qiyāma* too, *shafāʿa* will mean making available a means of salvation to individuals who would not succeed otherwise. The means in this instance will be the souls of great personalities who will take the hand of weaker souls and free them from perdition.

[296] Surat al-Taḥrīm, 66:8.

Help will be available only to those seekers of intercession who qualify for it; the great personalities cannot solicit God's mercy without cause.

Some imagine that intercession is a matter of personal choice and that the great personalities can decide to intercede for whomever they want and ignore those whom they do not want to assist. This view is correct from one aspect, but incorrect from another. It is incorrect because as we have seen, everything on the Day of Judgement is regulated by an orderly system that does not alter at the whim of individuals. Personal likes and dislikes have no effect on the Day. It is for this reason that God states in the Qur'an, "*Beware of a Day when a person shall not suffice for another; nor shall intercession on his behalf be accepted, nor shall compensation be received from him, nor shall he be helped by others.*"[297]; and, "*Remind them (by the Qur'an) lest an individual is destroyed due to his conduct. He shall have no guardian or intercessor except God. And even if he offered every compensation, it shall not be accepted from him.*";[298] and, "*When the trumpet is blown, then on that Day there will remain no kinship between them, nor will they enquire about each other.*"[299]

The Bible mentions that Jesus (a) said to the Jews, "Your conduct will show whether you have really repented or not. And do not tell yourselves that because Abraham (a) is your grandfather, you shall remain safe from God's wrath, because God can create children for Abraham (a) from the rocks in this very desert!"[300]

297 Surat al-Baqara, 2:48.

298 Surat al-Anʿām, 6:70.

299 Surat al-Mu'minūn, 23:101.

300 Gospel of Luke, 3:8.

However, from another aspect the view is correct because the love and hatred of these great personalities' mirrors that of God. Their friendship is only for God's friends and their enmity extends only to His enemies. Therefore, it is correct that they intercede for those whom they like, however these individuals are already people whom God desires to receive intercession. Therefore, "*they only intercede for those whom God approves, and they stand in awe of Him.*"[301] It is for this reason that God grants them permission to assist and intercede on behalf of those who are stuck on the path; "*The Day when no intercession will be of benefit except from the one whom the Merciful Lord has given permission, and with whose word He is pleased.*"[302] These great souls are those whose entire beings are suffused with the love of God and who are filled with knowledge and inner conviction; they only desire what God desires, and do not do anything except that which is righteous, "*And those whom they invoke besides Him have no power of intercession; only those (can intercede) who bear witness to the Truth and know (the qualities of the ones whom they want to intercede for).*"[303]

Those who shall Qualify for Intercession

Who will truly receive intercession and how will the process take place? Firstly, it must be appreciated that intercession will require some connection and relationship between the soul of the intercessor and the soul of the one seeking it. The stronger this relationship, the sooner the intercession is made, and the quicker salvation is achieved; and the weaker the connection between the two, the longer the process will take, because establishing a link between a pure soul and an impure one is a difficult task. It is for this

[301] Surat al-Anbiya', 21:28.

[302] Surat Ṭā Hā, 20:109.

[303] Surat al-Zukhruf, 43:86.

reason that intercession comes to some individuals quickly, and they do not reach the fires of Hell. For others though, it is very slow to take effect, and it is only achieved after they spend an extended period in Hell. However, what is absolutely necessary for intercession is the presence of some connection, and one whose soul cannot establish any bond with the great souls is cut off from intercession. It has been reported from the Prophet (s) that, "On the Day of Judgement I will intercede for anyone who has even an atom's weight of faith in their heart."[304] And if even this tiny amount of faith is absent, it is a sign that there was never even a remote bond between his soul and that of the Prophet (s).

In a famous tradition from the Prophet (s) it has been reported that, "Indeed, my intercession is for those from my nation who have committed the major sins; however, for the righteous there is no culpability."[305] The righteous referred to here are those who did not commit the major sins and the meaning of the tradition is that staying away from the major sins causes the consequences of the minor ones to be erased, just as the Qur'an states, "*If you avoid the major sins which are forbidden, We will do away with your minor sins and admit you (into Paradise) with honour.*"[306] It has also been reported from Imam al-Sadiq (a) that, "On the Day of Judgement, we will intercede for the sinners amongst our Shīʿa; as for the

304 Muttaqī al-Hindi, *Kanz al-ʿUmmāl*, trad. 39043 |

لَأَشْفَعَنَّ يَوْمَ الْقِيَامَةِ لِمَنْ كَانَ فِي قَلْبِهِ جَنَاحُ بَعُوضَةٍ إِيمَانٌ.

305 Muttaqī al-Hindi, *Kanz al-ʿUmmāl*, trad. 39549; Ṣadūq, *Kitāb al-Tawḥīd*, p. 407 |

إِنَّمَا شَفَاعَتِي لِأَهْلِ الْكَبَائِرِ مِنْ أُمَّتِي، فَأَمَّا الْمُحْسِنُونَ فَمَا عَلَيْهِمْ مِنْ سَبِيلٍ.

306 Surat al-Nisa', 4:31.

righteous amongst them, they will receive salvation from God Himself."[307]

A point that is worthy of consideration here is that in the foregoing traditions the Prophet (s) states that he will intercede for his nation and the Imam (a) states that he will intercede for his Shīʿa. As we had mentioned earlier this is only possible because of the relationship between their souls; a general affinity in the case of Prophet (s) and his nation, and a special affinity between the Imams (a) and their Shīʿa. In the same way, every Prophet (a) and Imam will intercede for his own nation and followers. It has been narrated from the Prophet (s) that, "The Prophets will intercede for anyone who had sincerely testified that there is no god but Allah, and they will bring them out of Hell."[308] In addition to the Prophets and Imams, who are the veracious (*ṣiddīqūn*), intercession will also be accepted from the faithful who had not indulged in major sins or who had repented for their sins. They will be able to intercede for people whose souls were connected to theirs. According to a tradition from Imam al-Sadiq (a), "The faithful (*mu'minūn*) are of two types: those who were true to the covenant they made with God and conducted themselves accordingly, and are referred to in the verse, "*Amongst the believers there are those who were true to their promise to God*".[309] They are the ones who will not experience the trials of *barzakh* and the *ākhira*; they will not require intercession and will intercede for others. The other type of believer is like a stalk of wheat

---

[307] Rayshahrī, *Mīzān al-Ḥikma*, 2:1474 |

إِذَا كَانَ يَوْمُ الْقِيَامَةِ نَشْفَعُ فِي الْمُذْنِبِينَ مِنْ شِيعَتِنَا، فَأَمَّا الْمُحْسِنُونَ فَقَدْ نَجَّاهُمُ اللهُ.

[308] Ibn Ḥanbal, *Musnad*, trad. 11081 |

يَشْفَعُ الْأَنْبِيَاءُ فِي كُلِّ مَنْ كَانَ يَشْهَدُ ﴿أَنْ لَا إِلَهَ إِلَّا اللهُ﴾ مُخْلِصًا، فَيُخْرِجُونَهُمْ مِنْهَا.

[309] Surat al-Aḥzāb, 33:23.

in the wind, sometimes bending one way and sometimes the other. They will be exposed to the terrors of the *barzakh* and the *ākhira*. They will receive intercession, but they will be unable to intercede for others."[310] It has also been reported from the Prophet (s) that, "Some believers will intercede for a large number of people, as many as the people of the tribes of Rabīʿa and Muḍar; the least number that a believer will intercede for will be thirty individuals."[311]

Everyone will need the Intercession of Prophet Muhammad (s)

All instances of intercession will be futile without the intervention of the Prophet (s); he is the main intercessor who possesses the greatest connection with God. As mentioned in the Qur'an, God is the actual source of intercession and it is only by His permission that others may intercede, "*Say: to God alone belongs (the right to grant) intercession in entirety; His is the dominion of the heavens and earth, and to Him will you all be returned.*"[312] Therefore, whoever desires to intercede for someone or receive intercession makes use of this Divine gift. God has granted this gift to His closest servant, in the sense that every intercession must pass by his intercession, because his soul is the closest to God. As a result, for intercession to occur, both those giving

---

310 Kulaynī, *al-Kāfī*, 2:248 |

الْمُؤْمِنُ مُؤْمِنَانِ: فَمُؤْمِنٌ صَدَقَ بِعَهْدِ اللهِ وَوَفَى بِشَرْطِهِ، وَذَلِكَ قَوْلُ اللهِ عَزَّ وَجَلَّ: ﴿رِجَالٌ صَدَقُوا مَا عَاهَدُوا اللهَ عَلَيْهِ﴾ فَذَلِكَ الَّذِي لَا تُصِيبُهُ أَهْوَالُ الدُّنْيَا وَلَا أَهْوَالُ الْآخِرَةِ، وَذَلِكَ مِمَّنْ يَشْفَعُ وَلَا يُشْفَعُ لَهُ، وَمُؤْمِنٌ كَخَامَةِ الزَّرْعِ، تَعْوَجُّ أَحْيَانًا وَتَقُومُ أَحْيَانًا، فَذَلِكَ مِمَّنْ تُصِيبُهُ أَهْوَالُ الدُّنْيَا وَأَهْوَالُ الْآخِرَةِ، وَذَلِكَ مِمَّنْ يُشْفَعُ لَهُ وَلَا يَشْفَعُ.

311 Rayshayhrī, *Mīzān al-Ḥikma*, 2:1467 |

فِي الْمُؤْمِنِينَ مَنْ يَشْفَعُ مِثْلَ رَبِيعَةَ وَمُضَرَ، وَأَقَلُّ الْمُؤْمِنِينَ شَفَاعَةً مَنْ يَشْفَعُ لِثَلَاثِينَ إِنْسَانًا.

312 Surat al-Zumar, 39:44.

and receiving intercession need his intercession and this is the praised rank (*maqāman maḥmūdā*) that God will grant His beloved Prophet (s) on the Day of Judgement; "*And stay awake in prayer in the small hours of the night as an additional worship for you, soon your Lord will resurrect you to a praised rank.*"[313] And so it has been reported that, "There is no one from the former or later generations except that he is in need of the intercession of Muhammad (s) on the Day of Judgement."[314]

The Last Spring of Mercy: The Pool of the Prophets (a)

Those who pass across the *ṣirāṭ* have managed to complete that which was deficient and shed that which was corrupt in their souls. However, these purified souls still require one finishing touch so that they can enter into Paradise. They need to eliminate the last traces of impurity and evil from the depths of the souls and establish in their hearts that state of tranquillity and serenity that is necessary for life in Paradise. This last cleansing can only be achieved through the purifying souls of the Prophets (a) connecting with the souls of the believers and transferring this tranquillity and serenity into their hearts. It is like an invigorating draught that the Prophets (a) pour into the hearts of their followers from the essence of their own lofty souls. For this reason, this station has been called the pool of the Prophets (a) and in the case of the Prophet (s) of Islam, it is called the pool of Kawthar. Before any believer can enter into heaven, he must drink at this pool so that the last vestiges of ignorance and insincerity, rancour and spite, vanity and greed and in short, every trace of evil and vice that would disrupt peaceful co-existence is eliminated. Now his entire being is suffused

[313] Surat al-Isrā', 17:79.

[314] Barqī, *al-Maḥāsin*, 1:293 |

مَا مِنْ أَحَدٍ مِنَ الْأَوَّلِينَ وَالْآخِرِينَ إِلَّا وَهُوَ يَحْتَاجُ إِلَى شَفَاعَةِ مُحَمَّدٍ يَوْمَ الْقِيَامَةِ.

with love for God and goodwill to others. In the words of the Qur'an, "*And we shall remove from their hearts every trace of ill-feeling; beneath them rivers will flow, and they will say: All praise is for God, Who has guided us to this, and we would never have been guided if it had not been for God's guidance.*"[315] This verse describes events just before entry into Paradise at the time when the believers will come to the end of their journey. It has been narrated from the Prophet (s) that he said, "I swear by the One in whose hand is my life! In *qiyāma* there exists a special water; know that the friends of God will all come to (drink that water at) the pool of the Prophets."[316] And he said, "On that Day every Prophet will be standing at a pool and will have a special staff by which he will signal whoever he recognizes from his nation to come forward and drink. Every nation will have a unique mark on their faces by which their Prophet will identify them."[317] He also said, "Every Prophet shall have a pool and I hope that I will have the most entrants into Paradise."[318] And, "My pool will span a vast distance, and its cups shall be as numerous as the stars in the sky. Whoever drinks from it will not be thirsty until he enters Paradise."[319]

---

[315] Surat al-A'rāf, 7:43.

[316] Muttaqī al-Hindi, *Kanz al-'Ummāl*, trad. 39009 |

وَالَّذِي نَفْسِي بِيَدِهِ إِنَّ فِيهِ لَمَاءً، أَلَا إِنَّ أَوْلِيَاءَ اللهِ لَيَرِدُونَ حِيَاضَ الْأَنْبِيَاءِ

[317] *Ibid*, trad 39118 |

وَإِنَّ كُلَّ رَجُلٍ مِنْهُمْ يَوْمَئِذٍ قَائِمٌ عَلَى حَوْضٍ مَلْآنَ مَعَهُ عَصًا، يَدْعُو مَنْ عَرَفَ مِنْ أُمَّتِهِ، وَلِكُلِّ أُمَّةٍ سِيمَاءٌ يَعْرِفُهُمْ بِهَا نَبِيُّهُمْ

[318] Ibn Kathīr, *Tafsīr*, 2:129 |

إِنَّ لِكُلِّ نَبِيٍّ حَوْضًا وَأَرْجُو أَنْ أَكُونَ أَكْثَرَهُمْ وَارِدًا

[319] Muttaqī al-Hindi, *Kanz al-'Ummāl*, trad. 39162 |

إِنَّ حَوْضِيَ مَا بَيْنَ أَيْلَةَ وَصَنْعَاءَ، ..... أَبَارِيقُهُ كَعَدَدِ نُجُومِ السَّمَاءِ، فَمَنْ شَرِبَ مِنْهُ لَمْ يَظْمَأْ حَتَّى يَدْخُلَ الْجَنَّةَ

A'rāf: Issuing Permission to Enter Paradise

At this point the people of Paradise and the people of Hell are completely separated by a heavy veil which has come down between them. Those who have been assigned to Hell have come to its doors while the people of Paradise are ready to enter into Paradise. As described in the Qur'an, at this final station, the close servants of God are arrayed at a location that is above the barrier that separates the two groups. They stand at the top of this wall (*a'rāf*) and can observe both groups simultaneously. They exchange some final words with them and issue the permission for the people of Paradise to be allowed to enter it. The significance of this final station is much more complex than we can comprehend, so here we will suffice ourselves by quoting the description mentioned in the Qur'an; "*And we shall remove from their hearts every trace of ill-feeling; beneath them rivers will flow, and they will say: All praise is for God, Who has guided us to this, and we would never have been guided if it had not been for God's guidance. Certainly, the messengers of God had come to us with the Truth. And it will be announced to them, "This is the Paradise that you have inherited due to your deeds!" And the dwellers of Paradise will call out to the inmates of Hell, "We have already found what our Lord had promised us to be true, have you also found what your Lord had promised to be true?" They shall say, "Yes." Then an announcer shall proclaim between them, "May the mercy of God be far from the wrongdoers, who hindered people from the path of God, seeking to make it crooked, and who disbelieved in the Hereafter."*

And between them shall be a partition; and on its elevations there are men who recognize everyone by their marks. They call out to the dwellers of Paradise, "Peace be upon you!" They have not yet entered it but are filled with hope. And when their eyes are turned on the inmates of Hell, they say, "O Lord! Do not let us be in the company of the wrongdoers." And the people on the elevations will call out to the people whom they recognize by their marks, "What use to you was your hoarded wealth and your arrogance? Are these (others) the ones about who you swore that God would never show His mercy? (They will then say to the people of Paradise) Now enter the Paradise without fear and sorrow."[320]

[320] Surat al-Aʿrāf, 7:43-50.

CHAPTER 5

ETERNITY

The Embodiment of Thoughts, Words and Deeds

In Paradise and Hell every experience that is encountered is governed by the inner state of the individual; as long as the inner state does not change, the outer environment and the quality of man's life does not improve either. Paradise and Hell are like magical realms in which everything that stems from the mind, soul and being of an individual finds an external existence that is real and tangible. This is called the embodiment of deeds (*tajassum al-aʿmāl*). Such a world may be difficult for us to imagine, but we must keep in mind that as we mentioned earlier, *ākhira* is the culmination of the hierarchy of existence; a world which has developed from primitive beginnings and developed to an unimaginable level of perfection, just as a tiny oak develops into a strong oak tree, "Objects in the realm of the dominion of God (*malakūt*) are like mustard seeds planted in a field. The mustard seed is the tiniest of seeds, yet it matures into a bush that is bigger than others. It becomes as big as a tree and birds' nest in its branches."[321]

The advice given to Qays ibn Mālik by the Prophet (s) is an affirmation of this embodiment, "Know that you have no choice, O Qays, except to be buried with a companion who is alive, while you are dead. If the companion is noble, then he will honour you, but if he is of evil character, then he will overpower you. He will only be resurrected with you, and you will only come forth with him. You will not be questioned about anything other than him. Therefore, do not allow your

---

[321] Gospel of Matthew, 13:31-32.

companion to be anything but good, so that you may form a close bond with him, because if he is evil, you will not be repulsed by anything more than by him... And he is nothing other than the embodiment of your actions.[322]

It has been mentioned in many verses of the Qur'an that whatever is received in that world is the product of one's own hands; it is the acquisition of a character and form that one has shaped himself in the *dunyā*, "*This is due to what your own hands have sent forth and God is not unjust to His servants*",[323] and, "*Indeed, We have warned you of an imminent punishment, a Day when man will see that which he has sent forth with his own hands and the disbeliever will cry, "O how I wish that I was dust!*"[324] They will find the act itself present, not just a report of it, "*The day when every soul shall find present whatever good it has done and whatever evil it has done.*"[325]

It has also been mentioned repeatedly that when people return to God, He will inform them of the meaning of their deeds, "*In the end your return is to your Lord, and He will inform you about what you used to do. Indeed, he is well aware of what is hidden in the hearts.*"[326] Therefore, whatever we do in this world and whatever we harbour in our hearts will acquire a different meaning in the Hereafter and God will inform us about it. Here, "informing" means showing us its reality

---

[322] Ṣadūq, *al-Khiṣāl*, p. 114 |
وَإِنَّهُ لَا بُدَّ لَكَ يَا قَيْسُ مِنْ قَرِينٍ يُدْفَنُ مَعَكَ وَهُوَ حَيٌّ، وَتُدْفَنُ مَعَهُ وَأَنْتَ مَيِّتٌ، فَإِنْ كَانَ كَرِيمًا أَكْرَمَكَ، وَإِنْ كَانَ لَئِيمًا أَسْلَمَكَ، ثُمَّ لَا يُحْشَرُ إِلَّا مَعَكَ، وَلَا تُبْعَثُ إِلَّا مَعَهُ، وَلَا تُسْأَلُ إِلَّا عَنْهُ، فَلَا تَجْعَلْهُ إِلَّا صَالِحًا فَإِنَّهُ إِنْ صَلَحَ أَنِسْتَ بِهِ، وَإِنْ فَسَدَ لَا تَسْتَوْحِشُ إِلَّا مِنْهُ، وَهُوَ فِعْلُكَ.

[323] Surat Āl-'Imrān, 3:182.

[324] Surat al-Nabā', 78:40.

[325] Surat Āl-'Imrān, 3:30.

[326] Surat al-Zumar, 39:7.

in that world, where it will either place us in Paradise or in Hellfire.

Hell

It is impossible to describe the torments of Hell and the wretchedness of its inmates. "The inmates of Hell don't make a sound except to scream and wail, they experience no pleasure, and they know no hope and no relief from sorrow. All doors of escape are closed to them, and they have no saviour from amongst the angels and no consoler from amongst men. God does not pay attention to them and removes their memory from the hearts of others, so that no one ever thinks of them."[327] "It is a place devoid of mercy; no supplication is answered therein, and no grief is dispelled."[328]

Th relentless torment in this world full of pain and misery springs from the corruption in the hearts of men and *jinn*' who consider themselves above God; and as long as this egoism persists and their existence poses a threat to others, their pain and misery will not cease. The reason Hell is devoid of mercy is because of the inmates' remoteness from God, and every tribulation that ensues is because of this remoteness.

Hell is a place where corruptness and impurity is accumulated together and then set on fire, and then time is given to see if their owners are thus purified, "*And the disbelievers will be gathered together in Hell, so that God may separate the impure*

[327] Mufīd, *al-Ikhtiṣāṣ*, p.365, quoting Imam al-Baqir (a) |
فَلَيْسَ لَهُمْ فِيهَا كَلَامٌ إِلَّا أَنِينٌ، فَيُطْبَقُ عَلَيْهِمْ أَبْوَابُهَا، وَيُسَدُّ عَلَيْهِمْ عُمُدُهَا، فَلَا يَدْخُلُ عَلَيْهِمْ رَوْحٌ أَبَدًا وَلَا يَخْرُجُ مِنْهُمُ الْغَمُّ أَبَدًا، فَهِيَ عَلَيْهِمْ مُؤْصَدَةٌ - يَعْنِي مُطْبَقَةٌ - لَيْسَ لَهُمْ مِنَ الْمَلَائِكَةِ شَافِعُونَ وَلَا مِنْ أَهْلِ الْجَنَّةِ صَدِيقٌ حَمِيمٌ، وَيَنْسَاهُمُ الرَّبُّ وَيَمْحُو ذِكْرَهُمْ مِنْ قُلُوبِ الْعِبَادِ، فَلَا يُذْكَرُونَ أَبَدًا.

[328] *Nahj al-Balāgha*, Letter 27 |
دَارٌ لَيْسَ فِيهَا رَحْمَةٌ، وَلَا تُسْمَعُ فِيهَا دَعْوَةٌ، وَلَا تُفَرَّجُ فِيهَا كُرْبَةٌ.

from the pure; He will heap the impure one upon another and consign them all to Hellfire. Indeed, they are the losers."[329]

This verse is explained in a beautiful parable by Jesus (a); "That which occurs in the dominion of God is the simile of the person who sowed good seed in his field. One night while he was asleep, his enemy came and sowed weeds amongst his wheat seeds and left. When the wheat sprouted and formed heads, the weeds also appeared. His servants asked, "Do you want us to pull out the weeds?" He replied, "No, do not do that because while you pull out the weeds, you might uproot the wheat at the same time. Wait until the time when both are ready for harvest. At that time, I will tell the harvesters to collect the weeds in bundles and burn them; thereafter, they can bring the wheat in for storage."[330]

Hell is a place of torment that actually stems from God's mercy. With the extraordinary power that human beings acquire in the Hereafter, if the inmates of Hell were not contained in a fiery prison, not a single moment of peace would remain for anyone. One of the blessings that the dwellers of heaven are constantly thankful for is that those who have still not shed the corruptness of their souls - despite all the stations and stages of purification - are locked away. If they were left free, they would not hesitate to inconvenience every other creature. Therefore, heaping all the corrupt souls together and imprisoning them in Hell is nothing but an extension of God's mercy on the rest of His servants. "Once again, the dominion of heaven can be explained with the following parable: fishermen cast a net into the water and catch all kinds of fish. Then they pull it to the shore and separate the good fish from the bad. They place the good fish in baskets

[329] Surat al-Anfāl, 8:36, 37.

[330] Gospel of Matthew. 13:24-30.

and throw away the bad. At the end of the time this is what will happen also. The angels will come and separate the righteous individuals from the corrupt; they will throw the corrupt into Hell where they will lay weeping and gnashing their teeth."[331]

It is apparent that if any of the inmates of Hell abandons his obstinacy and egoism and his existence is no longer a threat to the wellbeing of others, then he will leave Hell and enter a life of bliss. The punishments of Hell are all designed to dissuade the inmates of Hell from their arrogance. It has been narrated from the Prophet (s) that, "On the Day of Judgement anyone who has testified to the creed "there is no god but Allah" and whose heart contains an atom's weight of virtue will be removed from Hell."[332] As for those whose hearts did not even have an atom's weight of goodness, they would never be able to abandon their arrogance and consequently must remain in Hell for eternity.

It has been reported from an exegete of the Qur'an of the first century by the name of Ḍaḥāk that, "I received a narration of the Prophet (s) in which I had doubt; to resolve this I set off for Medina. In the mosque of the Prophet (s), I saw that the people were seated in two groups; at the head of each sat an old man relating the traditions of the Prophet (s). I enquired about these two men and was informed that one of them was Abu Saʿīd al-Khudrī and the other was Abu Ḥurayra. I came to Abu Saʿīd and said that I had received a report from the Prophet (s) which seemed doubtful to me, and for this reason I had come to Medina to seek its verification. He asked, "What is this report?" I said, "That the Prophet (s) said that "A group will be brought out of Hell

[331] Gospel of Matthew. 13:47-50.

[332] Mulla Fatḥullāh Kāshānī, *Tafsīr Minhāj al-Ṣādiqīn*, 5:430.

after they will have been turned to coal."[333] Abu Saʿīd pointed to his ear and said, "May both my ears turn deaf if I lie! I have heard the Messenger of God (s) say that mankind will be in different groups on the Day of Judgement; some will enter Paradise without accounting, and these will be the Prophets (a). Others will have to give an account of their deeds, and if their good deeds outnumber their evil ones, then they too will be taken to Paradise; and if their good and evil deeds are equal, God shall be merciful to them and forgive them, and they will be taken to Paradise; and I or other qualified people shall intercede for some. And if the situation is different from these two, then they will be taken to Hell, where they will be punished to the extent of their evil, and then they will be brought to their Paradise...they will be brought to a spring which is named the "spring of life" (*ʿayn al-ḥayāt*) and be instructed to wash themselves in this spring. As they enter the spring, all the remaining corruption and arrogance will wash away from their bodies; however, on their forehead, there shall remain a sign saying, "These are the servants of God whom He has released from the fire of Hell." When the dwellers of Paradise see them, they shall say, "These are the people who have been released from their Hells". God then removes these signs as well so that they are not embarrassed or discomfited by its presence.[334]

After this brief introduction, we now present a general discussion about Hell as it has been described to us.

The Landscape of Hell

Hell is a land of plains and deserts, mountains and valleys, precipices and chasms, streams, rivers and seas; its weather

---

333 إِنَّ قَوْمًا يُخْرَجُونَ مِنَ النَّارِ بَعْدَمَا صَارُوا جَمِيعًا فَحْمًا.

334 Mulla Fatḥullāh Kāshānī, *Tafsīr Minhāj al-Ṣādiqīn*, 5:430.

is dry and harsh, its waters are hot and foul, and its winds are searing and cause the skin to blister. Its skies are cloaked in clouds of black smoke, which cast shadows and darkness everywhere; "*And the people of the left hand, how wretched they are! In (a land of) of scorching winds and boiling water, and a shade of black smoke that is neither cool nor refreshing.*"[335] "*(They will be instructed) Proceed to that which you used to deny. Proceed to the shadow of three columns of smoke that neither gives shade nor relief from the fire of Hell. Indeed, it throws out sparks as big as forts!*"[336] This place will be surrounded by fire from above and below and from the right and the left, like being enclosed in a fiery comet whose heat melts everything in its path, "*They shall have layers of fire above them and layers of fire below them.*"[337]

More precisely, it is like a land of erupting volcanoes whose burning lava spreads over a vast area, "*We have prepared for the wrongdoers a fire that will surround them like towering walls.*"[338] For this reason, this land has earned the adjectives of Hellfire and *Jahannam*. Its waters are scalding, its winds are searing, its ground is burning, and its inhabitants are roasted from inside and out.

Jesus (a) cautioned, "If your eye sins, pluck it out, for it is better for you to enter the dominion of God with one eye than to see the fire of Hell with both eyes. It is a place where the flesh-eating maggots shall never die, and the punishment of the fire shall never ease."[339]

---

335 Surat al-Wāqiʿa, 56:41-44.

336 Surat al-Mursalāt, 77:29-32.

337 Surat al-Zumar, 39:16.

338 Surat al-Kahf, 18:29.

339 Gospel of Mark, 9:47,48.

The fire that rages across this land has no light and covers everything in a dark pall of smoke, "God kindled this fire for a thousand years until it was white, and then another thousand years until it became crimson, then another thousand years until it turned black, a blackness whose flames do not emit light."[340] And this is why Hell is covered in dense black smoke.

The valleys and plains of this land are each hotter than the other. Here, "There exists a valley called "Lamlam", and the other valleys of Hell seek refuge in God from it";[341] "Within it exists a pit and if anyone was to stumble into it he would fall for seventy years.";[342] "There is a mountain in it called Ṣaʿūḍ,[343] next to which is a valley called Saqar, at the bottom of which there is a pit called Habhab; whenever the door of that pit is opened the inmates of Hell scream due to its heat. The homes of the tyrants are located in that pit."[344] As for Saqar itself, it is the place where the abodes of the arrogant have been constructed; "*And what do you think Saqar is? It does not spare anyone nor leave anything unburnt. It roasts the skins of*

---

340 Ibn Rajab al-Ḥanbalī, *al-Takhwīf min al-Nār*, p. 96 |
أَوْقَدَ عَلَيْهَا أَلْفَ عَامٍ حَتَّى ابْيَضَّتْ، ثُمَّ أَوْقَدَ عَلَيْهَا أَلْفَ عَامٍ حَتَّى احْمَرَّتْ، ثُمَّ أَوْقَدَ عَلَيْهَا أَلْفَ عَامٍ حَتَّى اسْوَدَّتْ، فَهِيَ سَوْدَاءُ لَا يَضِيءُ لَهَبُهَا.

341 Abdallah ibn al-Mubārak, *Musnad ibn al-Mubārak*, p. 65 |
إِنَّ فِي جَهَنَّمَ لَوَادِيًا يُقَالُ لَهُ لَمْلَمُ، إِنَّ أَوْدِيَةَ جَهَنَّمَ لَتَسْتَعِيذُ مِنْ حَرِّهِ.

342 Ibn Rajab al-Ḥanbalī, *al-Takhwīf min al-Nār*, p. 122 |
إِنَّ فِي جَهَنَّمَ لَآبَارًا، مَنْ أُلْقِيَ فِيهَا تَرَدَّى سَبْعِينَ عَامًا.

343 The following verse in Surat al-Muddaththir may be a reference to Ṣaʿūd: "And soon We will make him ascend Ṣaʿud (or a slippery slope)." (74:17)

344 *Barqī, al-Maḥāsin*, 1:123 quoting Imam al-Baqir (a) |
إِنَّ فِي جَهَنَّمَ جَبَلًا يُقَالُ لَهُ صَعُودٌ، وَإِنَّ فِي صَعُودَ لَوَادِيًا يُقَالُ لَهُ سَقَرُ، وَإِنَّ لَفِي قَعْرِ سَقَرَ لَجُبًّا يُقَالُ لَهُ هَبْهَبُ، كُلَّمَا كُشِفَ غِطَاءُ ذَلِكَ الْجُبِّ ضَجَّ أَهْلُ النَّارِ مِنْ حَرِّهِ وَذَلِكَ مَنَازِلُ الْجَبَّارِينَ.

mortals."[345] Occasionally, Saqar complains to God of its own stifling heat and asks Him for permission to draw breath, and when it draws breath, the entire *jahannam* is engulfed in roaring flames."[346] "Within it is a valley called Wayl in which flows a river of pus. If someone falls into it, it would be forty years before he reaches its bottom."[347]

In this land, there are beaches similar to the coastlines of oceans, with pits filled with insects and snakes as big as camels, and scorpions as big as mules."[348] Due to the severe heat, the inmates of Hell, will seek relief by coming to these beaches, but the snakes and scorpions will attack them so savagely that burning in the fire will seem more bearable to them. They will prefer to run back towards the heat of the fire."[349]

The winds that blow across this land are infected with various sicknesses; "They contain seventy types of illnesses, each of which is drawn from the depths of Hell."[350] The Qur'an comments, "*Death will come at him from every direction, but he does not die.*"[351]

---

345 Surat al-Muddaththir, 74:27-29.

346 *Barqī, al-Maḥāsin*, 1:123 quoting Imam al-Sadiq (a) |
إِنَّ فِي جَهَنَّمَ لَوَادِيًا لِلْمُتَكَبِّرِينَ، يُقَالُ لَهُ سَقَرُ، شَكَا إِلَى اللهِ عَزَّ وَجَلَّ شِدَّةَ حَرِّهِ، وَسَأَلَهُ أَنْ يَأْذَنَ لَهُ أَنْ يَتَنَفَّسَ، فَتَنَفَّسَ فَأَحْرَقَ جَهَنَّمَ.

347 Ibn Rajab al-Ḥanbalī, *al-Takhwīf min al-Nār*, p. 117, 118 |
وَيْلٌ وَادٍ فِي جَهَنَّمَ يَهْوِي فِيهِ الْكَافِرُ أَرْبَعِينَ خَرِيفًا قَبْلَ أَنْ يَبْلُغَ قَعْرَهُ .... وَعَنْ أَبِي عِيَاضٍ، قَالَ: وَيْلٌ وَادٍ يَسِيلُ مِنْ صَدِيدٍ.

348 Ibid, p. 142 |
إِنَّ لِجَهَنَّمَ جُبَابًا فِي سَوَاحِلَ كَسَوَاحِلِ الْبَحْرِ، فِيهِ هَوَامٌّ وَحَيَّاتٌ كَالْبَخَاتِي، وَعَقَارِبُ كَالْبِغَالِ.

349 Ibid, p.126.

350 Ibid, p.121 |
إِنَّ فِي جَهَنَّمَ سَبْعِينَ دَاءً، كُلُّ دَاءٍ مِثْلُ جُزْءٍ مِنْ أَجْزَاءِ جَهَنَّمَ.

351 Surat Ibrāhīm, 14:17.

The Levels of Hell

In our discussion about the Hell of *barzakh*, we mentioned that Barahūt is divided into two parts: lands covered in darkness and lands full of fire. Those who inhabit the lands in darkness are those who are under impure influences, while the lands of fire are inhabited by those who are the actual impure influences themselves, and their entire beings are transformed into impurity.

In the Hell of the Hereafter, there is a similar division; those who had become the embodiment of impurity will be the fuel that kindles the flames of Hell, while those who allowed themselves to be influenced by them will burn in that fire. About the first group, God says, "*Indeed, you and that which you worship besides God shall be the fuel of Hell; to it, you shall all come.*";[352] and "*Indeed those who disbelieve, neither their wealth nor their offspring shall avail them anything with God; they shall be the fuel of Hellfire.*"[353] About the second group, God says, "*O believers! Protect yourselves and your families from a fire whose fuel is men and stones, over which are appointed stern and severe angels; they do not disobey God in what He commands them and do (precisely) what they are commanded.*"[354]

The address to the believers suggests that it is they who could get caught up and burnt in the fire, which is fuelled by others.

Additionally, depending on the kind of corruptness of individuals, there are seven levels in Hell, each of which has its own doorway, through which the inmates of that level shall enter. According to the Qur'an, "*It has seven gates, and*

[352] Surat al-Anbiya, 21:98.

[353] Surat Āl 'Imrān, 3:10.

[354] Surat al-Taḥrīm, 66:6.

for each, there is a specific group (of sinners)."[355] These divisions are made according to the type and amount of evil within the population of Hell. Those who are more vicious will be in the lower levels of Hell, while those who are less vicious will occupy levels above them. And so, "the doorways of Hell are arrayed in levels, one above the other."[356] "The distance between each level will be equal to a journey of seventy years."[357]

The inner states of the people of Hell will determine the intensity of the punishment that they must endure in order to awaken and abandon their egoism. About the meaning of "specific group" (*juz'un ma'lūm*) in the verse, it has been reported that the Prophet (s) said, "There will be a group of those who associated other deities with God, and another group of those who entertained doubts about God, and a group of those who were heedless of God."[358]

In describing these levels, it has been narrated that,[359] "The uppermost level is *Jaḥīm*, and when its inhabitants stand on its rocks their brains boil over due to its heat. The next level is *Laẓā*, which, "*is a fierce fire (laẓā), blistering away the skin. It invites those who turned their back and averted their face (from the truth), and who collected wealth and hoarded it.*"[360]

---

[355] Surat al-Ḥijr, 15:44.

[356] Sh Ṭūsī, *Tafsir al-Tibyān*, 6:338 |
قَالَ عَلِيٌّ (ع) وَالْحَسَنُ وَقُتَادَةُ وَابْنُ جَرِيجٍ: أَبْوَابُهَا أَطْبَاقٌ بَعْضُهَا فَوْقَ بَعْضٍ.

[357] Ibn Rajab al-Ḥanbalī, *al-Takhwīf min al-Nār*, p. 84 |
بَيْنَ كُلِّ بَابَيْنِ مَسِيرَةُ سَبْعِينَ سَنَةً.

[358] Suyūṭī, *Tafsīr al-Durr al-Manthūr*, 4:100 |
قَالَ رَسُولُ اللهِ صَلَّ اللهُ عَلَيْهِ [وَآلِهِ] وَسَلَّمَ فِي قَوْلِهِ تَعَالَى: ﴿لِكُلِّ بَابٍ مِنْهُمْ جُزْءٌ مَقْسُومٌ﴾، قَالَ: جُزْءٌ أَشْرَكُوا بِاللهِ، وَجُزْءٌ غَفَلُوا عَنِ اللهِ.

[359] Qummī, *Tafsīr*, 1:376,377.

[360] Surat al-Ma'ārij, 70:15-18.

The phrase, "it invites" (*tadʿū*) in this verse is noteworthy and suggests that the inmates of every one of these levels are naturally drawn there. This attraction is experienced by those who willingly renounced God and turned away from Him. One may ask how someone would go towards a place of such torment of his own volition. The answer is simple; it is exactly like when we abandon the remembrance of God which is the true source of contentment for the heart and purification of the soul, and eagerly chase after possessions and wealth which only leads to discontentment, worry and stress. This attraction results from man forgetting the remembrance of God or mistaking the true objective of his life. Swedenborg says, "If the pursuit of wealth is for a noble cause, then in the Hereafter this sentiment is transformed into happiness and delight. However, if it is for the sake of wealth itself then it transforms into filth. The interesting thing is that just as in this world, that type of person was drawn to gold and jewels and money, in the next world he will be enchanted by this filth."[361]

This idea has been mentioned in the Qur'an in a beautiful allegory, "*Let not those who hoard that which God has granted them of His bounty imagine that it is good for them; rather, it is worse for them. Soon that which they were miserly with shall form a collar around their necks on the Day of Judgement...*"[362]

"The third level is *Saqar*, which, "*does not spare anyone nor leave anything unburnt. It roasts the skins of mortals.*"[363]

[361] Swedenborg, section 363.

[362] Surat Āl-ʿImrān, 3:180.

[363] Surat al-Muddaththir, 74:28-29.

"The fourth level is "*Ḥuṭama*" which, "*throws out sparks as big as forts.*"[364] Whoever approaches it is charred as black as coal. However, the soul does not die and every time his skin becomes scorched, it is returned to its former state." Here also the phrase, "whoever approaches it" is worthy of consideration, because it implies that people will choose to do so willingly. One might say that the Qur'an contains many verses that indicate that the inmates of Hell will ask God for salvation from Hell, and will be remorseful for their actions, and will be suffused with an indescribable sorrow and anguish; why then would they willingly choose to remain in Hell? Actually, human beings do the same thing in *dunyā* also. They want to be free of the trials and afflictions of this world and achieve the happiness and contentment of the pious and righteous; often they pray to God to relieve them of the troubles of *dunyā*, however, they are so enmeshed in it that they cannot separate themselves from its clutches. Most people realize that the source of all their difficulties is their excessive attention to the trivial matters of *dunyā*, yet they are not prepared to concern themselves with anything else for even a few moments.

Ḥuṭama, which means a fire that consumes the mind, has been mentioned in another chapter in the Qur'an also: "*Woe to every slanderer and back-biter! Who constantly collects wealth and counts on it. He imagines that his wealth will make him immortal. Never! He will be thrown into the consuming fire (ḥuṭama). And what do you think ḥuṭama is? It is a fire kindled by God, which consumes the minds (hearts). Indeed, it will envelop them entirely, in extended columns.*"[365]

---

[364] Surat al-Mursalāt, 77:32.

[365] Surat al-Humaza, 104.

"The fifth level is *Hāwiya,* in which there is an angel called *Mālik* in charge. The inmates of Hell will plead with him to come to their aid. But he will bring them a vessel of molten metal full of noxious liquid from their own bodies. The liquid will be as hot as molten copper, and when they try to drink from it, its tremendous heat will cause the flesh from the faces to peel away and fall into it. And this is what God has mentioned, "*And if (due to their extreme thirst) they will call out for relief they will be given a drink like molten copper, that will scald their faces. A terrible drink, and a wretched dwelling place.*"[366]

"The sixth level is called "*Saʿīr*". Within it are three hundred pavilions of fire, each of which contains three hundred buildings of fire. Each building has three hundred rooms of fire, and each room has three hundred varieties of chastisement. They contain fiery snakes and scorpions, and shackles and chains of fire." It is for this place that God says, "*Indeed, We have prepared for the disbelievers' chains and shackles and a burning fire.*"[367]

"The seventh level is *Jahannam.*[368] It contains a burning pit called *Falaq,* whose fiery heat stokes the fires of Hell every time it is opened. It is the location of the worst punishment in Hell."

The various levels of punishment in Hell have been described metaphorically in a tradition in this manner: "Some will be in the fire up to their ankles, others up to their thighs, some up to their backs and others up to their collarbones."[369]

---

366 Surat al-Kahf, 18:29.

367 Surat al-Dahr, 76:4.

368 This name is given to the entirety of Hell as well.

369 Ibn Rajab al-Ḥanbalī, *al-Takhwīf min al-Nār*, p. 181 |
عَنِ النَّبِيِّ صَلَّى اللهُ عَلَيْهِ وَآلِهِ وَسَلَّمَ قَالَ: مِنْهُمْ مَنْ تَأْخُذُهُ النَّارُ إِلَى كَعْبَيْهِ، وَمِنْهُمْ مَنْ تَأْخُذُهُ النَّارُ إِلَى

And in another tradition we read, "The least punishment experienced in Hell will be by the one who is made to wear a pair of slippers made of fire; due to its heat his brain will boil over, and this will be accompanied by other punishments. Others will be immersed in the fire up to their thighs, others up to their backs and yet others up to their chests, as well as receiving other punishments. And some will be plunged entirely into the fire."[370]

The Emotional State of the Inmates of Hell

1. Gloom and remorse

The inmates of Hell are filled with gloom, sorrow, pain and remorse. However, this remorse can no longer lead to their reform. They intensely regret that they did not change themselves when they had the chance to do so; but now that that opportunity has passed, they can only wail and lament. They do not know when the impurity that permeates their beings will be cleansed so that they can enjoy God's mercy again and when they can be free of the evil and hate-filled company of their companions in Hell.

They constantly remember the wasted opportunities during their days in *dunyā* and the Paradise that they could have had but lost, "*The Day when the wrongdoer shall bite his hand (in regret), saying, "Ah! How I wish I had taken a path with the Messenger!*"[371] They will say, "*Ah! How great is our regret over our neglect concerning it!" while they will carry their burdens on their*

رُكْبَتَيْهِ، وَمِنْهُمْ مَنْ تَأْخُذُهُ النَّارُ إِلَى حُجْزَتِهِ، وَمِنْهُمْ مَنْ تَأْخُذُهُ النَّارُ إِلَى تَرْقُوَتِهِ.

370 Ibid |

عَنِ النَّبِيِّ صَلَّى اللهُ عَلَيْهِ وَآلِهِ وَسَلَّمَ قَالَ: إِنَّ أَهْوَنَ أَهْلِ النَّارِ عَذَابًا رَجُلٌ مُنْتَعِلٌ بِنَعْلَيْنِ مِنْ نَارٍ، يَغْلِي مِنْهُمَا دِمَاغُهُ مَعَ إِجْزَاءِ الْعَذَابِ، وَمِنْهُمْ مَنْ فِي النَّارِ إِلَى رُكْبَتَيْهِ مَعَ إِجْزَاءِ الْعَذَابِ، وَمِنْهُمْ مَنْ فِي النَّارِ إِلَى أَرْنَبَتِهِ مَعَ إِجْزَاءِ الْعَذَابِ، وَمِنْهُمْ مَنْ فِي النَّارِ إِلَى صَدْرِهِ مَعَ إِجْزَاءِ الْعَذَابِ، وَمِنْهُمْ مَنِ اغْتَمَرَ.

371 Surat al-Furqān, 25:27.

backs. Indeed, evil are the burdens they bear."[372] They will say, "*If only we could be returned (to dunyā), we would not belie the signs of our Lord, and we would be amongst the believers." But what they used to conceal before has now become manifest before them. And even if they were returned they would revert back to that which was forbidden – they are indeed liars."*[373] They wish, "*If only I had another chance, I would be amongst those who do good."*[374] And, "*How great is my regret about my neglect in regards to God and that I was amongst the mockers!"*[375] "*They will call out from the depths of Hell, "Our Lord! Remove us so that we may do good, not acting as before." But did We not grant you enough life for whoever wanted to reflect to think about the admonition, and a Warner came to you also? So, taste (the punishment) because there shall be no helper for the wrongdoers!"*[376] They will plead, "*Our Lord! Our wretchedness overcame us, and we went astray. Our Lord! Remove us from this Hell and then if were to resume (our evil ways) then we are indeed wrongdoers." He will say, "Remain in it and do not talk to Me. Indeed, there was a group of My servants who would call to Me saying, "Our Lord! We have believed in You, so forgive us and be merciful to us, you are the most Merciful." But you mocked them, until they made you forget Me, while you laughed at them."*[377]

God's aloofness and dismissal of their constant pleading is because they need to truly change from within before they can achieve salvation; simply supplicating and making promises of reform is not enough. The Hereafter is not a

---

[372] Surat al-An'ām, 6:31.

[373] Surat al-An'ām, 6:27,28.

[374] Surat al-Zumar, 39:58.

[375] Surat al-Zumar, 39:56.

[376] Surat al-Fāṭir, 35:37.

[377] Surat al-Mu'minūn, 23:106-110.

place where lies achieve anything, and the true inner nature is always manifested as an external reality.

This remorse and sense of isolation and profound loss brings with it an indescribable sorrow and anguish, "*(The torment) is not eased for them, and they are plunged into despair. And We did not wrong them, but it was they who were the wrong-doers.*"[378] It has been reported from the Prophet (s) that, "They will seek refuge in God from the pit of their misery." He was asked, "What is the pit of misery?" He replied, "It is a valley of Hell from which Hell itself seeks refuge in God a hundred times daily."[379]

And it has also been narrated that, "The weeping of the inmates of Hell will become constant and they will weep to an extent that their tears will dry up and then they will weep tears of blood."[380] Their breaths are filled with sobs and groans, "*As for the wretched, they shall be in the fire; for them therein is sighing and wailing.*"[381]

2. Mutual Enmity and Belligerence

As we mentioned when discussing *barzakh*, there is one trait that is common amongst all the inmates of Hell and that is they loathe one another. Each of them desires to gain mastery over the other, seeking to get him to serve his needs. This is a matter that results from their deep-rooted egoism. The only thing that keeps them in check from preying on each other is their fear of retribution and punishment.

378 Surat al-Zukhruf, 43:75,76.

379 Ibn Rajab al-Ḥanbalī, *al-Takhwīf min al-Nār*, p. 122 |
تَعَوَّذُوا بِاللهِ مِنْ جُبِّ الْحُزْنِ، قَالُوا: وَمَا جُبُّ الْحُزْنِ؟ قَالَ: وَادٍ فِي جَهَنَّمَ، تَتَعَوَّذُ مِنْهُ جَهَنَّمُ كُلَّ يَوْمٍ مِائَةَ مَرَّةٍ.

380 Ibn Rajab al-Ḥanbalī, *al-Takhwīf min al-Nār*, p. 206 |
يُلْقَى الْبُكَاءُ عَلَى أَهْلِ النَّارِ، فَيَبْكُونَ حَتَّى تَنْقَطِعَ الدُّمُوعُ، ثُمَّ يَبْكُونَ الدَّمَ.

381 Surat Ḥūd, 11:106.

Angels constantly monitor the internal affairs of Hell, and anyone who is tormenting someone beyond limits is severely punished. "*Boiling water will be poured down over their heads, whereby their skin and their interiors will melt away; and in addition, there will be iron hooks prepared for them.*"[382] However the effect of this severe chastisement is short-lived, and it does not stop them from their belligerence for long. This is because oppression, cunning and bullying is ingrained in their nature and functions like the instinct in animals. As a result, they now undergo two types of punishment; one that they bring on to each other and another, more severe punishment that is visited on them by the angels in order to restrain them from their mischief.

Their enmity for each other rages in their hearts but their fear of each other forces them to a solitary and lonely existence. Each one tries to pass off the burden of his sins to someone else and blames them for his fate, "*Every time a nation enters (Hellfire) it curses its predecessors until they have all assembled together. The followers will say about their leaders, "Our Lord! It is these that misled us, so give them a double torment of the fire." He will say, "Every one of you shall have double but you do not understand." And the leaders will say to the followers, "You were no better than us, so taste the punishment for what you earned.*"[383]

When the leaders of the disbelievers are brought to Hell and their followers are brought in behind them, the former will be told, "*This is a group of your followers being herded to join you. (The leaders) will say, "No welcome for them! Indeed, they will burn in the fire." (Their followers) will say, "It is you who have no welcome! It is you who brought this upon us, what a wretched*

[382] Surat al-Ḥaj, 22:19-21.

[383] Surat al-Aʿrāf, 7:38,39.

destination." They shall say, "Our Lord! Double the punishment of fire for whoever has brought this upon us."[384]

"And the disbelievers will say, "Our Lord! Show us those who misguided us from the jinn *and mankind, we shall crush them under our feet so that they become among the lowest."*[385] Indeed, *"The quarrelling of the people of the fire is most surely true."*[386]

3. Desire for Death or Escape

Their only desire in Hell is to die and that too is denied to them. They say to the angel in charge of Hell, "*O Malik! Let your Lord take away our life." He shall reply, "Indeed, you shall remain."*[387]

Although any attempt to escape from the valleys and townships where they are housed is immediately met with severe chastisement, and despite their certainty that they can never cross out of the boundaries of Hell, their suffering and misery occasionally compels them to try to escape, but, "*Whenever they seek to get away from it due to their anguish, they are returned to it, (and it is said to them), "Taste the punishment of burning!"*[388] Their return is accompanied by a more severe punishment than before and as mentioned in the verse, they are returned to a burning and consuming fire (*ḥarīq*).

The Life of the Dwellers of Hell

The people of Hell have disfigured, ugly faces and large, unsightly bodies. It has been reported from the Prophet (s) that, "No one dies except that he is resurrected as a thirty-

[384] Surat Ṣād, 38:59-61.

[385] Surat Fuṣṣilat, 41:29.

[386] Surat Ṣād, 38:64.

[387] Surat al-Zukhruf, 43:77.

[388] Surat al-Ḥaj, 22:22.

year-old, whether he died as a miscarried foetus or at an old age. Then, if he is from the people of Paradise he will be resurrected with a body like that of Adam (a) and features like that of Yusuf (a) and a heart like that of Job (a); but if he is of the people of Hell, then he will grow in size until he resembles a large shapeless mountain."[389]

The large ghoulish creatures are unclothed, except for that which they fashion for themselves out of burning pitch, "*Their garments will be of pitch (qaṭirān) and their faces will be enveloped by fire.*"[390] Pitch is an odorous and combustible material that they rub on their skin to protect them against the heat, but it itself is a source of greater heat and putrefaction for them.

The dwellers of Hell live in scattered groups across the towns and valleys that we have already mentioned. Their houses resemble burnt out buildings and collapsed castles which in fact are embodiments of their innate goodness which they burned away and ruined by their own actions. The Qur'an states that, "*On the Day when the disbelievers are exposed to the fire, (it will be said to them),* "*You squandered every goodness that you possessed during your life in the world, and sought your pleasure therein.*"[391]

Some towns are heavily guarded because the conditions of life there are so extreme that its inhabitants try to escape to other parts of Hell. It has been reported from Imam Ali (a) that, "There is a city in Hell called *Ḥaṣīna* (protected). Will

---

389 Ibn Rajab al-Ḥanbalī, *al-Takhwīf min al-Nār*, p. 177 |
مَا مِنْ أَحَدٍ يَمُوتُ سِقْطًا أَوْ هَرِمًا - وَإِنَّمَا النَّاسُ بَيْنَ ذَلِكَ - إِلَّا بُعِثَ ابْنَ ثَلَاثِينَ سَنَةً، فَإِنْ كَانَ مِنْ أَهْلِ الْجَنَّةِ، كَانَ عَلَى مَسْحَةِ آدَمَ، وَصُورَةِ يُوسُفَ، وَقَلْبِ أَيُّوبَ، وَمَنْ كَانَ مِنْ أَهْلِ النَّارِ، عُظِّمُوا وَفُخِّمُوا كَالْجِبَالِ.

390 Surat Ibrāhīm, 14:50.

391 Surat al-Aḥqāf, 46:20.

you not ask me what the city contains? It houses a group of those who broke their covenant with me (*al-nākithūn*)"[392]

The houses and townships of Hell are full of harmful insects and animals. It has been reported from Imam al-Baqir (a) that, "There is a valley in Hell called Ghasāq. The valley contains 330 castles, each with 330 rooms and each room has within it 330 scorpions."[393] It has been reported from Jesus (a) that he described Hell thus, "A place where the flesh-eating maggots never die, and the fire is never quenched."[394]

The type of food and nutrition that the inmates of Hell receive depends on the level that they are assigned to and which valley they reside in. In some places there is nothing to eat except thorns, "*No food for them except bitter thorns* (*ḍarīʿ*)."[395] *Ḍarīʿ* refers to dry thorns that are bitter, foul-smelling and poisonous; they have no nutritious value but only fill the stomach, "*Which neither nourishes nor satisfies hunger.*"[396] It has been reported from the Prophet (s) that, "*Ḍarīʿ* is a substance in Hell that resembles thorns; it is more bitter than poison and more foul-smelling than a dead corpse and more blistering than fire."[397] It is called *ḍarīʿ*

---

392 Ṣadūq, *al-Khiṣāl*, p. 296 |

أَنَّ عَلِيًّا عَلَيْهِ السَّلَامُ قَالَ: إِنَّ فِي النَّارِ لَمَدِينَةً يُقَالُ لَهَا الْحَصِينَةُ، أَفَلَا تَسْأَلُونِي مَا فِيهَا؟ فَقِيلَ: وَمَا فِيهَا يَا أَمِيرَ الْمُؤْمِنِينَ؟ فَقَالَ: فِيهَا أَيْدِي النَّاكِثِينَ

393 Ḥusain ibn Saʿīd al-Kūfī, *Kitāb al-Zuhd*, p. 100 |

إِنَّ فِي جَهَنَّمَ لَوَادٍ يُقَالُ لَهُ غَسَّاقٌ، فِيهِ ثَلَاثُونَ وَثَلَاثُمِائَةِ قَصْرٍ، فِي كُلِّ قَصْرٍ ثَلَاثُونَ وَثَلَاثُمِائَةِ بَيْتٍ، فِي كُلِّ بَيْتٍ ثَلَاثُونَ وَثَلَاثُمِائَةِ عَقْرَبٍ

394 Gospel of Mark, 9:48.

395 Surat al-Ghāshiya, 88:6.

396 Surat al-Ghāshiya, 88:7.

397 Mulla Fatḥullāh Kāshānī, *Tafsīr Minhāj al-Ṣādiqīn*, 10:224 |

الضَّرِيعُ شَيْءٌ يَكُونُ فِي النَّارِ يُشْبِهُ الشَّوْكَ، أَمَرُّ مِنَ الصَّبْرِ، وَأَنْتَنُ مِنَ الْجِيفَةِ، وَأَشَدُّ حَرًّا مِنَ النَّارِ، سَمَّاهُ

because the one who eats it is forced to do so with pain and wailing (*taḍarru'*) due to its unpleasantness and bitterness;[398] however, he has no choice but to eat it due to his intense hunger, which only increases by eating it.

In some places in Hell there is no food to be found at all and its inhabitants are forced to eat their own or each other's filth and excrement and pus and blood; just as in the world they used each other's mischief and depravity to achieve their vile goals. This filth is referred to in the Qur'an as *Ghislīn* or sometimes *Ghassāq*, which is putrid pus, "*So there is no friend for him here today. Nor any food except for the noxious discharge of wounds (ghislīn), which none but the wrongdoers eat.*"[399] "*This is scalding water and foul pus, so let them taste it. And other (torments) of the same type!*"[400] "Same type" here is an indication that all the food available in that area is of a similar kind.

However, the worst of all is *Zaqqūm*. It is the fruit of, "*a tree that grows from the depths of Hell. Its shoots are like the heads of demons,*"[401] invoking terror and revulsion. "*Indeed, the tree of Zaqqūm shall be the food of the vicious sinner! It shall boil within the bellies like molten copper, just like the boiling of scalding water.*"[402] Due to their intense hunger, the inmates of Hell stuff their bellies full of the fruit of Zaqqūm, and it begins to ferment and simmer within their stomachs like boiling water. As a result, they become intensely thirsty and wander

---

الله الضَّرِيعَ

[398] Ṭabarsī, *Tafsīr Majma' al-Bayān*, 10:727.

[399] Surat al-Ḥāqqa, 69:35-37.

[400] Surat Ṣād, 38:57,58.

[401] Surat al-Ṣaffāt, 37:64,65.

[402] Surat al-Dukhān, 44:43-46.

about in search of a spring of water. They can only find hot springs, but they gulp down copious amounts as if they were drinking cool water, "*Then indeed you, O erring ones, O deniers! You shall surely eat from a tree of Zaqqūm and fill your bellies with it and drink on top of it boiling water; and you shall drink like thirsty camels!*"[403]

These foul springs of scalding water are far from the tree of Zaqqūm and after they have found and drunk from the springs, the inmates of Hell return to their homes in the valleys of Hell, "*Is the welcome received by the people of Paradise better or the tree of Zaqqūm? Indeed, we have made it a torment for the wrong doers. Indeed, it is a tree growing from the depths of Hell. Its shoots are like the heads of demons. And indeed, they shall eat from it and fill their bellies with it. Then indeed they will have afterwards a drink of boiling water. And thereafter indeed, their return will be to the Hell fire.*"[404] They constantly move between their dwellings in Hell and the boiling springs, "*This is the Hell which the sinners deny. They will continually circle between it and the hot, boiling water.*"[405]

The environment, the food and drink, and this way of life suits the nature of the inmates of Hell; they cannot eat anything else and cannot live anywhere but here. That is not to say that they derive any pleasure from their circumstances, rather it is the only life they can tolerate. When we discussed the dimension of Hell in *barzakh*, we quoted Swedenborg as saying that as soon as the inmates of the Hell of *barzakh* come out from it they begin to suffocate, and the place becomes so unbearable for them that they quickly return to their *barzakhi* Hell. The same thing applies to the Hell of

---

[403] Surat al-Wāqiʿa, 56:51-55.

[404] Surat al-Ṣaffāt, 37:62-68.

[405] Surat al-Raḥmān, 55:43,44.

the Hereafter also. It has been reported by Ibn Abbas that, "The inmates of Hell pray for relief from the extreme heat and they are exposed to a cool wind, but its iciness nearly breaks their bones, so they ask for the heat to be restored again."[406] And it has also been reported that, "The inmates of Hell ask its supervisor to transport them to the borders of Hell. When they are taken there, the intense coldness causes them to swoon and they immediately hurry back to their homes in Hell."[407] And this is the same thing that has been reported by Ibn Abbas that, "There is an icy coldness in Hell called *Zamharīr* which plucks flesh away from bones, causing people to seek refuge in the fires of Hell."[408]

The Everlasting Paradise

When an individual enters Paradise, he has reached the true objective of his existence and becomes free of every fear and sorrow. In the words of the Qur'an, "*And whoever is drawn away from Hell and admitted into Paradise has triumphed.*"[409]

Paradise heralds the beginning of the life of a perfected human being. It is the end of transience and the beginning of permanence; an opportunity to grow without the danger of slipping or going astray ever again. Life here is not monotonous although it progresses in one direction. There are no concerns or sorrows or fears or anxieties;

---

[406] Ibn Rajab al-Ḥanbalī, *al-Takhwīf min al-Nār*, p. 101 |

يَسْتَغِيثُ أَهْلُ النَّارِ مِنَ الْحَرِّ، فَيُغَاثُونَ بِرِيحٍ بَارِدَةٍ يَصْدَعُ الْعِظَامَ بَرْدُهَا، فَيَسْأَلُونَ الْحَرَّ

[407] Ibid |

عَنْ عَبْدِ الْمَلِكِ بْنِ عُمَيْرٍ قَالَ: بَلَغَنِي أَنَّ أَهْلَ النَّارِ يَسْأَلُونَ خَازِنَهَا أَنْ يُخْرِجَهُمْ إِلَى جَانِبِهَا، فَيُخْرِجُهُمْ، فَيَقْتُلُهُمْ الْبَرْدُ وَالزَّمْهَرِيرُ حَتَّى يَرْجِعُوا إِلَيْهَا، فَيَدْخُلُوهَا مِمَّا وَجَدُوا مِنَ الْبَرْدِ

[408] Ibid |

إِنَّ فِي جَهَنَّمَ بَرْدًا هُوَ الزَّمْهَرِيرُ، يُسْقِطُ اللَّحْمَ حَتَّى يَسْتَغِيثُوا بِحَرِّ جَهَنَّمَ

[409] Surat Āl-'Imrān, 3:185.

rather everyone is filled with excitement, longing and love. Whatever a person wants is made available to him but there is no sign of lethargy and inactivity. Of course, it is difficult for us to imagine such a life, while we have set our goals and ideals in acquiring life's necessities and amassing wealth, fame and fleeting power. Nevertheless, I will attempt here to depict the picture that has been outlined for us. To begin to analyse life in Paradise it will be useful to start by mentioning a somewhat elaborate narration so that we can get an idea of the concepts that we will discuss later.

In his work *al-Ikhtiṣāṣ*, Mufīd[410] records a tradition from Imam al-Sadiq (a) who has narrated from the Prophet (s) that when the believers will reach the doors of Paradise, "an announcer will call out in a voice loud enough for every person in the Hereafter to hear, that "so-and-so, the son of so-and-so has triumphed and will henceforth never face any misfortune." He will then be admitted to a garden called "*Riḍwān*" which will contain trees casting expansive shade and flowing water and orchards full of fruit. Next to the fruit trees there will be two rivers flowing. He will wash himself in one of them and his face will begin to glow with pleasure, and he will drink from the other and all illness and pain will depart from him forever, and this is what God mentions, "*And their Lord shall give them a purifying drink.*"[411]

"Thereafter, the angels will come to welcome him and say, "Now you have been purified so enter with everyone else." They will enter into a wide boulevard lined with trees whose trunks will be of pearls and whose branches will be covered in jewels."

[410] Mufīd, *al-Ikhtiṣāṣ*, p. 350-356.

[411] Surat al-Dahr, 76:21.

"Now, angels will come forward to greet them with mounts and jewelled robes and heavenly foods. They will say, "O friend of God! Ride on whatever you like, wear whatever you like and eat of whatever you like." He will choose a robe and mount on a speed of light while his clothes and jewels will be made of light, and he will proceed in the land of light. He will be accompanied by angels of light and attendants composed of light to an extent that the angels will be dazzled by his appearance and will say to one another, "Stand aside, the guests of the all-Forgiving, all-Forbearing have come."

"Then his eyes will fall on the first of the palaces that have been constructed for him; a palace of silver whose walls are edged with pearls and rubies. His wives who live in that palace will come towards him and say, "Welcome! Alight and stay with us." When he makes a decision to go to his palace, the angels say to him, "O friend of God! Continue on your tour because you have other palaces besides this one." He continues onwards until he arrives at a palace made of gold whose walls are edged with pearls and rubies. His wives who live in that palace will come towards him and say, "Welcome, O friend of God! Alight and stay with us." When he decides to go to his palace, the angels say to him, "O friend of God! Continue on your tour because you have other palaces besides these two."

"Then he will come to a palace made of red ruby whose walls are edged in pearls and rubies. When he decides to enter that palace, the angels once again advise him, "O friend of God! Continue on your tour because you have other palaces besides these." He will continue in this manner until he has seen a thousand palaces in total. He sees their entire contents from outside and completes the survey of his holdings in less than a blink of the eye. When he reaches the last palace, his head droops. The angels ask him, "What is the matter, O friend of God?" He replies, "I swear by God! My eyes are nearly blinded with all this light." They say, "O friend of God! Know that in Paradise there is no blindness and no deafness."

"Then he comes to a palace whose interior is visible from outside and whose exterior can be seen from inside. It is constructed of slabs of silver, gold, rubies and pearls. Its mortar is made of musk and its walls glitter with a radiant light such that a person can see his own reflection in them."

"And in Paradise there is a river on whose two banks are seated maidens. God reveals to them, "Let My servant hear you praise Me, Glorify Me and eulogize Me." So, their voices ring out with a melody and sweetness the like of which no one has ever heard before, causing the people of heaven to become spellbound."

"Rivers with sweet and limpid waters flow all across the land of Paradise. Some are rivers of ever fresh milk which has not come from the udders of animals; there are rivers of pure honey, which has not come from the bellies of bees; and there are rivers of wine of unsurpassed taste, which have not come from grapes crushed by any hand. And as soon as they desire food white birds come to them and raise their wings and the dwellers of heaven eat from them what they want, while they sit or recline. And when they desire any fruit the branches of that fruit tree extend towards them, and they eat whichever fruit they like."

"*And the angels approach them from every door saying, "Peace be on you for your steadfastness. And how excellent is the final abode!*"[412] They live in this way until when suddenly a voice is heard from below the Throne of God saying, "O inhabitants

412 Surat al-Ra'd, 13:24.

of Paradise! How do you find the place you have returned to?" They reply, "We have returned to the best of places and our reward is the most generous of rewards. However, now that we have heard this voice, we have a keen desire to gaze at Your Magnificence, and that would be the best reward for us and one that You have promised us Yourself, and You never go back on Your word." So, God issues a command, and seventy thousand veils are lifted away. The inhabitants of Paradise climb onto their mounts, and dressed in luxurious and jewelled garments, ride in the shade of the trees until they reach the abode of peace (*dār al-salām*) which is the abode of God - the abode of light and glory and felicity."[413] "And there, when they hear the voice of God, they exclaim, "O our Master! We have heard the sweetness of Your speech, so manifest to us Your light. So, God reveals Himself to them and they gaze at His countenance which is hidden from every eye."[414] They cannot help but fall immediately into prostration saying, "Glory be to You! We did not worship You the way You truly deserved, O Most High!"

"God shall say, "O my servants! Raise your heads because this is not a place of deeds and worship, rather it is a place of blessings and petition and benevolence. You will no longer

---

413 وَالْمَلَائِكَةُ يَدْخُلُونَ عَلَيْهِمْ مِنْ كُلِّ بَابٍ ﴿٢٣﴾ سَلَامٌ عَلَيْكُمْ بِمَا صَبَرْتُمْ فَنِعْمَ عُقْبَى الدَّارِ ﴿٢٤﴾. فَبَيْنَا هُمْ كَذَلِكَ إِذْ يَسْمَعُونَ صَوْتًا مِنْ تَحْتِ الْعَرْشِ: يَا أَهْلَ الْجَنَّةِ، كَيْفَ تَرَوْنَ مُنْقَلَبَكُمْ؟ فَيَقُولُونَ: خَيْرُ الْمُنْقَلَبِ مُنْقَلَبُنَا، وَخَيْرُ الثَّوَابِ ثَوَابُنَا، قَدْ سَمِعْنَا الصَّوْتَ وَاشْتَهَيْنَا النَّظَرَ إِلَى أَنْوَارِ جَلَالِكَ وَهُوَ أَعْظَمُ ثَوَابِنَا وَقَدْ وَعَدْتَهُ وَلَا تُخْلِفُ الْمِيعَادَ، فَيَأْمُرُ اللهُ الْحُجُبَ، فَيَقُومُ سَبْعُونَ أَلْفَ حِجَابٍ، فَيَرْكَبُونَ عَلَى النُّوقِ وَالْبَرَاذِينِ وَعَلَيْهِمُ الْحُلِيُّ وَالْحُلَلُ، فَيَسِيرُونَ فِي ظِلِّ الشَّجَرِ حَتَّى يَنْتَهُوا إِلَى دَارِ السَّلَامِ، وَهِيَ دَارُ اللهِ، دَارُ الْبَهَاءِ والنُّورِ وَالسُّرُورِ وَالْكَرَامَةِ.

414 Clearly the meaning of this seeing is the gaining of new cognizance of the Majesty (*jalāl*) and Beauty (*jamāl*) of God, which had previously been hidden from the inhabitants of Paradise. It is obvious that God is not a body with a countenance that can be viewed by the physical eyes.

have to toil or endure pain." They raise their heads while their faces have become seventy times more radiant after being exposed to the countenance of God. At this time God says to the angels, "O my angels! Give them food and drink." A variety of food is brought for them, of a kind that they had never seen before. The food is as sweet as honey, as white as snow and as soft as cream. And when they eat of it, some of them say to others, "Truly the food that we ate in Paradise was nothing compared to this."[415]

Then He will say, "O My angels! Perfume them." So, they will bring to them a fragrant breeze that is whiter than snow and is called "*Muthīra*" which passes over their faces, backs and sides. They gaze towards the light of God's countenance as much as they are able to and say, "Our Master! Hearing Your sweet speech and seeing the light of Your countenance is enough delight for us, we do not desire or seek anything else. But God says, "I know that you are eager to meet with your wives, and they long to see you. "Go now to your wives."

They ask God to give them an appointment to come to this place again. God says, "You shall have a meeting every Friday. From one Friday to the next there is a span of seven thousand years by your reckoning." As they leave each is given a green pomegranate containing seventy garments the like of which no eye has seen before. When they return, their attendants go ahead and give the good news of their arrival to their wives who are waiting at the gates of their gardens. As he approaches and his wife looks at his face, she hardly recognizes him and says, "My dear! When you departed your face looked different." He will reply, "My dear! Do not be amazed at my appearance for I have gazed

[415] This is spiritual nourishment which fills them with new cognizance and increased love for God.

at the countenance of my Lord and my face has become illuminated by His light." He looks at the face of his wife again and says, "My dear! When I departed from you your face seemed different." And she will reply, "My dear! Do not be amazed at my appearance for I have looked at the face of one who has gazed at the countenance of God, and my face has become seventy times more radiant as a result. And they will embrace each other."

"At this time God will summon the Prophets (a) to present themselves. A man will come forth escorted by mounted attendants and rows of angels bathed in dazzling light will be arrayed in his honour. The people of Paradise will stretch out their necks to get a better view of him and ask each other, "Who is he? Indeed, he must have a great station before God." The angels will say, "This is the man that God fashioned with His own hands and breathed into him of His soul and taught him all the names. This is Adam who has been given permission to present himself."

"Thereafter, another man will come forward escorted by mounted attendants and rows of angels bathed in dazzling light will stand in his honour. The people of Paradise will stretch their necks to get a better view of him and ask, "Who is he?" The angels will reply, "This is Abraham, the friend of God, who has been given permission to present himself." Thereafter another man will come forward escorted by mounted attendants and rows of angels bathed in dazzling light will stand in his honour. The people of Paradise will stretch out their necks to get a better view of him and ask, "Who is he?" The angels will reply, "This is Moses' son of ʿImrān, who conversed with God. He has now been given permission to present himself." Another man will come forward escorted by mounted attendants and rows of angels bathed in dazzling light will stand in his honour. The people of Paradise will stretch out their necks to get a better view of him and ask, "Who is this who has been permitted to present himself?" The angels will reply, "This is Jesus' son of Mary, the spirit of God and His word."

At this time a man will come forward escorted by mounted attendants and rows of angels bathed in dazzling light will stand in his honour. Their number and resplendence will be seventy times greater than those who escorted the previous Prophets (a). The people of Paradise will stretch out their necks to get a better view of him and ask, "Who is this who has been permitted to present himself?" The angels will reply, "This is the man chosen for the final revelation and trusted with God's message and the greatest son of Adam. This is Muhammad (s), who has been permitted to present himself." Finally, another man will come forward escorted by mounted attendants and rows of angels bathed in dazzling light will stand in his honour. The people of Paradise will stretch out their necks to get a better view of him and ask, "Who is he?" The angels will reply, "This is the brother of the messenger of God, in the world and in the Hereafter."

"At this time all the Prophets (*nabiyyūn*), the veracious (*ṣiddīqūn*) and the witnesses (*shuhadā*) will be granted permission to present themselves. The Prophets (a) shall have pulpits of light, the veracious shall have thrones of light and the witnesses shall have chairs of light assembled for them. Then God will say, "Welcome to My guests, visitors and neighbours. O My angels! Give them food because for the longest time they remained hungry while other people ate, they remained thirsty while other people drank, they remained awake while other people slept, and they lived in anxiety while other people were oblivious."

The foregoing was an account of a lengthy tradition describing Paradise and its inhabitants which presented a lot of information about that life. The salient points can be summarized as below:

1. Although those who enter Paradise have passed through all the stages that lead to their perfection and have drunk from the fountain of the prophets (a), they still need to drink from the rivers of Paradise and bathe in them in order to prepare themselves for their lives there. Even if we take this preparation literally, it appears that the qualities of these rivers are amazing and wondrous and necessary for life there.

   A matter that must be always borne in mind is that when we speak of that world and attempt to describe it, it is not different from a foetus in the mother's womb attempting to describe this world. Just as the complexities and details of the *dunyā* are beyond its understanding and experience, we too are limited in our appreciation of the realities of the *ākhira.* Imagine trying to explain to a foetus that when it arrives in this world, it will chew food with teeth, or it will consume food that is similar to its own flesh, or that it will enter a world whose ends it cannot reach no matter how long it travels for, or that it may live there for eighty years, or that it will be able to write poems or fall in love, and so on. It is clear that the foetus would have a very basic and often mistaken understanding of these concepts; therefore, we should constantly remind ourselves that our own understanding of the Hereafter can be no more than an approximation of its true realities.

2. As we read in this tradition and as is repeatedly mentioned in the Qur'an also, the garments of Paradise are typically luxurious and bedecked with jewels and other finery,

"And eternally youthful servants shall serve them. When you see them, they will seem like scattered pearls. And all around, you shall see evidence of God's bounties and great kingdom. Their garments will be of fine green silk and brocade. They will be adorned with bracelets of silver.";[416] *"They will be adorned with bracelets of gold and they shall wear garments of fine silk and brocade and shall be reclining on thrones.";*[417] *"Within it are raised thrones, and goblets set at hand, and cushions placed in rows, and rich carpets spread out.";*[418] and, *"They recline on green cushions and rich carpets.";*[419] *"Trays and goblets of gold shall be circulated amongst them; therein they shall have whatever the hearts could desire and what delights the eyes.";*[420] *"They shall be on thrones encrusted with precious stones and seated opposite friends; with eternally youthful servants waiting on them with vessels and jugs and a cup from a pure spring. They shall not get a headache therefrom nor suffer intoxication."*[421]

As we will discuss later, all these descriptions are analogies and metaphors for the material and spiritual life that the inhabitants of Paradise will experience. And this is not just true for the bounties of Paradise, whose source and composition are unknown, but also true for its habitat and natural environment. For example, "the soil from the rivers of Paradise is of fragrant musk and its pebbles are pearls and rubies"[422] and, "God has constructed Paradise

416 Surat al-Dahr, 76:19-21.

417 Surat al-Kahf, 18:31.

418 Surat al-Ghāshiya, 88:13-16.

419 Surat al-Raḥmān, 55;76.

420 Surat al-Zukhruf, 43:76.

421 Surat al-Wāqiʿa, 56:15-19.

422 Majlisī, *Biḥār al-Anwār*, 8:219 |

طِينُ النَّهْرِ مِسْكٌ أَذْفَرُ، وَحَصَاهُ الدُّرُّ وَالْيَاقُوتُ

from two types of bricks; bricks of gold and bricks of silver. Its walls are made of ruby and its sky of turquoise and its pebbles of pearls and its soil of saffron and fragrant musk."[423] And in another part of Paradise, "there are walls made from bricks of gold, silver and ruby. Its mortar is of fragrant musk and its balconies are crusted with red, green and yellow rubies."[424]

3. The interconnection between the material and spiritual dimensions of life in the Hereafter is quite subtle, yet complex. As we read in the narration, "He will choose a robe, and mount on a speed of light while his clothes and jewels will be made of light, and he will proceed in the land of light. He will be accompanied by angels of light and attendants composed of light to an extent that he will be dazzled by his appearance." The question is that what is this light and how does it transform into clothes and jewels and mounts and attendants? This matter can only be properly understood and appreciated in that realm. It is worth noting that in Firdaws, the Paradise which is in the closest proximity of God, walls and houses and chambers are all made of light. However, in Eden, the Paradise which is lower, they are constructed of red rubies and pearls.[425]

---

423 Ṣadūq, *Man lā Yaḥḍuruhu al-Faqīh*, 4:355,356 |

خَلَقَ اللهُ عَزَّ وَجَلَّ الْجَنَّةَ مِنْ لَبِنَتَيْنِ، لَبِنَةٍ مِنْ ذَهَبٍ وَلَبِنَةٍ مِنْ فِضَّةٍ، وَجَعَلَ حِيطَانَهَا الْيَاقُوتَ، وَسَقْفَهَا الزَّبَرْجَدَ، وَحَصَاهَا اللُّؤْلُؤَ، وَتُرَابَهَا الزَّعْفَرَانَ وَالْمِسْكَ الْأَذْفَرَ

424 Ṣadūq, *al-Amālī*, p. 281 |

إِنَّ سُورَ الْجَنَّةِ لَبِنَةٌ مِنْ ذَهَبٍ، وَلَبِنَةٌ مِنْ فِضَّةٍ، وَلَبِنَةٌ مِنْ يَاقُوتٍ، وَمِلَاطُهَا الْمِسْكُ الْأَذْفَرُ، وَشُرَفُهَا الْيَاقُوتُ الْأَحْمَرُ وَالْأَخْضَرُ وَالْأَصْفَرُ

425 Ṣadūq, *Man lā Yaḥḍuruhu al-Faqīh*, 1:296. This narration will be examined in detail later.

4. The objects and substances of Paradise are not made of materials as we recognize them in our world; rather they originate from the immaterial world (*malakūt*). As we saw in the tradition, "there are rivers of ever fresh milk which has not come from the udders of animals; there are rivers of pure honey, which has not come from the bellies of bees; and there are rivers of wine of unsurpassed taste, which have not come from grapes crushed by any hand." The source of all these substances is the light of the immaterial world that is manifested in Paradise for the use of its inhabitants.
5. The expansiveness of Paradise is beyond imagination. The Qur'an states that Paradise is, "*as wide as the heavens and the earth.*"[426] If one considers that every inhabitant of Paradise has at least a thousand palaces as mentioned in this tradition, or that some may have as many as seventy thousand palaces as mentioned in other reports, then it appears that the domain of each individual would be the size of a large nation in our present world, because each palace would have its own lands. The Gospel of Barnabas quotes Jesus (a) thus: God shall say to the one who loved Him and worshipped Him sincerely, "O servant of Mine! Consider how many grains of sand there are in the sea. If the sea would give you just one grain of sand, would it not appear trivial to you? Of course, it would! But I swear by My Existence, as your Creator, that whatever I have bestowed to all the merchants and kings of the earth is less than a grain of sand compared to that which I shall grant to you in Paradise."[427]

[426] Surat Āl-'Imrān, 3:113.

[427] Gospel of Barnabas, 172:1-3.

Although such grandeur may be beyond our comprehension, nonetheless we can still appreciate the great difference in the scale of existence between that life and our lives in this world; and we can begin to imagine the expansiveness of the *ākhira* in comparison to *dunyā*. Therefore, we should not be surprised if we hear that in Paradise there is a tree that, "A rider can ride for a hundred years and still not leave its shade, and if a bird were to fly up from its base it would not reach its topmost branches until it falls down due to old age."[428] It has been reported that, "The doors of the heavens are opened on the nights of decree (*qadr*); so there is no worshipper who offers the ritual prayers (*ṣalāt*) that night except that for every single one of his prostrations (*sujūd*), God grants him a tree in Paradise such that if a rider travels under it for a hundred years he would still be in its shade."[429] Or that, "Whoever stays awake in the worship of God for an entire night, spending it in the recitation of the Qur'an, in prostration and in the remembrance of God... shall have a light established in his heart and sinfulness and jealousy shall be removed from it... and God shall say to the angels...give him a place in Paradise. And he shall have within it one hundred thousand cities; each city shall provide whatever the heart desires and the eyes take delight in and what the mind cannot even imagine. And

---

428 Kulaynī, *al-Kāfī*, 2:226 |

وَلَوْ أَنَّ رَاكِبًا مُجِدًّا سَارَ فِي ظِلِّهَا مِائَةَ عَامٍ مَا خَرَجَ مِنْهُ، وَلَوْ طَارَ مِنْ أَسْفَلِهَا غُرَابٌ مَا بَلَغَ أَعْلَاهَا حَتَّى يَسْقُطَ هَرِمًا.

429 Ḥurr al-ʿĀmilī, *Wasāʾil al-Shīʿa*, 8:2 |

تُفَتَّحُ أَبْوَابُ السَّمَاءِ فِي لَيْلَةِ الْقَدْرِ، فَمَا مِنْ عَبْدٍ يُصَلِّي فِيهَا إِلَّا كَتَبَ اللهُ لَهُ بِكُلِّ سَجْدَةٍ شَجَرَةً فِي الْجَنَّةِ، لَوْ يَسِيرُ الرَّاكِبُ فِي ظِلِّهَا مِائَةَ عَامٍ لَا يَقْطَعُهَا.

this is aside from the honour, closeness and abundance he gains in My estimation."[430]

All these reports indicate to us that we should not imagine that the realm of the Hereafter can be compared in any way to our present world. Moreover, it alludes to the sublime Qur'anic concept of limitlessness in the realm of God, "*There is not a thing but its treasures are with Us, and We do not send it down except in a known measure.*"[431] Treasures of God only find measures when they are relegated to the *dunyā*; there are no measures in the realm of God.

6. These enormous domains and vast distances and the grandeur of the personal property of every individual which include multitudes of servants and attendants, do not prevent the people of Paradise from their meetings, social activities and travel. It is true that everyone lives in his own domain as a noble king, however, they socialize and visit one other out of love and friendship and spend time together.

   We will speak again about this socializing and its objective; however, at this point we are concerned with the travel across great distances which, according to this narration, is done by travelling on mounts of light. What a mount of light is exactly remains to be seen, however this tradition indicates that as the angels show the inhabitants around

[430] Ṣadūq, *Amālī*, pg.368.

وَمَنْ أَحْيَا لَيْلَةً تَامَّةً تَالِيًا لِكِتَابِ اللهِ، رَاكِعًا وَسَاجِدًا وَذَاكِرًا، أُعْطِيَ مِنَ الثَّوَابِ مَا أَدْنَاهُ أَنْ يَخْرُجَ مِنَ الذُّنُوبِ كَمَا وَلَدَتْهُ أُمُّهُ، وَيُكْتَبُ لَهُ بِعَدَدِ مَا خَلَقَ اللهُ عَزَّ وَجَلَّ مِنَ الْحَسَنَاتِ ومِثْلَهَا دَرَجَاتٌ، وَيُثَبَّتُ النُّورُ فِي قَلْبِهِ، وَيُنْزَعُ الْإِثْمُ وَالْحَسَدُ مِنْ قَلْبِهِ، وَيُجَارُ مِنْ عَذَابِ الْقَبْرِ، وَيُعْطَى بَرَاءَةً مِنَ النَّارِ، وَيُبْعَثُ مِنَ الْآمِنِينَ، وَيَقُولُ الرَّبُّ تَبَارَكَ وَتَعَالَى لِمَلَائِكَتِهِ: يَا مَلَائِكَتِي، أُنْظُرُوا إِلَى عَبْدِي، أَحْيَا لَيْلَةً ابْتِغَاءَ مَرْضَاتِي، أَسْكِنُوهُ الْفِرْدَوْسَ، وَلَهُ فِيهَا مِائَةُ أَلْفِ مَدِينَةٍ، فِي كُلِّ مَدِينَةٍ جَمِيعُ مَا تَشْتَهِي الْأَنْفُسُ وَتَلَذُّ الْأَعْيُنُ، وَلَمْ يَخْطُرْ عَلَى بَالٍ سِوَى مَا أَعْدَدْتُ لَهُ مِنَ الْكَرَامَةِ وَالْمَزِيدِ وَالْقُرْبَةِ.

[431] Surat al-Ḥijr, 15:21.

their properties and holdings, they are mounted on steeds of light and, "complete the survey of their holdings in less than a blink of the eye."

7. In Paradise the praise and glorification of God is the most beautiful and pleasant melody that ears have ever heard. This is not the praise and glorification of worship; rather it is existential, just like love which has no reason but itself. The melody stems from the depths of the being and from sheer delight, "And in Paradise there is a river on whose two banks are seated maidens. God reveals to them, 'let My servant hear you praise Me, Glorify Me and eulogize Me'. So, their voices ring out with a melody and sweetness the like of which no one has ever heard before, causing the people of heaven to become spellbound."

8. Even greater than this is the feeling of mental ease, total contentment and mutual satisfaction that is enjoyed by the inhabitants of Paradise. Firstly, they are overjoyed because they have been given much more than they feel they deserve and in fact, they cannot imagine having anything more, because, "*They shall have therein whatever they desire, while with Us is still more.*"[432] This joy at what they have makes them more humble and grateful before God, and their perfect contentment with God's decree fills their hearts with an indescribable love for Him. And their happiness and contentment become complete when they realize that God is pleased with them too, and regards them in the same manner, "*And the angels approach them from every door saying, "Peace be on you for your steadfastness. And how excellent is the final abode!*"[433]

[432] Surat Qāf, 50:35.

[433] Surat al-Ra'd, 13:23,24.

In fact, the sure knowledge of God's pleasure is the greatest delight and one that gives them abiding tranquillity and contentment, "*God has promised the believing men and the believing women gardens beneath which rivers flow, wherein they shall abide eternally, and beautiful mansions in the Garden of Eden; but the greatest bliss is the pleasure of God - that is the supreme attainment.*"[434] This mutual regard has been mentioned several times in the Qur'an, "*God is pleased with them, and they are pleased with Him.*"[435]

It should be borne in mind that the substance of physical elements such as gold and silver and pearls in Paradise descends from *malakūt* and is different in nature and properties to what we know of them here in *dunyā*. Similarly, the nature of mental concepts and emotions such as peace, contentment and love will be quite different in Paradise. For example, peace in this *dunyā* can only be defined negatively as the absence of disturbance, while peace in Paradise is a positive existential concept which we yet have to experience.

9. The greatest gift of all however, is one that is even beyond the imagination of the inhabitants of Paradise. "*They shall have therein whatever they desire while with Us is still more.*"[436] This reference to "more" is something that God occasionally uses in order to stir their imagination and desire and increase their knowledge and perfection, love and longing, and their bounties and wealth. We read in the tradition that, "They live in this way until suddenly a voice is heard from below the throne of God saying,

[434] Surat al-Tawba, 9:72.

[435] Surat al-Mā'ida, 5:119, Surat al-Tawba, 9:100, Surat al-Mujādila, 58:22, Surat al-Bayyina, 98:8.

[436] Surat Qāf, 50:35.

"O inhabitants of Paradise! How do you find the place you have returned to?" They reply, "We have returned to the best of places and our reward is the most generous of rewards. However, now that we have heard this voice we have a keen desire to gaze at Your Magnificence." And of course, no sooner than they manifest this desire that it is accepted, because Paradise is a place of fulfilment of every desire, and whoever longs for more receives greater gifts; "So God issues a command, and seventy thousand veils are lifted away. The inhabitants of Paradise climb onto their mounts, and dressed in luxurious and jewelled garments, ride in the shade of the trees until they reach the abode of peace (*dār al-salām*) which is the abode of God - the abode of light and glory and felicity." And what comes to pass here cannot be imagined by any human being in this world or even in Paradise either.

10. When they go into His presence, the people of Paradise want nothing else except to remain forever witnessing the splendour of God and to be lost in the beauty of His countenance; "They gaze towards the light of God's countenance as much as they are able to and say, "Our Master! Hearing Your sweet speech and seeing the light of Your countenance is enough delight for us, we do not desire or seek anything else." However, they do not realize that what is still veiled from them of His Beauty is millions of times greater than what they have seen until now; yet at this moment this is the limit of their capacity to perceive. To see more they will have to evolve further and to do so, they will have to abide for a while with this new cognizance and rapture; they must experience further delights of Paradise so that they may mature further and qualify to be presented again. Therefore, God puts a desire in their hearts to visit their

spouses so that they willingly return; "But God says, "I know that you are eager to meet with your wives and they long to see you. Go now to your wives." They ask God to give them an appointment to come to this place again. God says, "You shall have a meeting every Friday. From one Friday to the next there is a span of seven thousand years by your reckoning." As they leave, each is given a green pomegranate containing seventy garments the like of which no eye has seen before." Do not wonder why garments should be in pomegranates because we are discussing a completely different world in which anything could be found in anything else, and every single feeling may feel like all feelings.

11. When the inhabitants of Paradise return from this journey, they have evolved and grown to such an extent that they seem to be different creatures altogether and are scarcely recognizable even to their spouses; "As he approaches and his wife looks at his face, she hardly recognizes him and says, "My dear! When you departed your face looked different." He will reply, "My dear! Do not be amazed at my appearance for I have gazed at the countenance of my Lord and my face has become illuminated by His light."

    This evolution and development and new radiance has transformed him, and he cannot be compared to his former self. In fact, his previous bounties and possessions no longer befit his new magnificence and are trivial to his new status. Consequently, everything must be enhanced to reflect his new stature and radiance. Everything around him changes as a result of the illumination of his own existence. That is why when he looks again at the face of his wife he says, "My dear! When I departed from you your face seemed different." And she will reply, "My dear!

Do not be amazed at my appearance for I have looked at the face of one who has gazed at the countenance of God, and my face has become seventy times more radiant as a result. And they will embrace each other."

12. Now he shall live in his new magnificence and capacity and beauty and enjoy the bounties that God has granted to him, until his new cognizance permeates his being completely; once that happens, he will be eager to journey to God again. And this desire, love and longing for the Lord, and the excitement and evolution and growth in beauty continue in a pleasant environment for eternity, "*Wherein they shall abide forever. They will not desire to leave therefrom.*"[437] And, "*For them there will be therein all that they wish for, and they will abide there eternally.*"[438]

Physical Pleasures in Paradise

As we have mentioned in the previous sections, in this world the human being has both a material as well as a spiritual dimension. In *dunyā* the soul perceived, learned and grew by living in a material body, while in *barzakh* it did the same in an imaginal body. However, the special quality of the human being in *qiyāma* is that there, the human soul can simultaneously make use of a physical body - which has been resurrected with vastly upgraded features - as well as the imaginal body. Actually, there is another higher means of perception than these two which the soul can also employ which presently is beyond our understanding. This means that the human being can experience spiritual as well as physical pleasure at the same time; in fact these two bodies are like two faces of the same coin.

[437] Surat al-Kahf, 18:108.

[438] Surat al-Furqān, 25:16.

While the imaginal body experiences the greatest pleasure by seeing and hearing the secrets of creation through the parallelism and correspondence (*tanāẓur*) that we have talked about at length, the physical body also experiences the highest level of pleasure through all its senses. The eyes see the most beautiful sights, the ears hear the most soothing melodies, the tongue tastes the most delicious food and drink, the touch feels the most pleasurable surfaces, and the nose smells the most delightful fragrances. Every sensation that can be experienced by the body is amplified to the utmost. Since these experiences are in synchrony with the experience of the imaginal body, which itself draws on the experience of the soul, the greater the soul's receptivity to God's mercy and grace, the more pleasurable will be the experience of the imaginal and physical bodies. In other words, the purer the soul is, and consequently the nearer it is to God, the more intensely it will experience the joys of Paradise.

This link between body and soul is not just one way and does not simply come from above; neither do these pleasures simply result in joy and happiness. Just as all pleasures experienced in *dunyā* had a particular purpose, in Paradise also they serve a very important function. In fact, it can be said that the ultimate purpose, which was to display gratitude, is realized in Paradise. Gratitude, which gives rise to love, is the highest connection that the human soul can have with God; it requires both true cognizance (*maʿrifa*) as well as submission (*khushūʿ*) and humble reverence (*khuḍūʿ*) in the heart. The Qur'an states that the true purpose of God's blessings – including the gift of sight, hearing and intellect – is to bring about gratitude, "*And God brought you out from the wombs of your mothers while you knew nothing, and He gave you hearing and sight and intellect so that perhaps you may give thanks.*"[439] Every physical or imaginal experience in Paradise creates further submission and appreciation in the soul, which in turn increases the love for God, and brings one even closer to Him; and this in turn intensifies the physical and imaginal pleasures. This mutual cause and effect process between the body and soul continues eternally.

The reason why seeking pleasure in the *dunyā* has been criticized in the Divine religions is not because of the pleasure itself, because all physical pleasures are creations of God and a part of the bounties, He has granted mankind; rather, it is because of the pursuit of illicit pleasures that results in neglect of the remembrance of God. In other words, the real philosophy behind these physical experiences is to bring about appreciation and gratefulness and consequently make man remember God. Conversely, the arrogant and defiant use of these bounties engenders the opposite outcome, and results in ungratefulness and neglect; ultimately this distances one from the Source of all grace and mercy.

In Paradise however, these pleasures are solely used to increase man's development and sublimity and are free of anything else. "*Say: Who has forbidden the adornment of God and the lawful provisions which He has produced for His servants? Say: They are for those who were believers in their life in the world, and exclusively for them on the Day of Judgement. Thus, We explain our revelation for people who understand. Say: My Lord has only forbidden immoral deeds whether committed openly or in secret, and sinful conduct, and wrongful oppression, and that you associate with God that for which He has not sent any authority, and that you speak about God that which you do not know.*"[440]

---

[439] Surat al-Naḥl, 16:78.

[440] Surat al-Aʿrāf, 7:32,33. The verse is saying that the correct ultilizaton of the pleasures of *dunyā* requires faith (īmān). Although those with no

Evolution in Paradise and Increase of Joy

Whatever we shall see in Paradise will be a representation of our inner state; and because that state will be continually changing as we grow wiser and love God more deeply, the nature, colour and fragrance of everything in Paradise will constantly improve and become more amazing and wondrous. The meaning of time in Paradise arises from this very evolution within us.

Wisdom and love have always been embedded in every human being because it is through these faculties that man's eternal soul – which God placed within the human being – is connected to Him. In Paradise man explores his soul every day and removes the veils that mask the beauty of that wisdom and love so that he can see himself more clearly, or rather see God more clearly; the two are the same in fact, because his ego does not exist anymore. What he sees now is his true self, which is one with his cognitive soul; and so, he will see and know God to the same degree as he knows himself. He is now a mirror that reflects the beauty of God. Whatever he sees inside himself is manifested externally too. It is similar to when the Names of God manifest themselves in the physical realm.

Therefore, with the removal of every inner veil, the flowers and gardens he sees externally are transformed as well. The appearance and decorations of his palaces and the elegance of his garments all take on a new beauty. His interactions with friends and neighbours and spouses change and become even more pleasurable. And all this increase in colour and fragrance and beauty, which he recognizes is from God,

---

faith also use these bounties, not only does it not result in anything lasting for them, but they transgress and use them wrongly and commit immoral acts, set up partners with God and became ungrateful.

increases his delight a hundredfold. His Lord helps him further by giving him nectar spiced with ginger (*zanjabīl*) to drink; this shall fill him with an excitement to see and understand more, "*And they will be given to drink a cup mixed with ginger from a fountain called Salsabīl.*"[441] His excitement will make him restless and even more eager to remove yet another veil and uncover greater wisdom and love. At this time, his Lord gives him wine mixed with soothing camphor to instil calm into his entire being and elevate him to a state of renewed wonderment, "*Indeed, the righteous shall drink from a cup mixed with camphor; a spring from which the true servants of God shall drink; making it flow in abundance (at will).*"[442] The wonders of Paradise will never cease. A wonderment that will not be transient like that of *dunyā*, but one which is accompanied by an abiding contentment and appreciation and an indescribable thankfulness, which in turn increases love and gives true meaning to one's existence.

These inner and outward transformations are also reflected in the face; the bounties of Paradise make the features of its inhabitants more beautiful and more youthful. It has been reported from Imam al-Sadiq (a) that, "When the Day of Judgment arrives, two believers, both of whom are destined for Paradise, will be stopped for accounting. One of them was poor in the world, while the other was wealthy. The one who was poor will say, "O Lord! Why have I been stopped here? I swear by Your honour, You know well that You had not granted me power and authority in the *dunyā*, so that You may see whether I acted justly or oppressively. And You had not granted me any wealth either that You may see whether I fulfilled the rights of others or neglected them.

---

441 Surat al-Insān, 76:17,18.

442 Surat al-Insān, 76:5,6.

My sustenance was meagre, as You know and You Yourself had apportioned for me." Then God will say, "This servant of Mine speaks truly, permit him to enter Paradise." But his companion will remain at that station for a long time; in that time, he will perspire so profusely that his sweat would be enough for forty thirsty camels to drink from; only then will he be entered into Paradise. The poor man who was his companion will say to him, "We were together, what delayed you so much?" The wealthy man will reply, "The length of the accounting. I was asked continuously about my possessions. They were presented one by one, and each time God kept pardoning and forgiving me until He enveloped me in His mercy and forgave me everything! However, tell me, who are you?" The poor man will say, "I am the same poor man who was at your side at the station of accounting."

The wealthy one will say in wonder, "The blessings of Paradise have altered your face beyond recognition!"[443]

The Doors of Paradise

People will not all enter Paradise through one gate or doorway; rather every group of believers will have a gate dedicated just for them, "*And those who were Godwary shall be*

---

[443] Ṣadūq, al-Amālī, p. 441 |

إِذَا كَانَ يَوْمُ الْقِيَامَةِ، وَقَفَ عَبْدَانِ مُؤْمِنَانِ لِلْحِسَابِ، كِلَاهُمَا مِنْ أَهْلِ الْجَنَّةِ، فَقِيرٌ فِي الدُّنْيَا، وَغَنِيٌّ فِي الدُّنْيَا، فَيَقُولُ الْفَقِيرُ: يَا رَبِّ، عَلَى مَا أُوقَفُ؟ فَوَعِزَّتِكَ، إِنَّكَ لَتَعْلَمُ أَنَّكَ لَمْ تُوَلِّنِي وِلَايَةً فَأَعْدِلَ فِيهَا أَوْ أَجُورَ، وَلَمْ تَرْزُقْنِي مَالًا فَأُؤَدِّيَ مِنْهُ حَقًّا أَوْ أَمْنَعَ، وَلَا كَانَ رِزْقِي يَأْتِينِي مِنْهَا إِلَّا كَفَافًا عَلَى مَا عَلِمْتَ وَقَدَّرْتَ لِي. فَيَقُولُ اللهُ جَلَّ جَلَالُهُ: صَدَقَ عَبْدِي، خَلُّوا عَنْهُ يَدْخُلُ الْجَنَّةَ. وَيَبْقَى الْآخَرُ حَتَّى يَسِيلَ مِنْهُ الْعَرَقُ مَا لَوْ شَرِبَهُ أَرْبَعُونَ بَعِيرًا لَكَفَاهَا ثُمَّ يَدْخُلُ الْجَنَّةَ. فَيَقُولُ لَهُ الْفَقِيرُ: مَا حَبَسَكَ؟ فَيَقُولُ: طُولُ الْحِسَابِ، مَا زَالَ الشَّيْءُ يَجِيئُنِي بَعْدَ الشَّيْءِ يَغْفِرُ لِي، ثُمَّ أُسْأَلُ عَنْ شَيْءٍ آخَرَ حَتَّى تَغَمَّدَنِيَ اللهُ عَزَّ وَجَلَّ مِنْهُ بِرَحْمَتِهِ، وَأَلْحَقَنِي بِالتَّائِبِينَ، فَمَنْ أَنْتَ؟ فَيَقُولُ: أَنَا الْفَقِيرُ الَّذِي كُنْتُ مَعَكَ آنِفًا، فَيَقُولُ: لَقَدْ غَيَّرَكَ النَّعِيمُ بَعْدِي.

led towards Paradise in groups; and when they come to it, its doors will be already open and its keepers will say, "Peace be upon you; you have done well, so enter and abide therein for ever."[444] It has been reported from the Prophet (s) that, "Paradise has eight doors and Hell has seven"[445] And it has been reported from Imam al-Baqir (a) that, "Have a good opinion (*ḥusn al-ḍann*) of God and know that Paradise has eight doors, the width of each would take forty years to cross.[446] And normally the size of doors is designed to accommodate the traffic of people who will enter through them.

It is beneficial to recount here a beautiful tradition reported by Bilāl which speaks both about the doors of Paradise as well as other aspects of that mysterious land. A man called ʿAbdallah ibn Ali reports, "I went from Basra to Egypt for trade and there I saw an old man; he was tall and had dark skin and white hair. He was wearing two worn out garments, one white and the other black. I asked who he was and was informed that he was Bilāl, a slave freed by the Prophet (s). So, I took a writing tablet and pen and approached him. I greeted him saying, "Salām on you, O Shaykh!" He replied to my salutation. I said, "May God have mercy on you, O Shaykh. Would you share with me something that you have heard from the Prophet (s)?" He asked, "How do you know who I am?" I said, "You are Bilāl, the *muezzin* of the Prophet (s)." When he heard the name of the Prophet (s), tears came to his eyes, and he wept. I wept also as did the people around me."

---

[444] Surat al-Zumar, 39:73.

[445] Ṣadūq, *al-Amālī*, p. 123 |

لِلْجَنَّةِ ثَمَانِيَةُ أَبْوَابٍ، وَلِلنَّارِ سَبْعَةُ أَبْوَابٍ.

[446] Ṣadūq, *al-Khiṣāl*, p. 408 |

أَحْسِنُوا الظَّنَّ بِاللهِ، وَاعْلَمُوا أَنَّ لِلْجَنَّةِ ثَمَانِيَةَ أَبْوَابٍ، عَرْضُ كُلِّ بَابٍ مِنْهَا مَسِيرَةُ أَرْبَعِينَ سَنَةً.

"Then he said, "Write down: In the name of God, the Beneficent, the Merciful. I heard the Prophet, peace be upon him, and his family say, "The walls of Paradise are made of bricks of gold, silver and ruby. Its mortar is of fragrant musk and its ramparts are crusted with red, green and yellow rubies." I asked how many doors it has. He replied, "It has several doors: the door of Mercy (*bāb al-raḥma*) is made of red ruby...the door of Perseverance (*bāb al-ṣabr*) is a small single door made from a sheet of red ruby. As for the door of Gratitude (*bāb al-shukr*) it is made of white ruby and has double doors the width of which is a distance of five hundred years' travel. It keeps calling out resoundingly and plaintively, "O Lord! Bring my people to me." I said, "Can a door speak?" He said, "Yes indeed, God, the Mighty and Gracious, gives it the ability to speak. Then there is the door of Trial (*bāb al-bala'*)." I asked, "Is the door of trial not the same as the door of perseverance?" He replied, "No." I asked, "What then is trial?" He said, "Calamities and sickness and disease and leprosy; and this is a single door made of a sheet of yellow ruby, very few people enter through it."

"As for the Great door (*bāb al-aʿẓam*), it is a door through which the righteous servants of God enter, those who were people of restraint, pious, eager to please God and intimate with Him." I said, "May God have mercy on you. Once they enter Paradise what do they do there?" He said, "They board boats of ruby with oars made of pearls and travel across the two banks of a river with transparent water. On the boat there are angels of light. They wear garments of an intense green colour." I asked, "May God have mercy on you. Can light be green?" He replied, "Their clothes are green, however a light from the light of the Lord of the worlds, Most Glorious, radiates from them." I asked, "What is the name of this place?" He replied. "It is called Jannat al-Ma'wā. (Garden of Refuge)" I asked, "Are there other gardens as well?" He replied, "Yes, Jannat al-ʿAdn (Garden of Eden) and it lies towards the middle of Paradise. Its walls are of red ruby and its pebbles are of pearls." I asked, "Are there any other gardens besides these?" He replied, "Yes. Jannat al-Firdaws (Garden of Paradise)." I asked, "And what are its walls like?" He said, "Enough! Leave me, you are hurting my heart." I said, "Rather, it is you who is doing this to me. I will not depart until you complete the description of its walls." He said, "Its walls are made from light." I asked, "What about its rooms?" He replied, "They are made from the light of the Lord of the worlds."[447]

The first thing that this narration makes clear is that the nature of those parts of Paradise that are more proximal to God are more unknown to us; for this reason, the construction material of Firdaws has been cryptically called light, whatever that may mean exactly. More familiar materials like red and yellow rubies, pearls, gold and silver have been mentioned as materials used to create the buildings and even trees and steeds found in the lesser levels of Paradise; but as we have mentioned, these are correspondences (*tanāẓur*), meaning that if we want to put a name from this world for these objects, they would be represented by gold, silver and pearls.

Secondly, the fact that there is a door called the door of Trial (*bāb al-balā'*) means that whoever continues to be steadfast in the face of severe and chronic illness and other difficulties in the life of *dunyā*, then a special door from the doors of Paradise will open itself just for them.

Thirdly, that Paradise has several doors due to the different states and qualities of the people who are admitted inside.

---

447 Ṣadūq, *Man lā yaḥḍuruhu'l Faqīh*, 1:295,296.

It is also because of this diversity that Paradise has been divided into different sections. In fact, everyone opens a door in Paradise that is befitting to the nature of their soul; they proceed to the level they deserve according to the predominant virtue that they possess. It has been mentioned in the traditions that, "When the month of Ramaḍān arrives, the doors of Paradise are opened and the doors of Hell are closed."[448] These doors refer to virtuous acts and are opened by the souls of the believers; and because there are many possible such acts, it follows that each of the eight doors of Paradise must be able to accommodate a wide variety of virtues. In other words, every good deed comes under one of the eight doors of goodness and virtue in the human soul and becomes a doorway for his entry into Paradise. Therefore, it must not come as a surprise if every act or worship and good deed is independently considered as a door from the doors of Paradise. As an example, in *Nahj al-Balāgha* we read, "Indeed, *jihād* is a door from the doors of Paradise which God has opened for His closest servants."[449] In another tradition it is mentioned that, "Be mindful of truthfulness (*ṣidq*) because truthfulness is a door from the doors of Paradise and beware of falsehood (*kidhb*) because falsehood is a door from the doors of Hell."[450] And, "Whoever feeds a hungry believer, God enters him into Paradise from a door through which only others who have done the same may enter."[451] And, "For every

448 Muttaqī al-Hindī, *Kanz al-ʿUmmāl*, trad. 23667 |

هَذَا شَهْرُ رَمَضَانَ قَدْ جَاءَكُمْ، تُفْتَحُ فِيهِ أَبْوَابُ الْجَنَّةِ وَتُغْلَقُ فِيهِ أَبْوَابُ النَّارِ.

449 Sharīf Raḍī, *Nahj al-Balāgha*, sermon 27 |

فَإِنَّ الْجِهَادَ بَابٌ مِنْ أَبْوَابِ الْجَنَّةِ، فَتَحَهُ اللهُ لِخَاصَّةِ أَوْلِيَائِهِ.

450 Muttaqī al-Hindī, *Kanz al-ʿUmmāl*, trad. 6862 |

عَلَيْكُمْ بِالصِّدْقِ، فَإِنَّهُ بَابٌ مِنْ أَبْوَابِ الْجَنَّةِ، وَإِيَّاكُمْ وَالْكَذِبَ فَإِنَّهُ بَابٌ مِنْ أَبْوَابِ النَّارِ.

451 Muttaqī al-Hindī, *Kanz al-ʿUmmāl*, trad. 16374 |

door from the doors of goodness, there is a corresponding door from the doors of Paradise, and the door of the fast is called Rayyān."[452] Naturally, if someone possesses all the good qualities, he may enter from any door that he chooses, "Whoever says *Lā ilāha illalāh* (there is no god but Allah) in a manner that his heart confirms what his tongue utters, may enter Paradise from any of its eight doors that he wishes."[453]

Fourthly, the entry from a particular door means living in the region that the door opens into, in the familiar company of other people of Paradise of similar dispositions and merits.

The Different Levels and Regions of Paradise

The levels of people vary from one another in Paradise, and in fact, each person is counted as his own level, "*They have varying degrees in the sight of God.*"[454] God says, "*See how We have favoured some of them (in provision in dunyā) over others; but in the Hereafter there are greater Degrees (of preference) and greater distinctions.*"[455] In the words of Imam Ali (a), "There are multiple stations and different levels of excellence."[456]

It is these multiple levels, which are arranged according to the proximity of a person to God, which make up the various regions and layers of Paradise; in fact, the regions

---

مَنْ أَطْعَمَ مُؤْمِنًا حَتَّى يُشْبِعَهُ مِنْ سَغَبٍ، أَدْخَلَهُ اللهُ بَابًا مِنْ أَبْوَابِ الْجَنَّةِ لَا يَدْخُلُهُ إِلَّا مَنْ كَانَ مِثْلَهُ.

452 Muttaqī al-Hindī, *Kanz al-ʿUmmāl*, trad. 23583 |

لِكُلِّ بَابٍ مِنْ أَبْوَابِ الْبِرِّ بَابٌ مِنْ أَبْوَابِ الْجَنَّةِ، وَإِنَّ بَابَ الصِّيَامِ يُدْعَى الرَّيَّانُ.

453 Muttaqī al-Hindī, *Kanz al-ʿUmmāl*, trad. 155 |

مَنْ قَالَ: ﴿لَا إِلَهَ إِلَّا اللهُ﴾، يُصَدِّقُ لِسَانَهُ قَلْبُهُ، دَخَلَ مِنْ أَيِّ أَبْوَابِ الْجَنَّةِ الثَّمَانِيَةِ شَاءَ.

454 Surat Āl ʿImrān, 3:163.

455 Surat al-Isrāʾ, 17:21.

456 *Nahj al-Balāgha*, sermon 85 |

دَرَجَاتٌ مُتَفَاضِلَاتٌ، وَمَنَازِلُ مُتَفَاوِتَاتٌ.

that are close to one another become specific colonies in which the inhabitants undergo similar experiences. We find in the traditions that, "Paradise has one hundred levels, each of which is separated by a distance greater than the distance between the heavens and the earth. The highest level of Paradise, which is located in its heart, is Firdaws; nothing exists higher than it except the throne of God, and all the rivers of Paradise originate from there. So, if you seek anything from God, ask Him for Firdaws."[457]

These levels themselves are distributed across wide regions, the choicest of which are the Paradise of the closest servants (*muqarrabūn*) and the Paradise of the righteous (*aṣḥab al-yamīn*, lit. people of the right hand). As we mentioned before, the *muqarrabūn* and the *aṣḥāb al-yamīn* are two groups of believers who differ in their aspect of faith. The faith of the *muqarrabūn* is based on love and the focus of their lives is God. The faith of the *aṣḥab al-yamīn* is based on obedience and the focus of their lives is to follow their beliefs in order to gain favour and protect themselves from harm in the Hereafter. Imam Ali (a) says, "A group worshipped God seeking His Paradise, and their worship is the worship of merchants; a group worshipped God out of fear of His punishment, and their worship is the worship of slaves; and a group worshipped God out of gratitude, and their worship is the worship of free men."[458] And it has been narrated from Imam al-Sadiq (a) that, "Believers are of three kinds; a group who

[457] Muttaqī al-Hindī, *Kanz al-ʿUmmāl*, trad. 39230 |

الْجَنَّةُ مِائَةُ دَرَجَةٍ مَا بَيْنَ كُلِّ دَرَجَتَيْنِ كَمَا بَيْنَ السَّمَاءِ وَالْأَرْضِ، وَالْفِرْدَوْسُ أَعْلَى الْجَنَّةِ وَأَوْسَطُهَا، وَفَوْقَهُ عَرْشُ الرَّحْمَنِ، وَمِنْهَا تُفَجَّرُ أَنْهَارُ الْجَنَّةِ، فَإِذَا سَأَلْتُمُ اللهَ فَاسْأَلُوهُ الْفِرْدَوْسَ.

[458] *Nahj al-Balāgha*, short sayings, 237 |

إِنَّ قَوْمًا عَبَدُوا اللهَ رَغْبَةً فَتِلْكَ عِبَادَةُ التُّجَّارِ، وَإِنَّ قَوْمًا عَبَدُوا اللهَ رَهْبَةً فَتِلْكَ عِبَادَةُ الْعَبِيدِ، وَإِنَّ قَوْمًا عَبَدُوا اللهَ شُكْرًا فَتِلْكَ عِبَادَةُ الْأَحْرَارِ.

worship God out of fear, this is the worship of slaves; and a group who worship God seeking reward, this is the worship of contractors; and a group who worship God out of love, this is the worship of free men, and the best form of worship."[459] The common factor amongst all these groups is their worship; however, what separates them is the motivation for their worship. The *muqarrabūn* have been cleansed of all egoism and are no longer concerned with thoughts of benefit or harm to themselves; the love of God has saturated their beings, and consequently both in *dunyā* as well as *ākhira* they experience God in a manner that is not possible for even the *aṣḥab al-yamīn*. Their worship was always full of humility and reverence and this qualified them for ascent into Firdaws, above which exists nothing but the throne of God, "*Indeed, the believers are successful. Those who are humble in their prayers and turn away from vain speech...they indeed shall be the inheritors, who will inherit Firdaws and dwell therein forever.*"[460] In Surat al-Wāqi'ā and Surat al-Raḥmān, the Qur'an distinguishes between the Paradise of the *muqarrabūn* and the Paradise of the *aṣḥāb al-yamīn* and places the former above the latter. It has been narrated from Imam al-Sadiq (a) that, "Do not talk of just one Paradise, because God has stated: *Some are raised higher in rank than others.*"[461] The difference in the levels is such that, "When the people of a lower level look towards a level higher than their own, it is like the inhabitants of the earth looking at the stars; they guess the identity of whom

[459] Kulaynī, *al-Kāfī*, 2:84 |
عَنْ أَبِي عَبْدِ اللهِ (عَلَيْهِ السَّلَامُ) قَالَ: إِنَّ الْعِبَادَ ثَلَاثَةٌ: قَوْمٌ عَبَدُوا اللهَ عَزَّ وَجَلَّ خَوْفًا فَتِلْكَ عِبَادَةُ الْعَبِيدِ، وَقَوْمٌ عَبَدُوا اللهَ تَبَارَكَ وَتَعَالَى طَلَبَ الثَّوَابِ فَتِلْكَ عِبَادَةُ الْأُجَرَاءِ، وَقَوْمٌ عَبَدُوا اللهَ عَزَّ وَجَلَّ حُبًّا لَهُ فَتِلْكَ عِبَادَةُ الْأَحْرَارِ وَهِيَ أَفْضَلُ الْعِبَادَةِ.

[460] Surat al-Mu'minūn, 23:1-11.

[461] Muḥammadi, Ray Shahrī, *Mīzān al-Ḥikma*, 1:431 |
لَا تَقُولُوا جَنَّةٌ وَاحِدَةٌ، إِنَّ اللهَ عَزَّ وَجَلَّ يَقُولُ: ﴿دَرَجَاتٌ بَعْضُهَا فَوْقَ بَعْضٍ﴾.

they see above the way the people on earth call out the name of the stars."[462]

From these descriptions, which are found in many traditions, we can conclude that the people of Paradise do not live in gardens next to each other; rather, each garden or group of gardens is separated by unimaginable distances just as the stars and galaxies are distant from each other. This is also mentioned in the Qur'an because according to it, the size of Paradise is as wide as the expanse of the heavens and the earth, "*Hasten towards forgiveness from your Lord, and a garden as wide as the heavens and the earth, prepared for the Godwary.*"[463] In fact, every level is separated from the one below it by the same expanse, and every higher level forms the heaven for the one lower than it.

As we have mentioned, these levels are according to the proximity of its inhabitants to God, and in reality, this is nothing except individual differences in cognizance (*maʿrifa*) and love of God. It has been reported from Imam Sajjad (a) that, "God enters a group into Paradise and bestows so much on them that all their desires are satisfied, while above them there is another group inhabiting a higher level of Paradise. When they look at them, they recognize them and say, "O Lord! These were our brothers, and we were together in *dunyā*; on what grounds have you favoured them over us?" They will be told, "How different you were from each other! They used to remain hungry while your bellies were full, they would remain thirsty while you drank, and they would stay awake in the night while you slept."[464]

462 Māzandarānī, Mawlā Muḥammad Ṣāliḥ, *Sharḥ Uṣūl al-Kāfī*, 9:79, quoting the *Tafsīr* of Qurṭubī.

463 Surat Āl-ʿImrān, 3:133.

464 Muḥammadī, Ray Shahrī, *Mīzān al-Ḥikma*, 1:432 |

The phrase that "all their desires are satisfied" is worthy of some consideration; it confirms that everyone in Paradise will receive bounties according to their desires and aspirations, and everyone will of course only aspire to the extent to their cognizance. However, God extends his aspirations so that he may dwell in His proximity and seek higher favours from Him.

It has also been reported from the Prophet (s) that, "In Paradise the separation of two successive levels is the distance between the heavens and the earth. Sometimes a servant raises his gaze and suddenly sees a shining light that almost blinds him. He is elated at the sight and asks, "What was that?" He is told, "That is the light of your brother from the believers." He says, "Is that the same brother with whom I stood to worship in *dunyā*? How has he been elevated so greatly over me?" He is told, "His worship was better than yours." Then his heart is inspired with gladness, and he becomes content."[465]

The fact that everyone is completely satisfied within their level in Paradise is a very important matter and worthy of deliberation. The reason for this satisfaction is that everyone has received every last thing he could wish for and cannot imagine or want anything more. In the Gospel of Barnabas, it has been mentioned that Bartholomew asked Jesus (a), "O Teacher! Will the reward in Paradise be the same for

---

إِنَّ اللهَ جَلَّ ثَنَاؤُهُ لَيُدْخِلُ قَوْمًا الْجَنَّةَ فَيُعْطِيهِمْ حَتَّى تَنْتَهِيَ أَمَانِيُّهُمْ، وَفَوْقَهُمْ قَوْمٌ فِي الدَّرَجَاتِ الْعُلَى، فَإِذَا نَظَرُوا إِلَيْهِمْ عَرَفُوهُمْ فَيَقُولُونَ: رَبَّنَا، إِخْوَانُنَا كُنَّا مَعَهُمْ فِي الدُّنْيَا فَبِمَ فَضَّلْتَهُمْ عَلَيْنَا: فَيُقَالُ: هَيْهَاتَ! إِنَّهُمْ كَانُوا يَجُوعُونَ حِينَ تَشْبَعُونَ، وَيَظْمَأُونَ حِينَ تَرْوَوْنَ، وَيَقُومُونَ حِينَ تَنَامُونَ.

[465] Ibid |

الدَّرَجَةُ فِي الْجَنَّةِ فَوْقَ الدَّرَجَةِ، كَمَا بَيْنَ السَّمَاءِ وَالْأَرْضِ! وَإِنَّ الْعَبْدَ لَيَرْفَعُ بَصَرَهُ فَيَلْمَعُ لَهُ نُورٌ يَكَادُ يَخْطِفُ بَصَرَهُ فَيَفْرَحُ، فَيَقُولُ: مَا هَذَا؟ فَيُقَالُ لَهُ: هَذَا نُورُ أَخِيكَ الْمُؤْمِنِ، فَيَقُولُ: هَذَا أَخِي فُلَانٌ، كُنَّا نَعْمَلُ جَمِيعًا فِي الدُّنْيَا وَقَدْ فُضِّلَ عَلَيَّ هَكَذَا؟ فَيُقَالُ: إِنَّهُ كَانَ أَفْضَلَ مِنْكَ عَمَلًا، ثُمَّ يُجْعَلُ فِي قَلْبِهِ الرِّضَا حَتَّى يَرْضَى.

everyone? If it is the same then that would be against justice, and yet if it is not the same, the lesser will envy the greater." Jesus (a) replied, "It will not be the same, because God is Just; however, everyone will be content with that which he has received from God, because there is no envy in that realm. O Bartholomew! Will a master who has many servants clothe them all with the same garment? Will the children who wear the clothes of children be saddened that they cannot wear the clothes of the adults? Rather, on the contrary, if the adults desire to clothe them with their large garments the children would become upset because by being forced to wear garments that are not of their size, they would think that they are being mocked. So, raise your heart, dear Bartholomew, to God in Paradise; you shall see that everyone has their reward, and the fact that it is more for one and less for another will not cause anyone to become jealous."[466]

As was mentioned, these levels are determined by the cognizance of individuals. It has been reported from Imam al-Sadiq (a) that, "I advise you to recite the Qur'an because the levels of Paradise are according to the verses of the Qur'an. On the Day of Judgement, the reciter of the Qur'an shall be told, "Recite and ascend higher!" So, for every verse he recites, he will be raised one more level."[467] It is obvious that the meaning of recital on that Day is not confined to mere verbal recitation; rather, it refers to the cognizance that every verse of the Qur'an inspires within the heart and soul of the individual. In fact, there are many in *dunyā* who

[466] Gospel of Barnabas,176:8-17.

[467] Ḥurr Āmilī, *Wasā'il al-Shī'a*,6:190 |

عَلَيْكُمْ بِتِلَاوَةِ الْقُرْآنِ، فَإِنَّ دَرَجَاتِ الْجَنَّةِ عَلَى عَدَدِ آيَاتِ الْقُرآنِ، فَإِذَا كَانَ يَوْمُ الْقِيَامَةِ يُقَالُ لِقَارِئِ الْقُرْآنِ: اِقْرَأْ وَارْقَ، فَكُلَّمَا قَرَأَ آيَةً يَرْقَ دَرَجَةً.

have committed the entire Qur'an to memory but will be unable to recite even a single verse on the Day of Judgement.

However, after reading all this, one must not imagine that the lower levels of Paradise are not worthy of appreciation. It has been reported from the Prophet (s) that "The person in the lowest level in Paradise is one whose kingdom would take a thousand years travel to see in its entirety; he himself, however, can survey his entire kingdom in one glance, just as he sees all his spouses, servants and thrones."[468] And it has been reported from Imam al-Sadiq (a) that "The person in the lowest level of Paradise will still be able to host the entirety of mankind and *jinn* and give them food and drink to their fill, without anything substantial being reduced from his possessions."[469]

The Levels of Paradise and Family Life

The Qur'an states, "*Those who believed, and their offspring followed them in (weaker) faith, We shall cause their offspring to join them (in Paradise).*"[470] This verse raises a question as to how will the members of one family who are on different levels of Paradise be joined together in one place? The apparent answer is that this joining comes about by the fulfilment of the desire of the strongest in faith in the higher levels, who are able, through the power of their souls, to raise the level of the weaker members of their family. It has been reported from the Prophet (s) that "Even if the offspring of a righteous

---

[468] Muḥammadī, Ray Shahrī, *Mīzān al-Ḥikma*, 1:433 |
إِنَّ أَدْنَى أَهْلِ الْجَنَّةِ مَنْزِلَةً لَرَجُلٌ يَنْظُرُ فِي مُلْكِهِ أَلْفَ سَنَةٍ، يَرَى أَقْصَاهُ كَمَا يَرَى أَزْوَاجَهُ وَخَدَمَهُ وَسُرُورَهُ.

[469] Muḥammadī, Ray Shahrī, *Mīzān al-Ḥikma*, 1:434 |
إِنَّ أَدْنَى أَهْلِ الْجَنَّةِ مَنْزِلًا لَوْ نَزَلَ بِهِ الثَّقَلَانِ - الْجِنُّ وَالْإِنْسُ - لَوَسِعَهُمْ طَعَامًا وَشَرَابًا، وَلَا يَنْقُصُ مِمَّا عِنْدَهُ شَيْءٌ.

[470] Surat al-Ṭūr, 52:21.

believer is located in a lower level of Paradise, God allows him to raise them to his own so that his heart is pleased."[471] It has also been reported from him that "When a person enters Paradise, he searches for his father and mother and asks about his family and children. He is told, "They have not reached your level, and they did not have your quality of deeds." He will say, "O my Lord! Whatever I did, I intended to do for myself and them." At that time, a command will be issued to join all of them with him."[472]

What can be understood from the foregoing is that love and regard for one's family exists, at least to the same extent, if not stronger, in Paradise as it did in *dunyā*, and one of the pleasures of Paradise is the coming together of families to live with each other. However, love for those family members who have become inmates of Hell is completely erased from the hearts of the people of Paradise because they cannot bear any pollution at all.

In addition to family life, Paradise also has a social system, which we discussed at length in the section concerning *barzakh*.

That which cannot be described about Paradise

Whatever we have said so far about Paradise was about that limited aspect of it that we can understand through the concepts and experiences that we are familiar with in this *dunyā*; however, there are things that exist there that cannot be explained through anything we know from our world or anything that we can imagine in our mind, "In Paradise, there are realities that no eye has seen and no ear has heard,

---

471 Fayḍ al-Kāshānī, *Tafsīr al-Ṣāfī*, 5:79 |
إِنَّ اللهَ يَرْفَعُ ذُرِّيَّةَ الْمُؤْمِنِ فِي دَرَجَتِهِ، وَإِنْ كَانُوا دُونَهُ، لِتَقَرَّ بِهِمْ عَيْنُهُ.

472 Suyūṭī, Jalāl al-Dīn, *al-Durr al-Manthūr*, 6:119.

and no human mind has ever conceived."[473] In the words of the Qur'an, "*No person knows what pleasures have been kept hidden for them as a reward for their good deeds.*"[474] They remain hidden because, due to the reduced capacity of human understanding, these blessings cannot yet be described and made clear.

A Final Word

Whatever you have read in the chapters of this book was just an approximation of what wonders lie in wait for creation in general and human beings, in particular, to witness and experience of the majesty, mercy and generosity of God. They all allude to one fact; our comprehension of God in this realm of *dunyā* is by no means proportionate to His greatness, grandeur and glory, and our understanding of ourselves is nowhere near what we really are. The vast expanse of the universe compared to what will come in *ākhira* is narrower and darker than the womb surrounding a baby, and the countless talents of humans in this world compared to what they will become in *ākhira* are like the abilities of a foetus compared to a grown-up human being.

Ākhira is a realm which shall transform the entire creation at the same time. It is not a place where human beings enter one at a time or one that only human beings go to; rather, the entire universe will enter into it in a single instant. Just like a larva emerges from its cocoon and becomes a beautiful butterfly, or just like a small seed grows from the ground into a strong tree, the universe of *dunyā* will one Day shed its skin and emerge into the universe of *ākhira*.

---

473 Muttaqī al-Hindī, *Kanz al-ʿUmmāl*, trad. 39241 |
إِنَّ فِي الْجَنَّةِ مَا لَا عَيْنٌ رَأَتْ، وَلَا أُذُنٌ سَمِعَتْ، وَلَا خَطَرَ عَلَى قَلْبِ بَشَرٍ.

474 Surat al-Sajda, 32:17.

The characteristics of the new realm will be entirely different; it is as if God has created a new world or that creation has been recreated anew: "*God originates the creation, then repeats it; then you shall be brought back to Him.*"[475] However, just as the butterfly is born from the larva and cannot exist without it, the world of *ākhira* is also born of *dunyā* and cannot come about without it.

The qualities of *ākhira* are completely different from those of *dunyā*, and consequently, whatever descriptions we come up with for that world can be no more than metaphors that approximate its reality. It is like trying to explain to a larva in its cocoon what it will be like to sprout wings and fly or to explain the colour red or green to a blind person.

Everything that transpires before *ākhira* is a journey we must undertake, while the world of *ākhira* represents the destination and journey's end. We began as dust, became water, then an embryo, then we came into the world, and then we shall leave it; we will thereafter travel along until we reach *ākhira*, where we will rest for eternity, "*The Hereafter (ākhira) is the home of permanent settlement.*"[476] This is why God calls it "home", "*Make a mention of Our servants Abraham, Isaac and Jacob, men of strength and insight. We chose them for an exclusive quality, the keeping in mind of the final home.*"[477]

Real life and meaningful existence can only take place in the Hereafter; what we experience in this world is a pale shadow and fleeting fragrance of it in comparison. The life of this world is no more than a kind of play, which prepares us for the real life that is to follow; "*And the life of this world is nothing*

[475] Surat al-Rūm, 30:11.

[476] Surat al-Ghāfir, 40:39

[477] Surat Ṣād, 38:46.

more than diversion and play! And the abode of the Hereafter is indeed life if only they knew."[478] Of course, just as the playing of children has an important role in the development of their character, the game of life also plays a very important role in shaping the destiny of the human being. In *dunyā*, our souls are in an embryonic state, just as our bodies were when we were in the wombs of our mothers, and the play and diversions of life are essential for the nurturing of this growing soul.

The single factor that grants man a lofty status in the Hereafter is the remembrance and reverence of God in this world. It is like a seed which grows and bears its fruit in the soul. "*Do you not consider how God sets forth a parable? A good word is like a good tree: its roots are steady, and its branches are in the sky. It gives its fruit every moment by the leave of its Lord. God draws these parables for mankind so that they may take admonition.*"[479]

On the other hand, the single factor that brings about man's downfall is egoism and self-centredness, which disrupts his relationship with the rest of the creation; it makes him give undue importance to the trivial matters of *dunyā* and ultimately waste the potential of his soul altogether.

If we wish to live in harmony with the rest of creation and progress into the next stage of our existence with peace and contentment, we have to take away our attention from our lower selves and direct it towards the Creator of all things. This is the way, and this is the truth.

---

478 Surat al-ʿAnkabūt, 29:64.

479 Surat Ibrāhīm, 14:24-25.

BIBLIOGRAPHY

Abd al-Futtūḥ, Ḥusain ibn ʿAlī. 1408 AH. *Rawḍ al-Jinān wa Rūḥ al-Jinān fī Tafsīr al-Qur'ān*. Mashad: Asṭan-i Quds-i Raḍawī.

Barqī, Aḥmad ibn Muḥammad ibn Khālid. 1303 Shamsi. *Al-Maḥāsin*. Tehran: Dār al-Kitāb al-Islāmiyya.

Bible. 2002. Translation and exegesis, Anjuman Bayna'l Milali Kitāb-i Muqaddas.

Bukhārī, Muḥammad ibn Ismāʿīl. 1401 AH. *Ṣaḥīḥ al-Bukhārī*. Beirut: Dār al-Fikr.

Fayḍ al-Kāshānī, Mullā Muḥsin. 1415 AH. *Tafsir al-Ṣāfī*. Tehran: Intishārat-i Ṣadrā.

Gospel of Barnabas. Internet Edition

Ḥanbalī, ibn Rajab. 1404 AH. *Al-Takhwīf min al-Nār*. Damascus: Dār al-Rushd.

Ḥurr ʿĀmilī, Sh Muḥammad ibn al-Ḥasan. *Wasā'il al-Shīʿa ilā Taḥṣīl Masā'il al-Sharīʿa*.

Ḥusainī Tehrānī, ʿAllama Muḥammad Ḥusain. 1381 Sh. *Maʿād Shināsī*. Mashad: *Nūr-i Malakūtiy-i Qur'ān*.

Ibn ʿArabī, Muḥyi al-Dīn Muḥammad. 1422 AH. *Tafsīr ibn ʿArabī*. Beirut: Dār Iḥyā' al-Turāth al-ʿArabī.

Ibn Ḥanbal, Aḥmad. (Not dated). *Musnad*. Beirut: Dār al-Ṣādir

Ibn Kathīr, Ismāʿīl ibn ʿAmr. 1419 AH. *Tafsīr al-Qur'ān al-ʿAẓīm*. Beirut: Dār al-Kitāb al-ʿIlmiyya

Ibn Mubārak, ʿAbdallāh. 1411 AH. *Musnad ibn Mubārak*. Beirut: Dār al-Kitāb al-ʿIlmiyya

Kāsḥānī, Mullā Fatḥullāh. 1336 Sh. *Tafsīr Manhaj al-Ṣādiqīn fī'l Zam al-Mukhālifīn*. Tehran: Intishārāt-i ʿIlmī.

Kūfī, Ḥusayn ibn Saʿīd. 1399 AH. *Kitāb al-Zuhd*. Qom: Al-ʿIlmiyya.

Kulaynī, Muḥammad ibn Isḥāq. 1363 Sh. *Al-Kāfī*. Tehran: Dār al-Kutub al-Islāmiyya.

Madanī, Syed ʿAlī Khān. 1415 AH. *Riyāḍ al-Sālikīn fī Sharḥ Ṣahifatu Sayyid al-Sājidīn*. Qom:

Al-Majlisī, ʿAllāma Muḥammad Bāqir. 1403 AH. *Biḥār al-Anwār*. Beirut: Dār Iḥyā al-Turāth al-ʿArabī.

Mauro, James, "Bright lights, big mystery", *Psychology Today*, July 1992.

Māzandarānī, Mawlā Muḥammad Ṣāliḥ. 1421 AH. *Sharḥ Uṣūl al-Kāfī*. Beirut: Dār Iḥyā al-Turāth al-ʿArabī.

Moody, Raymond. 1975. *Life after Life: The Investigation of a Phenomenon, Survival of Bodily Death*. Seattle: Mockingbird Books.

Mufīd, Sh. Abū ʿAbdillāh Muḥammad ibn Nuʿmān. 1414 AH. *Al-Ikhtiṣāṣ*. Beirut: Dar al-Mufīd.

Muḥammadī Ray Shahrī, Muḥammad. 1375 Sh. *Mīzān al-Ḥikma*. Qom: Dār al-Ḥadīth.

Mu'assasay-i Nashr-i Islāmī.

Muslim Nishābūrī, Abū'l Ḥusayn. Not dated. *Al-Jāmiʿ al-Ṣaḥīḥ*. Beirut: Dār al-Fikr.

Muttaqī al-Hindī, ʿAlī ibn Ḥisam al-Dīn. 1409 AH. *Kanz al-ʿUmmāl fī Sunan al-Aqwāl wa'l Afʿāl*. Beirut: Mu'assasat al-Risāla.

Qāḍī Nuʿmān al-Miṣrī, Abū Ḥanīfa Nuʿmān ibn Muḥammad. 1383 AH. *Daʿā'im al-Islām*. Cairo, Dār al-Maʿārif.

Qummī, Sh. Abbas. 1417 AH. *Mafātīḥ al-Jinān*. Beirut: Dār al-Thaqalayn.

Qummī, ʿAlī ibn Ibrāhīm. 1404 AH. *Tafsīr al-Qummī*. Qom: Dār al-Kitāb.

Rāzī, Imām Fakhr al-dīn, Muḥammad b. ʿUmar. 1420 AH. *Mafātīḥ al-Ghayb*. Beirut: Dār Iḥyā al-Turāth al-ʿArabī.

Rūmī, Maulana Jalāl al-Dīn Muḥammad. 1386 Sh. *Mathnawiy-i Maʿnawī*. Tehran: Intishārāt Qaqnūs.

Ṣadrā Shīrāzī, Mulla Ṣadr al-Dīn Muḥammad. 1990 CE. *Al-Ḥikmatu'l Mutaʿāliya fī'l Asfār al-ʿAqliya al-Arbaʿa (Asfār)*. Beirut: Dār al-Turāth al-ʿArabiyya.

Ṣadūq, Muḥammad ibn ʿAlī ibn Bābawayh. 1414 AH. *Iʿtiqādāt*. Beirut: Dār al-Mufīd.

------ 1417 AH. *al-Āmālī*. Qom: Mu'assasat al-Biʿtha.

------ 1368 Sh. *Thawāb al-Aʿmāl*. Qom: Intishārāt Amīr.

------ 1403 AH. *Al-Khiṣāl*. Qom: Manshūrāt Jāmiʿat al-Mudarrisīn.

------ 1385. ʿIlal al-Sharāyaʿ. Najaf: al-Maktabat al-Ḥaydariyya.

------ 1379 Sh. *Maʿāni al-Akhbār*. Qom: Mu'assay-i Nashr-i Islāmī.

------ not dated. *Man lā Yaḥḍuruhu'l Faqīh*. Qom: Mu'assasay-i Nashr-i Islāmī.

Sharīf Radī, Abū'l Ḥasan Muḥammad ibn al-Ḥasan. 1384 Sh. *Nahj al-Balāgha*. Qom: Dār al-Ḥadīth.

Swedenborg, Emanuel. 2000. *Heaven and Its Wonders and Hell Drawn from Things Heard & Seen*. US: Swedenborg Foundation

Suyūṭī, Jalāl al-Dīn. 1404 AH. *Al-Durr al-Manthūr fī'l Tafsīr bi'l Ma'thūr*. Qom: Library of Ayatullah Marʿashī Najafī.

Al-Ṭabarānī, Abū'l Qāsim Sulaymān ibn Aḥmad. 1412 AH. *Al-Aḥādīth al-Ṭiwāl*. Beirut: Dar al-Kitāb al-ʿIlmiyya.

Ṭabarsī, Faḍl ibn al-Ḥasan. 1372 Sh. *Majmaʿ al-Bayān fī Tafsīr al-Qur'ān*. Tehran: Intishārāt-i Nāṣir Khusro.

Ṭūsī, Muḥammad ibn al-Ḥasan. Not dated. *Al-Tibyān fī Tafsīr al-Qur'ān*. Beirut: Dār Iḥyā al-Turāth al-ʿArabī.

Ṭūsī, Syed Khalīl al-Raḥmān. Unpublished. *Mabāniy-i Falsafey-i Akhlāq-i Mulla Ṣadrā*.

------ 1386 Sh. *Al-Shawāhid al-Rububiyya fī'l Manāhij al-Sulūkiyya*. Intishārāt-i Mawlā.

------ 1354 Sh. *Al-Mabda' wa'l Maʿād*. Introduction and revision by Syed Jalāl al-Dīn Āshtiyānī. Intishārāt-i Anjuman-i Shahanshahīy-i Falsafey-i Iran.

Zamakhsharī, Muhammad. 1407 AH. *Al-Kashshāf ʿan Ḥaqā'iq Ghawamiḍ al-Tanzīl*. Beirut: Dār al-Kitāb al-ʿArabī.

www.ingramcontent.com/pod-product-compliance
Lightning Source LLC
Chambersburg PA
CBHW071417090426
42737CB00011B/1491
9781789910780